Antoni Nadbrzeżny

From Mother of the Redemption
to Mother of All Believers

The Mariology of Edward Schillebeeckx

VANDENHOECK & RUPRECHT

The book is a part of the project funded by the Ministry of Education and Science, Republic of Poland, "Regional Initiative of Excellence" in 2019–2023, 028/RID/2018/19, the amount of funding: 11 742 500 PLN.

Publishing reviews:
Prof. Marek Gilski, The Pontifical University of John Paul II in Krakow
Prof. Bogdan Ferdek, Pontifical Faculty of Theology in Wroclaw

Bibliographic information published by the Deutsche Nationalbibliothek:
The Deutsche Nationalbibliothek lists this publication in the Deutsche Nationalbibliografie; detailed bibliographic data available online: https://dnb.de.

Translator: Dominika Bugno-Narecka
Proofreading: Thaddaeus Lancton
Index: Dawid Mielnik
Typesetting: le-tex publishing services, Leipzig
Cover design: SchwabScantechnik, Göttingen
Printed and bound: Hubert & Co, Ergolding
Printed in the EU

Vandenhoeck & Ruprecht Verlage | www.vandenhoeck-ruprecht-verlage.com
E-Mail: info@v-r.de

ISBN 978-3-525-50107-8

Lublin Theological Studies

in connection with
The John Paul II Catholic University of Lublin

edited by
Adam Kubiś (The John Paul II Catholic University of Lublin)

Volume 14

Table of Contents

Introduction

A significant decline in the interest in Mariology was observed in the academic centers of Western Europe shortly after the conclusion of the Second Vatican Council (1962–1965). Despite the richness of innovative content and methodological impulses stemming from Chapter VIII of the Dogmatic Constitution on the Church *Lumen Gentium*, frequently referred to as *Magna Carta* of contemporary Mariology, European theological circles did not respond with an immediate reflection on the mystery of Mary, the Mother of God. The decades-long *moratorium* on Mariological thought and work was an extreme reaction to the dominance of uncritical maximalist Mariology which immediately preceded the Council and was not rooted in the Bible, but was overly abstract, ignorant of its historical-salvific dimension and expressed in an outdated language.

From the outside, this period of "Mariological silence," characterized by the evident decline in the number of publications on Mariology, can be perceived as an expression of the relegation of Mariological issues to the margins of theological thought. However, looking at the phenomenon from the point of view of the fundamental changes which have been taking place within the Mariological paradigm, one can notice the phases of gradual maturation of theological reflection on the Mother of God. The renewal of Catholic Mariology in the spirit of the Second Vatican Council has surely required some time and reflection.

The secularization of European societies, the positive phenomenon of women's emancipation, radical cultural, political and religious changes, as well as the crisis of Thomistic metaphysics and the neo-scholastic theological method have become reasons for questioning and rejecting traditional Mariology which is now perceived as an obstacle for the credibility of Christianity. Many contemporaries strongly object to the outdated interpretations of basic Mariological themes, which are often idealistic and legendary. Marian piety is sometimes considered to be a manifestation of human frustration and complexes. In the context of the negative experiences of modern man, such as the rejection of the God hypothesis, a pessimistic sense of one's own finitude, disappointment with and doubts about the meaning of human life and death, theology must present Mary as a real challenge (*Maria – een uitdaging*) and as a person who has universal meaning for human culture.[1]

In October 1990, during the international congress for Dominicans on Mariology in Huissen, the leading Flemish theologian, Edward Schillebeeckx, said the following words: "Authentic Marian devotion belongs to the essence of Christianity

---

1 Wiel Logister, *Maria, een uitdaging* (Baarn: 1995), 6–7.

in which only Jesus Christ, referring all people to the one God, being the guide for all people on the path to the one God, can be called the central or focal point. Mary – the mother of this Jesus, the Christ, the Son of God, our Lord – reflects in her gift of faith some of the splendor of her Son – of the *Kyrios Christ*."[2]

Edward Schillebeeckx's standpoint quoted above clearly indicates that after the period of putting aside Mariological issues, the time has come to recognize Mariology as an important field of theology, one that requires a refined theological and anthropological meaning. The statement quoted above not only indicates a renaissance of Mariological reflection in European theology which comes after the phase of "Mariological silence," but it is also an intellectual encouragement to undertake thorough research into the Mariology of one of the most outstanding contemporary theologians, Edward Schillebeeckx. A short presentation of his biography allows one to capture the essential ideological connections between his theology and other theological and philosophical trends mentioned already at the beginning of this study.

Edward Schillebeeckx[3] was born on 12 November 1914 in Antwerp, Belgium. At the age of 20 he entered the Dominican Order in Ghent. He studied in Leuven, where the Flemish Province of the Dominicans had its own research center. After the Second World War, he continued his studies in France at the Dominican center Le Saulchoir, where he met Father Marie-Dominique Chenu[4] and Father

---

2 "[…] Waarachtige Mariaverering behoort tot het wezen van het christendom, waarbinnen alleen Jezus Christus, verwijzend naar de al-enige God van alle mensen, in zijn van zichzelf weg-wijzen naar de enige God van alle mensen, centrum en focus mag worden genoemd. Maria: moeder van deze Jezus, de Christus, zoon Gods, onze Heer, weerspiegelt in haar gelovige overgave iets van de glans van haar zoon: Kurios Christos." MGVM, 57–8.

3 Stephan van Erp, "Tussen traditie en situatie. Edward Schillebeeckx voor een volgende generatie," *Tijdschrift voor Theologie* 1 (2010): 8–18; Annekatrien Depoorter, "Tussen denken en leven. Een beknopte biografie van Edward Schillebeeckx," *Tijdschrift voor Geestelijk Leven* 1 (2009): 5–12; Battista Mondin, "Schillebeeckx," in Battista Mondin, *Dizionario dei teologi*, (Bologna: Edizioni Studio Domenicano, 1992), 530–9; Erik Borgman, *Edward Schillebeeckx: een theoloog in zijn geschiedenis* (Baarn: Nelissen, 1999); John Bowden, *Edward Schillebeeckx. Portrait of a Theologian* (London: SCM Press, 1983); Richard Auwerda, *Dossier Schillebeeckx. Theoloog in de kerk der conflicten* (Bilthoven: Nelissen, 1969); Mark Schoof, "The Later Theology of Edward Schillebeeckx. The New Position of Theology after Vatican II," *The Clergy Review* 55 (1970): 943–60; Boniface Willems, "Edward Schillebeeckx," in *Tendenzen der Theologie im 20. Jahrhundert. Eine Geschichte in Porträts*, ed. Hans J. Schulz, (Stuttgart: Kreuz-Verlag, 1966), 602–7; Robert Schreiter, "Schillebeeckx," in *The Modern Theologians*, ed. David F. Ford (Cambridge: Blackwell, 1997): 152–61; Antoni Nadbrzeżny, "Schillebeeckx Edward," in *Encyklopedia Katolicka*, vol. 17, ed. Edward Gigilewicz (Lublin: Towarzystwo Naukowe KUL, 2012), 1224–6.

4 Cf. Edward Schillebeeckx, "In memoriam M.-D. Chenu (1895–1990)," *Tijdschrift voor Theologie* 30 (1990): 184–5; Edward Schillebeeckx, *Je suis un théologien heureux* (Paris: Cerf, 1995), 149–152.

Yves Congar.[5] Then, he studied at Collège de France and at L'École des Hautes Études at the Sorbonne, where he improved his knowledge of patristics, medieval studies and contemporary philosophy. His early work was strongly influenced by the "nouvelle théologie."[6] After defending his PhD on the basis of the dissertation *De Sacramentele heilsekonomie*,[7] Schillebeeckx briefly lectured at Hoger Instituut voor Godsdienstwetenschappen at Leuven. In 1957, he took over the department of dogmatic theology and history of theology at the Catholic University of Nijmegen (now Radboud University), the Netherlands. The then Cardinal Bernard Jan Alfrink (1900–1987)[8] wanted the Theological Faculty of that university to be an intellectual partner in the ecclesiastical dialogue; hence, the Catholic University of Nijmegen was characterized by great independence from the Dutch episcopate.

The Second Vatican Council opened a new phase in Schillebeeckx's life. He was appointed theological expert and advisor to the Dutch episcopate during the Council sessions.[9] Then, he became known as one of the organizers of the Dutch Pastoral Council held in Noordwijkerhout in 1966–1970, which considered the idea of the Second Vatican Council's *aggiornamento* on a national scale.[10] At the same time, as editor-in-chief, Schillebeeckx actively participated in the work of the quarterly of Dutch and Flemish theologians, *Tijdschrift voor Theologie*, and was the head of the dogmatic section of *Concilium: International Journal for Theology*. His closest collaborators were his conciliar colleagues: Y. Congar, H. Küng, H. de Lubac and K. Rahner.

Two periods can be distinguished in Schillebeeckx's theological work. The first period covers the years 1946–1967, when his theological reflection followed phenomenological Thomism. Schillebeeckx discussed here the problems of sacramentology, Mariology and spiritual theology. His works from this period are characterized by the continuation of the method adopted at Le Saulchoir, which consists in the historical reconstruction of positive data, and the acceptance of the gnoseo-

---

5 Cf. Edward Schillebeeckx, "In memoriam Yves Congar (1904–1995)," *Tijdschrift voor Theologie* 35 (1995): 271–3.

6 Jürgen Mettepenningen, *Nouvelle Théologie – New Theology. Inheritor of Modernism, Precursor of Vatican II* (London: T&T Clark, 2010), 120–2.

7 Cf. Edward Schillebeeckx, *De sacramentele heilsekonomie. Theologische bezinning op S. Thomas' sacramentenleer in het licht van de traditie en van de hedendaagse sacramentsproblematiek* (Antwerpen: Nelissen, 1952).

8 See Ton H.M. van Schaik. *Alfrink: Een biografie* (Amsterdam: Anthos, 1997).

9 Cf. Edward Schillebeeckx, *Het Tweede Vaticaans Concilie, I* (Tielt: Lannoo, 1964); Edward Schillebeeckx, *Het Tweede Vaticaans Concilie, II* (Tielt: Lannoo, 1966).

10 Cf. Schillebeeckx, *Je suis un théologien heureux*, 58–60.

logical perspective which he adopted from the Dominican philosopher D. M. De Petter.[11]

The second period, which began around 1967, is characterized by a radical change in theological interests and the adoption of new methods. A research trip to the USA was the particular inspiration for this change.[12] During this period, Schillebeeckx abandoned the academic version of Thomism characterized by excessive abstraction, and, as a theologian, confronted intellectually modern hermeneutics. His interests focused on the dialogue between theology and the broadly understood experience of contemporaneity.[13] As a result, the Flemish theologian, as one of the first Catholic thinkers, introduced hermeneutic problems to systematic theology, developing new concepts of Christology, ecclesiology and Mariology.[14]

Some of Schillebeeckx's theological theses became the subject of doctrinal examination on the part of the Vatican Congregation for the Doctrine of the Faith. The first official investigation within the Congregation took place in 1968 and concerned some ambiguities in the interpretation of the idea of secularization. A renewed investigation was undertaken in 1978 after the publication of two monumental works on Christology: *Jezus, het verhaal van een levende* (1974) and *Gerechtigheid en liefde. Genade en bevrijding* (1977). Summoned by the Congregation, Schillebeeckx came to Rome in December 1979 to explain his innovative theological views. The third official investigation at the Congregation began in 1984 and concerned Schillebeeckx's writings on Church ministry.[15] Although ecclesiastical disciplinary sanctions were never imposed, the explanations provided by Schillebeeckx were not considered sufficient.[16] In this period, he received many honorary doctorates (also from the Catholic University of Leuven in 1974) and the prestigious European Erasmus prize in 1983.

---

11 Cf. Dries Bosschaert and Stephan van Erp, "Schillebeeckx's Metaphysics and Epistemology: The Influence of Dominicus De Petter," in *T&T Clark Handbook of Edward Schillebeeckx*, eds. Stephan van Erp and Daniel Minch (London: Bloomsbury, 2019), 29–44.

12 Cf. Edward Schillebeeckx, "Katholiek leven in de Verenigde Staten," *De Bazuin* 51, no. 17 (1968): 1–6; Schillebeeckx, "De schok van de toekomst in Amerika," *De Bazuin* 41, no. 41 (1971): 1–8.

13 Rosino Gibellini, "Préface. Honnêtes envers le monde. La théologie de frontière d'Edward Schillebeeckx," in Schillebeeckx, *Je suis un théologien heureux*, 9–14.

14 Cf. Ted Schoof and Jan van de Westelaken, *Bibliography 1936–1996 of Edward Schillebeeckx O.P.* (Nijmegen: Nelissen, 1997).

15 Cf. Edward Schillebeeckx, *Kerkelijk ambt. Voorgangers in de gemeente van Jezus Christus* (Bloemendaal: Nelissen, 1980); Edward Schillebeeckx, *Pleidooi voor mensen in de kerk. Christelijke identiteit en ambten in de kerk* (Baarn: Nelissen, 1985).

16 Schillebeeckx, *Je suis un théologien heureux*, 67–77; Edward Schillebeeckx, *Theologisch testament. Notarieel nog niet verleden* (Baarn: Nelissen, 1994), 59–66; Ted Schoof, *De zaak Schillebeeckx* (Bloemendaal: Nelissen, 1980); Pierre Grelot, *Église et ministères. Pour un dialogue critique avec E. Schillebeeckx* (Paris: Cerf, 1983).

From the second half of the 1960s, Schillebeeckx developed and propagated hermeneutic theology understood as a reflection on Christian experience. By hermeneutics he meant not only the art of interpreting specific passages from the Bible or Tradition, but also the interpretation of the totality of faith in order to obtain its credible actualization in a given cultural context. Until the end of his life, the Flemish theologian focused on Christological, hermeneutic and ecclesiological problems. He died in Nijmegen on 23 December 2009.[17]

After analyzing Schillebeeckx's bibliography, it must be said that due to the relatively small number of published Mariological texts, he is not considered as one of the most prominent contemporary Mariologists, who include G. Roschini, C. Balić, W. Beinert, R. Laurentin, G. Philips, F. Courth, S. de Fiores, and B. Forte. In lexicons, encyclopedias and textbooks of theology, Schillebeeckx is presented mainly as an outstanding theologian in the field of Christology, sacramentology and ecclesiology. He is known internationally as the author of the comprehensive Christological trilogy which has been translated into many languages.[18] It should be remembered, however, that the extensive bibliography of Schillebeeckx's works reveals a wide spectrum of his interests, including issues directly related to Mariology.

When conducting research on Schillebeeckx's Mariology, one should bear in mind the fact that most of his Mariological works had been written before the Second Vatican Council, which does not mean, however, that the neo-scholastic model of theology had been uncritically adopted by him. Schillebeeckx clearly refers in his Mariology to Augustinianism, existentialism, phenomenology, philosophy of dialogue, hermeneutics, and even structuralism, wishing to develop a biblical and historical-salvific perspective which was seriously neglected by Catholic theology in the first half of the 20th century. In the face of intellectual confrontation with Hegelianism, evolutionism and historical materialism, there was a growing need to develop an in-depth theological reflection on history, which could contribute to the construction of a diachronic theology. Research on the Mariological works of Edward Schillebeeckx confirms that also in this field he turned out to be a creative, courageous and innovative theologian. The Latin maxim *non multa sed multum* (not quantity but quality) describes perfectly his achievements in the field of Mariology, which might be small in terms of quantity, but are rich in terms of their content.

---

17 Antoni Nadbrzeżny, "Edward Schillebeeckx OP (1914–2009) als een pionier van de hermeneutische theologie," in *Plurima sub falso tegmine vera latent. The Embarrassments of Interdisciplinarity*, ed. Agnieszka Flor-Górecka (Lublin: Towarzystwo Naukowe KUL, 2022), 185–6; Nadbrzeżny, "Teolog w świecie konfliktów. *In memoriam* Edward Schillebeeckx (1914–2009)," *Roczniki Teologii Dogmatycznej* 57, no. 2 (2010): 119–29.

18 Edward Schillebeeckx, *Jezus, het verhaal van een levende* (Bloemendaal: Nelissen, 1974); Edward Schillebeeckx, *Gerechtigheid en liefde. Genade en bevrijding* (Bloemendaal: Nelissen, 1977); Edward Schillebeeckx, *Mensen als verhaal van God* (Baarn: Nelissen, 1989).

This book aims to reconstruct, present and evaluate Edward Schillebeeckx's Mariology, to demonstrate the discipline's development from the pre-Vatican II concepts to contemporary approaches, while taking into account the importance of Schillebeeckx's ideas for the renewal of this theological field.

The following specific questions arise from the intellectual encounter with Schillebeeckx's Mariology: What is the significance of the biblical image of Mary for contemporary systematic Mariology? Is the pluralism of biblical Mariologies true? Which biblical themes should be developed in the construction of modern Mariology? Why is Mary's dynamic faith a hermeneutic key to the understanding of her unique place in the history of salvation?

Moreover, it is worth inquiring about the fundamental issue of Mary's participation in the redemption accomplished by Christ: Is the description of Mary as an intermediary, used in the Catholic tradition, theologically correct? In what sense does Mary act as the representative of all humanity before God? An in-depth analysis of Schillebeeckx's Mariological achievements also prompts us to seek answers to the question about the meaning of Mary's universal spiritual motherhood. Should Mary's motherhood continue to be the leading idea in Mariology? What is Mary's relationship with Christ, the Holy Spirit, the Church and humanity?

In researching Schillebeeckx's Mariology, issues related to the veneration of the Mother of God cannot be ignored. Hence, theological analysis in this book include Marian piety, its theological and psychological justification, the meaning of popular piety and the extremely interesting function of the so-called private Marian apparitions. In the context of the issues discussed, the following additional questions arise: What is Mary's meaning for the contemporary practice of Christian life? How does the broadly understood human experience influence the shape of contemporary Marian piety? What ways of renewing Marian devotions does Edward Schillebeeckx propose?

Fundamental questions about the merits of Mariology are inevitably accompanied by the issues related to meta-Mariology. They concern not so much the substantial image of Mary, but rather the issues related to the way of practicing Mariology. Again, it is worth asking: Why does the historical-salvific Mariology promoted by Schillebeeckx reflect better the truth about the person and life of Mary than the static, speculative pre-Vatican II Mariology? What are the tasks of contemporary exegesis and hermeneutics in developing Mariology? What methods are induced by the modern way of thinking about reality? Which theological sources (*loci theologici*) should be valued and appreciated in Mariological reflection? What factors influence the shape of Mariological language? What determines the universalistic character of Mariology? Should contemporary Mariology be constructed on the basis of specific systems, trends or philosophical ideas? What context is required for Mariological reflection? What is the role of modern experience in creating a theological image of Mary? Ultimately, one must attempt to indicate the methodological directions for the future developments in Mariology.

Research into Schillebeeckx's thought conducted for the sake of this book attempts to find reasonable answers to the above questions or, at least, to create theological premises for solving the outlined problems. The results of this search not only draw attention to the importance of Mariological issues in the current cultural context and report on Edward Schillebeeckx's Mariological views, but also show their genesis, development, and connection with the changes typical of our era and with other areas of theology. They also demonstrate consistency or inconsistency with the latest trends in the Catholic doctrine and attempt to evaluate Schillebeeckx's thought.

The book also undertakes the task of exploring the personalistic aspect of Schillebeeckx's thought and presenting his Mariological reflection as a solid basis for developing a dynamic, historical-salvific and realistic Mariology. A significant problem arises at this point: Is it methodologically correct to use the term "personalism" in relation to Schillebeeckx's theology? In this book, I try to prove the thesis that in the period immediately preceding the Second Vatican Council Schillebeeckx sought to develop a phenomenological and personalistic Mariology inspired by Augustinian thought. It was only in the post-conciliar years that his tendency to construct Mariology based on philosophical anthropology weakened. For this reason, it is difficult to talk about Schillebeeckx's personalism understood as a modern version of that philosophical and theological system. Instead, one can discern in his thought a valuable anthropological sensitivity in the appreciation for the conscious subjective side of the personal being (the internal personal dynamism, the dialogic way of being, the freedom-oriented structure of being), which may be at least a starting point for the creation of a coherent personalistic Mariology. An in-depth analysis of Schillebeeckx's entire Mariological work performed in a dynamic relationship with other areas of theology and science allows for the discovery of a whole range of the so-called "personalistic moments" in his Mariology. These are characteristic fundamental themes that may constitute important ideas for building a strictly personalistic Mariology.

In order to achieve my research goal, I had to analyze thoroughly the basic source material which consists of Edward Schillebeeckx's book publications in the field of Mariology and a number of his articles in theological and popular science journals as well as specialized dictionaries. On the occasion of the Marian Year (1954) announced by Pope Pius XII, Schillebeeckx wrote a book on Mariology entitled *Maria, Christus' mooiste wonderschepping*[19] (*Mary, Christ's Most Beautiful*

---

19 Edward Schillebeeckx, *Maria, Christus' mooiste wonderschepping. Religieuze grondlijnen van het Maria-mysterie* (Antwerpen: Apostolaat van de Rozenkrans, 1954).

Creation). Soon, the work was extended and given a new title: *Maria, moeder van de verlossing*[20] (*Mary, Mother of the Redemption*). In the following years, the work was translated into many languages.[21] It was enthusiastically received among the supporters of Mariological renewal and undoubtedly contributed to the preparation of Chapter VIII of the constitution *Lumen Gentium*. Due to the historical-salvific, sacramental and personalistic dimension of the proposed Mariology, Schillebeeckx, like M. Schmaus and R. Laurentin, is included among the precursors of the Conciliar concept of Mariology.[22]

The theology of the Flemish Dominican is of particular interest to Western European and American research centers, although it is also necessary to emphasize the growing interest in Schillebeeckx's thought among theologians from Asia.

The authors of the few Polish studies of Schillebeeckx's thought (Andrzej Zuberbier, Czesław Bartnik, Alfons Nossol, Stanisław Napiórkowski, Alfons Skowronek) focus almost exclusively on sacramentological and Christological issues. Particularly noteworthy are the books and articles by Antoni Nadbrzeżny,[23] which are entirely devoted to Schillebeeckx's ecclesiology and soteriology.

The authors of many foreign studies on Edward Schillebeeckx's ideas focus mainly on issues related to sacramentology, Christology, ecclesiology, hermeneutics, eschatology, soteriology and theological anthropology. The works of Stephan van Erp,[24]

---

20 Edward Schillebeeckx, *Maria, moeder van de verlossing. Religieuze grondlijnen van het Maria-mysterie* (Antwerpen: Apostolaat van de Rozenkrans, 1955).

21 Edward Schillebeeckx, *Marie, mère de la rédemption* (Paris: Cerf, 1963); *Mary, Mother of the Redemption* (New York: Sheed & Ward, 1964); *Maria, madre della redenzione* (Catania: Paoline, 1965); *Maria, madre de la redención* (Madrid: Fax, 1969).

22 "Schmaus e Laurentin, Schillebeeckx rappresentano la punta dei mariologi che preparano la posizione del Concilio e aprono la strada ad ulteriori traguardi." Stefano de Fiores, *Maria nella teologia contemporanea* (Roma: Centro di Cultura Mariana "Mater Ecclesiae," 1987), 107.

23 Cf. Antoni Nadbrzeżny, "Kerk en bevrijding in het denken van Edward Schillebeeckx," *Roczniki Teologiczne* 64, no. 7 (2017): 97–107; "De receptie van de de theologie van Edward Schillebeeckx in Polen (1965–2016)," in *De Lage Landen en de religie. De positie van de religie in verschillende culturele aspecten*, ed. Bas Hammers and Muriel Waterlot, 65–76 (Lublin: Wydawnictwo KUL, 2017); "Tussen sacralisatie en banalisering. Lijden in de theologie van Edward Schillebeeckx," *Roczniki Teologiczne* 45, no. 2 (2018): 47–61; *Filozofia zbawienia. Soteriologia egzystencjalna Paula Tillicha i Edwarda Schillebeeckxa* (Kraków: Wydawnictwo WAM, 2020); "Kościół jako sakrament dialogu według Edwarda Schillebeeckxa," *Roczniki Teologiczne* 50, no. 2 (2003): 229–42; *Sakrament wyzwolenia. Zbawcze posłannictwo Kościoła w posoborowej eklezjologii holenderskiej* (Lublin: Wydawnictwo KUL, 2013).

24 Cf. Stephan van Erp, Martin G. Poulsom, and Lieven Boeve, eds. *Grace, Governance and Globalization* (London: T&T Clark, 2018).

Erik Borgman,[25] Robert Schreiter,[26] Lieven Boeve,[27] Philip Kennedy,[28] Ignace D'hert,[29] Hadewych Snijdewind,[30] Pim Valkenberg,[31] Raymond Winling,[32] Mary Catherine Hilkert,[33] Ted Schoof,[34] and Roger Haight[35] are of great help in interpreting Schillebeeckx's theological views. They present the main ideas of Schillebeeckx's theology in the broad context of current religious, theological, ecclesiastical and non-ecclesiastical experiences. The works of the above authors present the basic epistemological assumptions of the narrative and phenomenological manner of practicing theology, which is also visible in the Mariology he created.

No attempt has been made in theological research so far to comprehensively describe the issues of Mariology developed by Edward Schillebeeckx . This monograph fills the gap. It was written by a Polish theologian and is an extended version of his doctoral dissertation defended at the John Paul II Catholic University of Lublin (Poland) in 2002. It is safe to say that the book is an expression of the contextual reception of Edward Schillebeeckx's Mariology in Poland, where Marian piety – supported and shaped by Cardinal Karol Wojtyła (1920–2005), the later Pope John Paul II,[36] and the Cardinal Primate Stefan Wyszyński (1901–1981) – was a significant spiritual force in a largely Catholic society and an important factor that united the Church community against the pressure of the communist regime.[37]

---

25 Cf. Erik Borgman, *Edward Schillebeeckx. A Theologian in His History*, (London: Bloomsbury, 2006).

26 Cf. Mary Catherine Hilkert and Robert J. Schreiter, eds., *The Praxis of the Reign of God. An Introduction to the Theology of Edward Schillebeeckx* (New York: Fordham University Press, 2002).

27 Cf. Lieven Boeve, Frederiek Depoortere and Stephan Van Erp, eds. *Edward Schillebeeckx and Contemporary Theology* (London: T&T Clark International, 2010).

28 Cf. Philip Kennedy, *Schillebeeckx* (Collegeville: Liturgical Press, 1993).

29 Cf. Ignace D'hert, *Een spoor voor ons getrokken. De Jezustrilogie van Edward Schillebeeckx* (Baarn:Nelissen, 1997).

30 Cf. Hadewych Snijdewind, *Leeswijzer bij "Jezus, het verhaal van een Levende" van Edward Schillebeeckx* (Baarn: Nelissen, 1994).

31 Cf. Pim Valkenberg, *Leeswijzer bij "Mensen als verhaal van God" van Edward Schillebeeckx* (Baarn: Nelissen, 1991).

32 Cf. Raymond Winling, *Teologia współczesna 1945–1980* (Kraków: Wydawnictwo ZNAK, 1990), 349–53.

33 Cf. Mary Catherine Hilkert. "Hermeneutics of History in the Theology of Edward Schillebeeckx," *The Tomist* 51, no. 1 (1987): 97–145.

34 Cf. Ted Schoof, "Edward Schillebeeckx – De laatste twintig jaar," *Tijdschrift voor Theologie* 50, no. 1 (2010): 144–152.

35 Cf. Roger Haight, "Engagement met de wereld als zaak van God – Christologie & postmoderniteit," *Tijdschrift voor Theologie* 1 (2010): 73–94.

36 Cf. Kazimierz Pek, Stanisław C. Napiórkowski and Wacław Siwak, eds., *The Debate about Mariology of John Paul II* (Stockbridge, MA: Marian Heritage, 2018); Pek, *Totus Tuus Renewed – John Paul II* (Lublin: Towarzystwo Naukowe KUL, 2021).

37 Cf. Ryszard Ficek, "Mariological Dimension of the Theological and Pastoral Concepts of Cardinal Stefan Wyszyński, Primate of Poland," *Studia Sandomierskie* 27 (2021): 229–49.

Although Schillebeeckx's Mariological thought waited a rather long time to be elaborated upon in the form of a monograph, it cannot be argued that it has been overlooked or underestimated in the past decades. It is necessary to notice and appreciate the few minor studies that have been written so far on the Mariology of this outstanding Flemish theologian. A mini-synthesis of Schillebeeckx's Mariology was provided by Stefano de Fiores in the book *Maria nella teologia contemporanea*,[38] which presented historical circumstances of the creation of Schillebeeckx's basic Mariological work, *Maria, moeder van de verlossing* (*Mary, Mother of the Redemption*), and provided a short theological description that can serve as a good introduction to the reflection on Schillebeeckx's Mariology practiced in the context of meta-dogmatic (functional) Christology. Unfortunately, the theologically reliable publication by Stefano de Fiores does not include the analysis of a number of Mariological articles written by Schillebeeckx and does not take into account his latest bibliography.

The first part of Carl Straeter's book *La mariologia secondo la "nuova teologia" olandese*[39] presents quite extensively the hermeneutic principles of theology developed by Edward Schillebeeckx, while the second part contains only an outline of the theological image of Mary contained in the historical-salvific orientation of the "Dutch Catechism" written by P. Schoonenberg and E. Schillebeeckx.[40] Straeter's study is limited to a brief and schematic overview of the most important Mariological themes: Mary's divine motherhood, her virginity, the Immaculate Conception, the Assumption and the relationship of the Mother of God to the Church. Apart from Schillebeeckx's views, the author presents, in a rather general way, Mariological concepts of other representatives of the so-called "Dutch school": P. Schoonenberg, F. Mamlberg, W. Bless, and F. Haarsma.

An article by D. Fernández entitled "María en las recientes cristologías holandesas"[41] contains a comparative analysis of Mariological views of the representatives of "Dutch Christology." It emphasizes biblical, historical-salvific and functional dimension of the theological image of Mary as the fundamental implication of Christology practiced from a meta-dogmatic perspective by such theologians as E. Schillebeeckx, P. Schoonenberg, or A. Hulsbosch.

---

38 Cf. de Fiores, *Maria nella teologia contemporanea*, 103–7.

39 Cf. Carl Straeter, *La mariologia secondo la "nuova teologia" olandese* (Roma: Edizioni Paoline, 1972).

40 Cf. *De Nieuwe Katechismus. Geloofsverkondiging voor volwassenen* (Antwerpen: Paul Brand, 1966). German translation: *Glaubensverkündigung für Erwachsene. Deutsche Ausgabe des Holländischen Katechismus* (Nijmegen-Utrecht: Dekker & Van De Vegt, 1968).

41 Cf. Domiciano Fernández, "María en las recientes cristologías holandesas," *Estudios Marianos* 47 (1982): 47–72.

The article "Op zoek naar Maria ... en verder! Schillebeeckx' mariologie en haar actuele betekenis" authored by Dutch theologian Erik Borgman is worthy of note.[42] It provides useful and inspiring ideas to be studied in my research on the Mariology of Schillebeeckx. Presenting the main lines of Schillebeeck's theological thinking, the article encourages us to develop a renewed Mariology in the spirit of Christian personalism and humanism.

A recently published article by American author Julia Feder from Creighton University in Omaha, Nebraska, entitled "Mary, Model of Eschatological Faith" is particularly noteworthy.[43] Based on a thorough analysis of Schillebeeckx's Mariology, the article is an example of a deep reflection on the mystery of the person of Mary from the perspective of her dynamically developing faith. The presentation of Mary's eschatological faith as a model for all believers corresponds perfectly to the directions for the renewal of Catholic Mariology indicated by the Second Vatican Council.

Despite the fact that the above-mentioned scientific works undoubtedly contain many interesting and inspiring threads, they are by definition only aspectual approaches to Schillebeeckx's Mariology. This monograph aims to be an integral presentation of Schillebeeckx's Mariological thought and to justify the statement that his thought constitutes a solid basis for building axiological Mariology, in which the person of Mary is a fascinating example of fidelity to values such as dialogue, responsibility, cooperation and solidarity. The most prominent commentators on Schillebeeckx's theology include S. van Erp, E. Borgman, R. Schreiter, Ph. Kennedy, L. Boeve, M.C. Hilkert, K. McManus, I. D'hert, H. Snijdewind, T. Schoof, F. Depoortere, D. Minch, and many others.[44] Review of the theological bibliography confirms the lack of a monograph on Edward Schillebeeckx's Mariology.

The method used in this book is a complex one. According to the classical approach to general methodology, research methods should be distinguished from the methods of a lecture on academic material. In the research process that has led to the writing of this book, I used the analytical and heuristic method at the stage of studying literature. The method covers the entirety of cognitive measures aimed at

---

42 Cf. Borgman, "Op zoek naar Maria ... en verder! Schillebeeckx' mariologie en haar actuele betekenis," *Tijdschrift voor theologie* 33 (1993): 241–66.

43 Cf. Julia Feder, "Mary, Model of Eschatological Faith," in *T&T Handbook of Edward Schillebeeckx*, eds. Stephan van Erp and Daniel Minch (London: Bloomsbury, 2019), 326–39.

44 Cf. Stephan van Erp, Christopher Cimorelli and Christiane Alpers, eds., *Salvation in the World. The Crossroads of Public Theology* (London: Bloomsbury, 2017); Stephan van Erp and D. Minch, eds., *T&T Handbook of Edward Schillebeeckx* (London: Bloomsbury, 2019); Daniel Minch, *Eschatological Hermeneutics. The Theological Core of Experience and Our Hope For Salvation* (London: Bloomsbury, 2020); Marijn de Jong, *Metaphysics of Mystery. Revisiting the Question of Universality through Rahner and Schillebeeckx* (London: Bloomsbury, 2021).

determining the scope of the sources, the aspect of research and the identification of the content that constitutes the narrow context of the analyzed issues. After a thorough analysis of the extensive source material, I used the method of interpreting Schillebeeckx's Mariological views in relation to the philosophical assumptions accepted by him, namely, the phenomenological, existentialist, structuralist and personalistic assumptions, and then comparing them to the basic tendencies of contemporary Mariology. Such a methodological procedure allowed me to determine the ideological orientation of the analyzed contents and enabled me to show the interdisciplinary aspects of Schillebeeckx's theology, as well as to outline the possibilities for the development of Mariology as a theological sub-discipline. In the next stage, I made an attempt to identify personalistic elements in Schillebeeckx's Mariology. The main point here was to highlight the fundamental ideas that can constitute a reliable basis for the development of historical-salvific and personalistic Mariology recommended by the Second Vatican Council (cf. LG 55, 24, GS 62).

Upon the completion of the analytical stage, the content obtained was systematized in terms of the concept adopted for this work. For this purpose, I used the method of critical synthesis, which aimed at creating a coherent theological structure that would solve the problems confronted in this work, along with the evaluation of the views discussed. This critical approach, necessary to maintain the scientific nature of this book, allowed me to show the dynamics of the developments in Edward Schillebeeckx's Mariological thought, to define the directions of change in content and methodology, to notice modifications in the field of theological language, and to show the influence of innovative, relational concepts of theological sources (*loci theologici*) on the shape of the theological icon of Mary in the future (such as his original concept of experience, the liturgy, and the Church).

The systematization of the researched material required integration of various types of theological language typical of the subsequent stages of Schillebeeckx's work and reflecting his fascination with many contemporary philosophical, theological and cultural trends, including Thomism, phenomenology, existentialism, philosophy of dialogue, structuralism, liberation theology, feminist theology, hermeneutics, experience, and secularization.

This book consists of six chapters. In each of these chapters, the first section deals with important methodological issues which affect the meritorious originality in the field of Mariology presented in the subsequent parts. The first chapter presents the biblical image of the Mother of God, which allows us to see the essential revelatory and transcendent dimension in the individual story of Mary of Nazareth. Exegetical analysis of the relevant fragments of the Bible allows us to discover the developmental character of faith in the person of the Mother of God, which constitutes the hermeneutic key in determining her role in the history of salvation.

The second chapter addresses the problem of defining Mary's place and role in the history of salvation. Mary's participation in the objective and subjective redemption is the central subject of analysis here. Theological research allows us to conclude that the category of salvation history constitutes a fundamental idea in the renewal of Mariology postulated by the Second Vatican Council. Departure from a purely biographical Mariology, which is often legendary or static, unrealistic and excessively abstract, is a *sine qua non* condition for a credible presentation of the Catholic doctrine of the Mother of God to contemporary people who are more open to narrative Mariology.

Mary's relationship with the Church is the subject of the third chapter. Due to the relational concept of the Church as a "sacrament of dialogue," Mary can be presented as the Mother of Christ not only from an individual perspective, but also from a universal perspective as the spiritual Mother of all believers. The universal spiritual motherhood of Mary, which is deeply rooted in the Church understood as *communio*, does not exclude the assumption that Mary, as the Mother of the Church, remains for us and with us as our great Sister in faith.

The fourth chapter is a theological reflection on the complex reality of Marian veneration in the context of the basic structure of Christian prayer which is based on the scheme: to the Father through Christ in the Holy Spirit. It also discusses the phenomenon of Marian apparitions and popular piety which is only a subjective "theological source" (*locus theologicus*) within theological methodology.

In the fifth chapter, I attempt to present the directions for the development of Edward Schillebeeckx's Mariology, both in terms of content and methodology. At the same time, I emphasize the need to take into account the biblical dimension more fully, to appreciate the pneumatological and ecclesiological issues in Mariological research and to develop a new theological language, adequate for the mentality and intellect of modern man.

The structure adopted for this book allows for an exhaustive presentation of the results of research on this topic which is the analysis of Edward Schillebeeckx's Mariology in the context of contemporary cultural, social and religious changes. Individual chapters create a coherent system and allow for a comprehensive presentation of the issues discussed and for highlighting the factors that determine both the development of Mariological thought in the work of Edward Schillebeeckx, and its inspiring value for the contemporary reader who experiences difficulties in understanding the deeper meaning of theological statements about the role of Mary in the life of Christ and the Church.

I. A Biblical Icon of Mary

Pre-Vatican II Mariology, which was mainly constructed on the grounds of the speculative method, had gradually reached the state of deep crisis that manifested itself in the extreme autonomization and isolation from other fields of theology, and the abstraction of theological language. Despite the intellectually high level of rationally presented, revealed truths, speculative Mariology did not take into account the proper hierarchy of theological sources *(loci theologici)*. Excessive exposition of the doctrinal statements made by the Magisterium of the Catholic Church had led to a depreciation of biblical sources. As a result, biblical statements, recognized and accepted only as external theological arguments, were completely subordinated to systematic assumptions. They were treated instrumentally as an exemplification of previously adopted Mariological theses. Biblical Mariology, understood as a systematic, historical and critical elaboration of Mariological topics based on biblical literature, was expected to be the remedy for the crisis.

In the mid-1950s, Edward Schillebeeckx showed appreciation for biblical content in Mariological reflection and presented Mary in a new light. The return to the Bible resulted in Schillebeeckx's work in the revival of Mariological language as far as the formal aspect is concerned and, as regards the meritorious aspect, in the identification of Mary's epiphanic character and the presentation of the dynamic development of her faith.

1. The Biblical Foundation of Mariological Language

Within modern methodology of theology, more and more attention is paid to the problem of language. The latter is recognized not only as an instrument of cognition and organization of acquired knowledge, but also as the subject of thorough theological reflection. Research into language undertaken by analytical philosophy, structuralism and hermeneutics led to a "linguistic revolution," which in theology resulted in an increase in semiological sensitivity.[45]

Each scientific discipline uses its own specialist language, which is a function of both the research subject matter and the adopted method. Specialization within the sciences entails appropriate language specification. This is also the case in theology, in which smaller language units are distinguished within the individual areas of theology. Hence, one can reasonably speak of Mariological language as a linguistic substructure of dogmatic language.

The language of Mariology is not an autonomous system of signs isolated from dogmatic language and nor governed by an independent set of rules, although it should be remembered that, due to its subject matter, Mariological language uses distinctive vocabulary. Under the pressure of numerous contemporary linguistic and hermeneutic trends, Mariology must pose a critical question about the *status quo* of its own language, a language it wishes to use in order to describe the reality it studies.

The construction of Mariological language, although often done in an intuitive way, cannot be the result of chance or randomness. Instead, it requires methodological discipline which will ensure correctness, soundness, orthodoxy, and coherence of the constructed language. These, in turn, are indispensable conditions for objectivity, precision and clarity of communication of theological knowledge.[46] The post-conciliar revival associated with the enhancement of Mariology's biblical character inclines us to address the problem of the relationship between the modern language of Mariology and the language of the Bible.

The theologian, Edward Schillebeeckx, sees an urgent need to connect the entirety of dogmatic thought with thorough biblical exegesis. At the same time, the

---

45 Cf. Edward Schillebeeckx, "The Crisis in the Language of Faith as a Hermeneutical Problem," *Concilium* 9, no. 5 (1973): 31–45; Edward Schillebeeckx, *God the Future of Man* (London: Sheed & Ward, 1969); John Shea, *Religious Language in a Secular Culture. A Study in the Theology of Langdon Gilkey* (Mundelein, IL: University of St. Mary of the Lake, 1976); Langdon Gilkey, *Naming of Whirlwind: The Renewal of God-Language* (Indianapolis: The Bobbs-Merrill Company, 1969); Anton Grabner-Haider, *Glaubenssprache. Ihre Struktur und Anwendbarkeit in Verkündigung und Theologie* (Wien: Herder, 1975); Paul Ricoeur, *Hermeneutics and the Human Sciences: Essays on Language, Action and Interpretation* (Cambridge: Cambridge University Press, 1981); Józef Życiński, *Three Cultures: Science, the Humanities and Religious Values* (Tuckson: Pachart Publishing House, 1990); Günther Schiwy, *Neue Aspekte des Strukturalismus* (München: Kösel Verlag, 1971); Czesław Bartnik, "Możliwość stosowania analizy strukturalistycznej w teologii," *Znak* 25 (1973): 720–38; Peter Richardson, Charles Mueller and Stephen Pihlaja, *Cognitive Linguistics and Religious Language* (New York: Routledge, 2021).

46 Stanisław C. Napiórkowski, *Matka naszego Pana* (Tarnów: Biblos, 1992), 97–9; cf. Stanisław C. Napiórkowski, "Où en est la mariologie?" *Concilium* 3 no. 29 (1967): 97–112.

connection between dogmatic theology and biblical theology acquires the necessary character and results from the very essence of Christian revelation, which by definition has a dialogic dimension.[47]

Revelation is not a static code of truths of faith, but a vivid dialogue between a human being and God held within a historical context; a dialogue which leads to the formation of the language that communicates redemption and takes the form of things, words, texts, people, and events.[48] The awareness of the revelation – constituted by God's words and deeds, and handed down in the Tradition – is gradually growing in the People of God. This awareness consistently tends to be expressed in scriptural language, which, as an important element, co-creates the Church.[49] Due to the Bible, theology from the very beginning seems to have had a pre-existing language, which constitutes the basis for the further shaping of dogmatic language.

Mariology arises from biblical exegesis, although it is not identified with it. By analogy, Mariological language is created on the basis of the biblical language, but is not limited to it, because it cannot treat the Bible in an instrumental way as a formal, external or literary justification for the theses expressed as a result of previous speculation. Within theological *topoi*, the Bible always comes in the first place, being a constitutive source of knowledge and argumentation as well as the norm of every theological undertaking (*norma normans non normata*). Biblical Mariology has a critical function in dogmatic theses which are a systematic expression of God's revelation by means of a new, more adequately formulated contemporary language. The reception of the Word of God can take different forms, depending on the historical and social context of the particular era. The way that Divine Revelation is being reinterpreted again and again is called "Tradition."[50]

The Bible is read and interpreted in a dual context. The first context is specifically biblical and remains unchanged. It is the subject of exegetical analysis and leads to the emergence of biblical theology. Research on this context is intended to answer the question of how the Word of God addressed to the Chosen People and the original Church was heard, understood and expressed in the language of faith appropriate to the mentality of the time. The second context concerns the historically changing cultural and social environment. The purpose of dogmatic research into this context is to determine the conditions necessary for a modern, faithful understanding of the biblical message and to express the message in a

---

47 OTh, 127.

48 MMV, 19–20.

49 Edward Schillebeeckx, "Verschillend standpunt van exegese en dogmatiek," in *Maria in het boodschapsverhaal. Verslagboek der zestiende Mariale Dagen 1959* (Tongerlo: Secretariaat der Mariale dagen – Norbertijner Abdij, 1960), 57.

50 OTh, 127–8.

sound and understandable language of faith. Both contexts are in a close and inseparable relationship with each other; however, the understanding of the Word of God contained in the Bible, by virtue of belonging to the constitutive phase of Revelation, is the norm for a faithful understanding of this reality in the post-apostolic Church. In addition to the written Word of God, Schillebeeckx also notices the Word's current reality, present in the human subject, which is the work of the Holy Spirit and which he calls *locutio interna*. The language of faith and theology is born of an internal encounter *here and now* between God revealing Himself and the *anamnesis* of reality confirmed by the Bible and Tradition.[51]

Applying the Flemish theologian's principle to Mariology, one can easily conclude that the shape of Mariological language is determined not only by the scriptural language of the Bible, but also by the Holy Spirit currently working within the Church, which, in the context of modernity, reveals what is important in the biblical message. The Holy Spirit becomes the creator of contemporary horizons of understanding and a hermeneut of the biblical meaning for the needs of the language of faith.

The language of Mariology does not stop at expressing the literal understanding of the biblical text, but wishes to add a deeper reality defined by the term *sensus plenior*.[52] Extraction and expression of the fuller meaning of the text assumes the use of historical, philological and literary methods. Due to the fact that the Word of God was expressed in a human way, there is a specific semantic split between the literal sense or meaning (*sensus litteralis*) and the fuller sense or meaning (*sensus plenior*). The typology of meanings results from the very structure of the biblical word which is divine in a human way. The task of Mariological language is then (1) to discover and express clearly the Mariological sense of the biblical images of the Church contained in the book of Revelation and the Gospel of John; (2) to highlight the relationship between the Old Testament motifs concerning the dwelling of God among His people and the infancy gospels; and (3) to connect the eschatological understanding of the Daughter of Zion and the holy city of Jerusalem with the figure of Mary.[53] The Old Testament ideas thus become a prism in the theological view on Mary, and their transposition onto the Mother of God is an expression of the gradual increase in the Mariological awareness of the Church. The use of biblical categories in the language of Mariology is the effect of these procedures.

Schillebeeckx recognizes the objective dynamics of the biblical *sensus plenior*, which has an important internal relationship with the dogma. "Church dogmas are not some theologically expressed conclusions drawn from the New Testament data;

---

51 OTh, 144.

52 OTh, 148; Schillebeeckx, "Verschillend standpunt van exegese en dogmatiek," 64.

53 OTh, 135: cf. Hugolin Langkammer, *Maria in der Bibel. Was will die Offenbarung von der Mutter Jesu sagen?*, (Wien: Rozenkranz-Sühnekreuzzug, 1988), 95–115. See Aristide Serra, *Myriam, fille de Sion* (Paris: Mádiaspaul, 1999).

they are not *sensus consequens,* but have a much more internal connection with the *sensus plenior* of the Bible. They are an expression of what already existed vaguely in the apostolic consciousness. Theological thinking has an irreplaceable role in making this expression possible in the life of the faith of the Church directed by the Magisterium of the Church."[54]

Taking into account the *sensus plenior* of the relevant biblical texts, Mariological language undertakes the task of expressing *explicitly* those dogmatic contents which in the apostolic consciousness were formally revealed by God and thus formally, and not only virtually, revealed. It should be remembered that the knowledge of *sensus plenior* is not acquired in a single act of exegetical analysis of the selected texts, but extends in time onto the entire hermeneutic process implemented in Tradition. This gradual increase in the dogmatic awareness, which takes place due to the work of the Holy Spirit and under the guidance of the Magisterium of the Church, leads to the search for a new form of language based on the results of exegetical analysis. Dogma expressed in a particular type of theological language might have changed its wording throughout the history, without, however, violating the essential biblical content that constitutes its core.[55]

The literal sense, which actually exists and has its own autonomy, does not exhaust the depth of meaning of the Old Testament texts, because the entire Old Testament remains internally oriented to Christ and that meaning is fulfilled in Christ (Luke 24:44). Jesus is a hermeneutic prism in reading all Old Testament literature. Thanks to its objective dynamics, the literal sense becomes the carrier of a deeper sense. In the context of awaiting the Messiah (*Messias-verwachting*), the books of the Old Testament gain a new and deeper interpretation already in the translation of the Septuagint.[56]

For the language of Mariology, the Holy Bible has a particular significance because it is the source and the testimony of the reality which we theologically call Tradition (*caput divinae traditionis*).[57] Hence, dogmas formulated in a particular type of language do not constitute theologically simple conclusions of exegesis, but can be known as a vivid reality, truly existing in the Bible. Due to the universal purpose of the Bible for people of all times, Mariology must make a permanent reinterpretation of the experience of faith recorded in the books of the Bible.[58]

---

54 OTh, 135. [translation mine]
55 Edward Schillebeeckx, "O katolickie zastosowanie hermeneutyki. Tożsamość wiary w toku jej rein-terpretacji," *Znak* 20 (1968): 980.
56 Schillebeeckx, "Verschillend standpunt van exegese en dogmatiek," 70–1.
57 OTh, 138–140.
58 "De Schriftuur blijft immers een *levend* boek van alle gelovigen. Zij werd in de postexilische tijd gelezen en herlezen in het licht van nieuwe volksgebeurtenissen en in het licht van de steeds meer gespannen Messias-verwachting, zodat door het synagogale bidden van wellicht in vroeger tijden

Reliable exegetical and historical research is the basis for creating an adequate Mariological language which would convey a substantially proper image of Mary. According to Schillebeeckx, the source of dogmatically erroneous Mariological views lies in the so-called "Protoevangelium of James" (or "Infancy Gospel of James") and other apocryphal writings.[59] Apocryphal literature, despite its Christian origin and known pietistic values, contains many elements of folk fantasy that lead to Gnostic and Docetic Mariological interpretations. They stand in clear opposition to the image of Mary conveyed by the Gospels.[60] Therefore, realizing the conciliar postulate of returning to the sources (*redditio ad fontes*), one should build the language of Mariology on the solid foundations of contemporary exegesis which is a methodological safeguard against the temptation of uncritical maximalism.

Schillebeeckx is clearly in favor of pneumatology and Christology in Mariology (*een pneuma-christologische mariologie*). In other words, he approves of the primacy of the pneumatological perspective in the language of Mariology and of the need to take into account the entire plan of salvation, in which Christ occupies the central place. Starting from an authentically evangelical interpretation of Mary, an updated Mariology (*een geactualiseerde Mariologie*) with an ecclesio-typical profile should be created. The starting point for the renewal of Mariological language is the question about the relationship between the theological image of Mary crystallized in the course of Tradition and her biblical image. This constitutes an attempt to show Mary from a critical and historical point of view. The result of such an adopted method would be the achievement of the golden mean between Mariological minimalism and maximalism, which would avoid both theological and sentimental exaggeration, as well as the rationalist reduction of the mystery of Mary.[61]

---

geschreven psalmen deze gebedshymnen aan messiaanse uitdrukkelijkheid wonnen. De Septuaginta-vertaling is niet zelden de getuige van een dieper begrijpen en interpreteren van Schriftuur naar aanleiding van het geëvolueerde geloofsbewustzijn van het Judaïsme, en daarom een hulp bij het opsporen van de <sensus plenior>, zo zelfs dat er in de laatste jaren weer stemmen opgingen ter verdediging van het geïnspireerd karakter van deze vertaling." Schillebeeckx, "Verschillend standpunt van exegese en dogmatiek," 71.

59 MGVM, 38.

60 Cf. Józef Kudasiewicz, *Matka Odkupiciela* (Kielce: Wydawnictwo "Jedność," 1996), 182–5; Czesław Bartnik, *Matka Boża* (Lublin: Wydawnictwo KUL, 2012), 104–6; Stanisław C. Napiórkowski, *Mariologia polsko-syberyjska* (Lublin: Wydawnictwo KUL, 2023), 29–34.

61 MGVM, 30; cf. Gérard Philips, *Dogmatische Constitutie over de Kerk "Lumen Gentium." Geschiedenis, Tekst, Kommentaar*, vol. II (Antwerpen: Patmos, 1968), 229–31; Peter Hünermann, "Theologischer Kommentar zur dogmatischen Konstitution über die Kirche *Lumen gentium*," in *Herders Theologischer Kommentar zum Zweiten Vatikanischen Konzil II*, eds., Peter Hünermann and Bernard J. Hilberath (Freiburg im Breisgau: Herder, 2004), 263–563; Joseph Ratzinger, "The Ecclesiology of the Constitution *Lumen Gentium*," in Joseph Ratzinger, *Pilgrim Fellowship of Faith. The Church as Communion* (San Francisco: Ignatius Press, 2005), 123–52; Salvatore M. Perrella, "Concilio Vaticano II," in *Mariologia*, eds., Stefano de Fiores etc. (Cinisello Balsamo: Edizioni San Paolo, 2009), 308–19.

Historical changeability is an important feature of the language of faith. The reality of Divine Revelation was expressed in the New Testament by means of words and terms taken from pre-Christian society. By giving those terms a specifically Christian meaning, Revelation took the form of a "linguistic event."[62] It follows that the reality of Christian Revelation can be perceived only by means of the historical language of faith.

According to Schillebeeckx, the language of faith is created on the basis of the common human language which constitutes a "form of human life." Historically speaking, Revelation did not take place in social and historical isolation, but in the context of the already existing, frequently different and conflicting interpretations, concepts and expectations. That is why the linguistic aspect in the presentation of Revelation cannot be defined as a non-temporal category, because there are different interpretative language models already within the New Testament. Hence, the shaping of Mariological language appears to be a historical and hermeneutic undertaking. Ignoring the historical dimension of the Revelation leads to the aberrations within the language of faith.[63]

The contemporary language of faith, which is a matrix for the language of Mariology, must take into account an important reference both to the past and to the future. It must be noted that the relationship with the past is not only theoretical but also practical. The past has a dynamic, internal, developmental dimension oriented towards the future. "Language will strive to realize what it expresses because there is an internal logic and a transition between orthodoxy and orthopraxy."[64] The attempt to create a comprehensible language of faith cannot rely on a simple, direct and passive evocation of the biblical language of the past treated as source material, because it is significantly conditioned by the historical, political, social and cultural background of the era in which it was created. Therefore, no historically conditioned language of faith can be absolutized.[65]

Mariological language based on the biblical language cannot remain closed to the broadly understood experience of modern reality. The task of Mariological language is to recall critically the past expressed in the biblical experience and to juxtapose it with the current experience. In this way, the language of Mariology would grow out of two sources simultaneously. "It has been understood better than before that Christian theology draws not from one, but from two sources, which must constantly remain in a mutual and critical relationship; namely on the

---

62 Schillebeeckx, "The Crisis in the Language of Faith as a Hermeneutical Problem," 31.

63 Ibid., 34–5.

64 Edward Schillebeeckx, "Die Theologie," in *Kirche in Freiheit. Gründe und Hintergründe des Aufbruchs in Holland*, eds., Edward Schillebeeckx et al. (Freiburg im Breisgau: Herder, 1970), 14–18. [translation mine]

65 Schillebeeckx, "The Crisis in the Language of Faith as a Hermeneutical Problem," 43.

one hand, it draws from the entire tradition of great Judeo-Christian experience, and on the other, from the modern human experience, which is Christian and non-Christian."[66]

Schillebeeckx clearly emphasizes that the world of human experience in the current existential situation is becoming an indispensable and determining condition which enables us to understand Divine Revelation in the context of the modern realities. The multitude and the diversity of concepts, interpretative models and literary genres used by the biblical authors have become the basis for attempts to create a new language of faith, which, taking into account the current wealth of experience, nevertheless remains faithful to the essence of the biblical message.[67]

The contemporary human experience is shaped, to a large extent, by the results and achievements of other sciences that provide theology not only with cognitive methods but also with substantive information that internally and directly regards the Christian faith. Rightly, then, the language of Mariology, shaped by history and becoming history, requires a renewal through dialogic openness towards other scientific disciplines. "Biblical interpretation of reality requires a new update, because the reality in which the believer now lives and which he or she is a part of is no longer the same as the reality actually interpreted in the Bible and the Tradition derived from the Bible. Besides, this phenomenon can be found already in the Bible itself: *relectures bibliques* – a re-reading of the original mission in the light of the changed historical, social and cultural conditions. That is why other sciences make an irreplaceable contribution to the expression of faith."[68]

On account of this, the language of Mariology acquires an interdisciplinary character, treating other sciences as *loci theologici*. These sciences, using their own types of knowledge and interpretive models, contribute to the broadening of the scope of experience. They change the current picture of the world and of man, and affect significantly the content of theology. In this sense, they should be considered

---

66 Schillebeeckx, *Menschliche Erfahrung und Glaube an Jesus Christus* (Freiburg im Breisgau: Herder, 1978), 13; cf. Walter Kasper, *Glaube und Geschichte* (Mainz: Matthias-Grünewald-Verlag, 1970), 120–38. [translation mine]

67 Edward Schillebeeckx, *Interim Report on the Books Jesus & Christ* (New York: Crossroad, 1981), 3; cf. Schillebeeckx, *Jezus, het verhaal van een levende*, 328–58.

68 Edward Schillebeeckx, "Krytyczny status teologii" (*Critical Status of Theology*), *Concilium* (Materiały Kongresu "Przyszłość Kościoła," Brussels, September 12–17, 1970) special issue, Poznań-Warszawa 1971, 48. [translation mine]

a critical instance (authority) vis-a-vis theology and interpretations provided by theology.[69]

In light of the above analysis, it can be easily noticed that the language of Mariology, similar to the language of faith in general, can be a carrier of both meaning and non-sense in a specific historical human context. The great danger to the language of Mariology is posed by linguistic alienation consisting in the hermetic self-enclosure to the results of other auxiliary sciences; ideologization limited to a purely ideological and historical interpretation without showing any praxeological dynamics; and biblicism consisting in the mechanical translation of biblical language into contemporary language.

Mariological language must curb all the tendencies of exclusivity in order not to become a kind of "language ghetto" – closed to the reality of human experience.[70]

An important problem here consists in maintaining a sufficiently critical tension in the relationship between the message of faith conveyed by Tradition and the social environment in which this relationship takes place. Therefore, the task of Mariology is to constantly verify such language in terms of its significant connection with the experience of contemporary society in order to ensure sensibility, communication and cultural adaptation.

For Schillebeeckx, the entirety of theology takes the form of a hermeneutic process of updating and revising the content of faith.[71] The need for theological application of hermeneutics also in Mariology is the implication of this assumption. Faith requires understanding, and the truth was not revealed by God as *nuda vox Dei*, but was expressed in human words recorded in the Old and the New Testaments, which in themselves are already an interpreted response of faith to God's initiative. Reinterpretation of biblical texts is an attempt to rediscover the essential content of faith which can also communicate divine truth outside its original historical context and be expressed in the contemporary language of faith appropriate to the current situation of man. This hermeneutic situation, which consists of this awareness and the way of understanding human existence appropriate for each historical period, has become the basis for the reinterpretation of faith, the evolution of dogmas and the development of theological language. In this way, a "hermeneutic circle" arises from the historicity of human existence, in which the question, while arising from

---

69 Ibid., 48–9; cf. Edward Schillebeeckx, "Interdisciplinarity in theology," *Theology Digest* 24 (1976): 137–142; Stanisław C. Napiórkowski, *Jak uprawiać teologię?* (Wrocław: Wydawnictwo Wrocławskiej Księgarni Archidiecezjalnej, 1996), 37–51.

70 Schillebeeckx, "The Crisis in the Language of Faith as a Hermeneutical Problem," 34–6.

71 Schillebeeckx, "Krytyczny status teologii," 50.

the current historical situation, in a sense determines the answer, which after some time becomes the basis for new questions.[72]

The answer to the contemporary questions cannot be a literal repetition of the biblical text. At this point, there is a significant difficulty in identifying the "invariable or the unchangeable element" in the reinterpretation of faith while maintaining its identity. Traditionally, a distinction was made between the central dogmatic affirmation, which is a permanent core (*id quod*), and an external, variable or changeable way of presenting a given truth (*modus cum quo*). The biggest problem, however, is the accurate grasp of the essence of truth, which cannot be isolated from a historically variable interpretation. The hermeneutic problem becomes a dogmatic problem at this point, as it concerns the issue of the identity of faith in its contemporary attempt at reinterpretation and linguistic expression.[73]

Schillebeeckx proposes three basic hermeneutic principles that should be applied in the process of reinterpreting faith. They have a significant impact on the shape of Mariological language.

a) The Past in the World of the Present

A look into the past always originates from the present moment which in itself is already shaped by that past. The consequence of this statement is the fact that the history of the contemporary language of faith and theology influences the profile of the modern language of Mariology. Only in a narrowed meaning is the past a closed reality, because it concerns the present in one way or another; moreover, it would be otherwise cognitively elusive. The time distance between the biblical text and the contemporary interpreter is no longer seen as an obstacle to an objective interpretation, but rather as an ontological condition of this objectivity. This time distance cannot be erased in the contemporary attempt to interpret the Bible. The tradition of faith is a necessary hermeneutic bridge extending between the array of modern questions and the interpreted reality of the past. "Objectivity in terms of history is the truth of the past in the light of the present, not a reconstruction of the past in its incommunicable factuality. The literal repetition of the old formulas of faith is to familiarize us with the historicity of our human existence, and thus poses a deadly danger to strictly biblical orthodoxy."[74]

The tradition of faith is a necessary condition for the understanding of that faith. Through the future-oriented present, humans want to understand the past in a

---

72 Schillebeeckx, "O katolickie zastosowanie hermeneutyki," 979–83; cf. Czesław Bartnik, *Hermeneutyka personalistyczna* (Lublin: Wydawnictwo "Polihymnia," 1994), 192–6; Herbert Hammans, "Recent Catholic Views on the Development of Dogma," *Concilium* 21 (1967): 109–31.

73 Cf. Lothar Steiger, *Die Hermeneutik als dogmatisches Problem* (Gütersloh: Verlagshaus Gerd Mohn, 1961).

74 Schillebeeckx, "O katolickie zastosowanie hermeneutyki," 997. [translation mine]

creative way. At present, it is not possible to express the essential content of faith in a language other than the language of the present. Hence, the language of Mariology must take into account the fact that today's understanding of oneself directly participates in the interpretation of an old text. There is the phenomenon of the accumulation of tradition in the Bible, in which the older layers were reinterpreted in the light of the then present that expressed new experience(s). Depending on the historically changing experience, the very understanding of the text underwent significant modifications, creating the history of Tradition.[75]

Schillebeeckx rightly observes that "we cannot first delve into the past and only then, as if in the second instance, translate the result into our today's language, and express that past in terms of our contemporary consciousness. These two phases run in parallel. The task of reinterpretation is to find the right language in which the text can speak, because there is no interpretation *an sich* which would be valid for all times. The text gains an inner fullness in the present moment. Fertile creativity and simultaneous its relation with Tradition are present in the very act of understanding."[76]

The truth is always learned through interpersonal dialogue, hence the shape of Mariological language is the result of human cooperation. The language of Mariology is co-created as a result of the dialogue with the Bible and the Tradition of faith within the Church, not as a consequence of the solipsism of one's own beliefs.

b) The Present and the Past from the Perspective of the Promise

Schillebeeckx is against the so-called "new hermeneutics" represented mainly by Bultmann and Gadamer and based solely on the *hermeneia* of the humanities. The one-sidedness or partiality of the new hermeneutics approach, already recognized in part by W. Pannenberg and J. Moltmann, consists primarily in omitting the fundamental questions concerning the development of the future.[77] According to Schillebeeckx, it is a serious mistake of the "new hermeneutics" to limit the interpretation of the biblical text by referring it only to the present moment, and not taking into account its significantly internal future dimension. The present has been mistakenly treated here as an *eschaton*. The Bible clearly indicates the primacy of the future eschatological element over the present and the past, for the deposit of faith contained in the biblical texts does not constitute a closed reality, but is a

---

75 Edward Schillebeeckx, "Z hermeneutycznych rozważań nad eschatologią," *Concilium* 1–5 (1969): 36.

76 Schillebeeckx, "O katolickie zastosowanie hermeneutyki," 1002. [translation mine]

77 Cf. Krzysztof Góźdź, *Jesus Christus als Sinn der Geschichte bei Wolfhart Pannenberg* (Regensburg: Verlag Friedrich Pustet, 1988), 42; Jürgen Moltmann, *Theologie der Hoffnung* (München: Kaiser, 1965); Wolfhart Pannenberg, *Offenbarung als Geschichte* (Göttingen: Vandenhoeck & Ruprecht, 1967).

Promise which is constantly actualized in history and which takes on the shape of the future.[78]

The language of Mariology, arising from its biblical foundation and transforming itself in the stream of historical experience contained in Tradition, should take into account the element of Divine Promise, in the spirit of which the present must be interpreted. Due to its orientation toward the reality of the Divine Promise, the Bible-based orthodox language of Mariology takes on a futuristic character and becomes a *conditio sine qua non* of orthopraxy, which is an internal verification of the dogma referring in its essence to the eschatological future.

c) A Permanent Element of the Present, the Past and the Future

In the hermeneutics of history, one cannot ignore an important aspect of temporality that is essential for human existence, namely the awareness of time.[79] The past, which is present in the present and facing the future, leads consequently to the shift from interpretation to reinterpretation. The question that arises is to what extent the language of Mariology will be able to express the objective element of the continuity of faith in the dynamic reinterpretation of the reality which is heading towards eschatological finalization. The language of Mariology, intending to express precisely the understanding of faith, cannot be a pure description, an existential analysis of reality or a projection into the future. Instead, it must be an echo of obedience to the silent call of Divine Revelation as a still living reality. *Mystery-which-is-a-Promise*, which is indefinable but present throughout history, is the guarantor of the identity of faith in all consecutive ecclesiastical interpretations. The continuity of faith and of religious language realized in the course of history does not occur automatically, thoughtlessly, or without action, but requires a constant, confident, human activity oriented towards the future. An important condition for the proper and faithful relay of the biblical message is the deep embedding of the language of faith, and hence of Mariological language, in the context of the Church. The ecclesiastical nature of the language of faith determines, to a great extent, whether the new reinterpretation will be approved by the Magisterium of the Church as an expression of an understanding of the faith that is relevant for the given era. The language expressing faith has the element of development in it due to the fact that an understanding of faith has a historical character and therefore is not something final.[80]

---

78 Schillebeeckx, "Z hermeneutycznych rozważań nad eschatologią," 33.

79 Schillebeeckx, "O katolickie zastosowanie hermeneutyki," 1007; cf. Kasper, *Glaube und Geschichte*, 68–82.

80 Schillebeeckx, "O katolickie zastosowanie hermeneutyki," 1007–8; cf. Piet Schoonenberg, "Wierzę w życie wieczne," *Concilium* 1–5 (1969): 60–2.

Summing up the analysis carried out in this section, it should be emphasized that, according to Schillebeeckx, Mariology, like other fields of theology, does not use a formal, artificial language, but one that arises from the real, natural and colloquial religious language, which gradually, in the complicated process of transformation, reaches the level of language applicable to theological knowledge. The language of Mariology grows out of biblical language, but it does not identify with it and does not constitute its simple extension. Biblical language, similar to the language of each epoch, is conditioned by social and cultural factors, and therefore it cannot be uncritically transferred and mechanically woven into the modern language of Mariology which must remain open to the current experiences that shape natural, human language. Hence, the postulate of dialogue seems to be of particular importance. One could even think of confronting the language of Mariology with the results and achievements of other theological and non-theological disciplines in order to ensure its soundness and comprehensibility.

An important feature of Mariological language is constituted by its social and ecclesiastical character. The language of Mariology reasonably assumes the history of Tradition, i. e. the sequence of reinterpretations, which are treated as a condition for understanding the biblical message in the modern world. Schillebeeckx's appreciation for the historical dimension of human existence prompts the use of the hermeneutic method in Mariological research, which leads to the creation of a dynamic language that employs the categories of the past and the present in their essential connection with the eschatologically understood future. Language with a semantic leaning towards the future makes orthopraxy an important component of the revised and updated interpretation.

Despite many significant and theologically attractive conclusions, it seems that Schilleebeeckx's concept of the relationship between the language of Mariology and biblical language also has several weaknesses. The distinction between the colloquial language of faith and the language of Mariology, where the latter is a higher, systemically organized form of religious language, has not been made clearly enough. The language of Mariology, as a specialized language of theology, cannot be reduced to the status of a colloquial language, although it must maintain real contact with a specific living language as its base.

Schillebeeckx's thinking reveals an anti-philosophical tendency that does not allow for the construction of Mariological language within a coherent system. The sound postulate of linking Mariological language with the experience of the modern existential conditions without philosophical mediation will not achieve the intended result, as it will lead to linguistic particularization, confusion of the levels and the types of language, and to the weakening of its functional and cognitive efficiency. Resignation from developing a systematic language of theology carries the threat of semantic chaos.

Taking into account the fact of the historical development of any language, the relationship between morphological and content-related changes within the contemporary language of Mariology has not been presented in a very clear way. The problem of the contextual nature of Mariology, and thus its relation to the achievements of other sciences, requires a more thorough study, because, on the one hand, it would be a mistake to treat any field of theology as a synthesis of the results from other sciences, while on the other hand the hermetic closure of Mariology to dialogue with other sciences could lead to primitive conclusions and the disappearance of critical reflection. Hence, the question concerning the method of rebuilding the old language of Mariology into a new one remains open.

2. Mary's Epiphanic Function

A theologically correct understanding of Mary's epiphanic function in the light of the written Word of God contained in the Old and the New Testament requires us first to present, in its broad context, the relationship of the human person with the redemptive work of God which takes place in history.

The phenomenological category of an "encounter" (*ontmoeting*) taken from natural, colloquial language becomes particularly useful for the expression of the relationship between man and the living God in the mystery of revelation. Schillebeeckx states that "revelation and religion, that is, the encounter of the created and time-bound man with the uncreated God, constitute history by their very own nature."[81] The ontological result of this encounter is a community of grace which does not need an objective element of mediation. "This means that the community of grace constitutes a real inter-subjectivity between God and man – a partnership in which God personally addresses man and man personally responds to Him in faith. Meeting with God in faith is a modern, proper and suitable expression of the dogma of grace."[82]

Revelation is not a divine monologue, but a real meeting of persons during which God freely gives Himself in the act of encountering man. For Schillebeeckx, the experience of human encounter is the basis for a more precise definition of the semiotic content of the concepts of revelation and faith. Divine Revelation, like any other human encounter, has two constitutive elements: the presence of persons and faith understood as mutual trust embedded in the atmosphere of love.

---

81 Edward Schillebeeckx, *Christus sacrament van de Godsontmoeting* (Bilthoven: Nelissen, 1964), 15.
82 OTh, 22.

The act of faith is the opening of the human being towards the God Who reveals Himself, while experiencing the internal action of grace which is an invitation to take the initiative of a personal self-giving in faith. Divine Revelation and its human response remain in a dialogical correlation. God reveals Himself in history and brings salvation in it. Not only does He convey the message about salvation, but He also works in a salvific way in history whose meaning is simultaneously interpreted by means of the prophetic word.[83]

Edward Schillebeeckx strongly rejects the ahistorical Platonic way of understanding revelation that would come without any significant connection with the world, the human person and history. Christianity is not a static doctrinal reality but, above all, an event of God revealing Himself in a salvific way in human history. This revelation takes the form of an existential event in which divine reality enters human reality in a visible form.[84] God's entry into the course of human history causes a transformation which is significant in terms of quality. Secular history reaches the level equal to the history of salvation. As a result, according to Schillebeeckx, human history can be understood as the sequence of all historical facts and events through which God reveals Himself as our Savior.[85] Hence, God's activity in human history should be treated as one of the basic paradigms, because both the Old and the New Testament focus on the fundamental reality of the Kingdom of God which originates in the world, realizes itself in the person of Jesus Christ and in some way completes itself in the perspective of human history.[86]

Divine Revelation has a dialectical character. On the one hand, as an absolutely free initiative of divine love, it transcends every subjective human experience; while on the other, it can only be perceived in the context of human experience in which it manifests itself. As far as the genetic aspect is concerned, Revelation has its richest source in God and is in no way the effect of human efforts, plans, ideas or achievements. However, this does not exclude the fact that human intentions, plans, expectations and experiences were included in Divine Revelation.[87] Schillebeeckx emphasizes the necessary relationship between Revelation and experience. The sequence of human experiences throughout history becomes the medium for

---

83 Schillebeeckx, "Verschillend standpunt van exegese en dogmatiek," 55–7.

84 MMV, 19.

85 "Juist omdat God zelf onze geschiedenis is binnengetreden werd tot *heilsgeschiedenis* gemaakt: tot een zinvol verloop van historische feiten waarin en waardoor God zich als *onze verlossende God* toont." MMV, 19.

86 "In de godsdienst gaat het om het <rijk van God> dat *komt*. Het oude Testament spreekt slechts van <de komende God>. Het Nieuwe Testament is gecentreerd rond de komst van Christus: zijn geboorte en vertoeven bij ons. Zijn heengaan en zijn zending van de Heilige Geest en zijn wederkomst. De Kerk is dit wordende rijk Gods." MMV, 19.

87 Schillebeeckx, *Interim Report on the Books Jesus & Christ*, 11–12.

Divine Revelation. Schillebeeckx states openly that, "Revelation is communicated by means of a long process of events, experiences and interpretations."[88] In this way, experience becomes such an important part of the concept of revelation that one can reasonably speak of its experiential structure.[89] This means that transcendent reality manifests itself dynamically through human experience which is historically conditioned and broadly understood here.[90]

God's salvific action takes place in a significant and tangible connection with time, space, events, and human persons. All these components play an important role in the course of the history of salvation and have a universal meaning for all humanity. The focal point in the history of salvation is the Person of the man Jesus Christ, Who, being the living God, simultaneously acts in a human and historical form. In the story of Jesus, the human world and the divine world meet *par excellence*. The supra-historical dimension is integrated into the historical figure of Jesus Christ, in Whom the Trinity is revealed. As a result, the story of Jesus takes on a dual character. On the one hand, He is totally involved in the entire drama of the human fate which ultimately leads to death. On the other hand, from the point of view of plan for our salvation, the story of Jesus is a theophany, that is, a historically conditioned Divine Revelation in the context of earthly reality.[91]

In this way, Schillebeeckx unquestionably gives the event of Jesus Christ an absolute priority, exceptionality, uniqueness and irreducibility in the work of Divine Revelation. This, however, does not indicate an extreme revelatory exclusivity of Jesus Christ, according to which, Divine Revelation would be limited only to the phenomenon of Jesus and would be devoid of any connection with other created realities. In other words, considering the concept of revelation presented by the Flemish theologian discussed here, there is a sufficiently justified basis to give other persons a suitable function in the act of Divine Revelation. Undoubtedly, this applies above all to Mary as the Mother of Jesus.

According to Schillebeeckx, Mary is the most important person, after Jesus Christ, in the historical sequence of events. This means that Mary's role in the divine plan was determined by her maternal relationship with one particular Person – Jesus

---

88 Ibid., 11.

89 "De openbaring heeft plaats in de historische menselijke ervaringen in deze wereld, maar tegelijk roept zij ons uit de vanzelfsprekendheden van onze beperkte wereld. [...] Deze ervaringsstructuur van de openbaring zal op een uiterst pregnante wijze tot uiting komen in de christelijke openbaring die zijn aanvang heeft genomen in een historische ontmoeting van mensen met een medemens: Jezus van Nazaret. In hem verschijnt juist op de meest verrassende wijze in onze geschiedenis wat wij, mensen, nooit hadden kunnen bedenken." Schillebeeckx, *Gerechtigheid en liefde. Genade en bevrijding*, 54.

90 Cf. D'hert, *Een spoor voor ons getrokken. De Jezustrilogie van Edward Schillebeeckx*, 36–9.

91 MMV, 20.

of Nazareth. Such an important relationship between Mary and her Son, in whom the fullness of Revelation took place, means that her life has also gained revelatory value. That is why it is justified to treat Mary's life story as a personal and individual form of Divine Revelation. The earthly history of the Virgin of Nazareth becomes, due to God's choice, a history of salvation, i. e. a socially and culturally conditioned personal epiphany of God Who acts to redeem humanity.[92]

Schillebeeckx sees in Mary two irreducible and incomparable dimensions: historical and supra-historical. The historical dimension, related to a specific place of birth, way of upbringing, work, and lifestyle, is closely related to and remains in correlation with the supra-historical salvific dimension. The supra-historical dimension of Mary does not depreciate in any way her fully human personal world, her subjectivity, the dynamics of her religious experience, her feelings, or her participation in the hardships of everyday life, or in the history and the fate of her own nation. Many of the historical facts from Mary's daily life cannot be reconstructed and verified due to insufficient biblical documentation. The Bible presents only facts from Mary's life in which the supra-historical dimension, the one that plays a decisive role, is revealed. Certain events in her life take on the function of a privileged means of communication in the visible form of the act of salvation, constituting a blessed *kairos* in Mary's earthly history. The remaining minor tangential events build a natural background for the working of divine grace in the Virgin of Nazareth's daily existence. Schillebeeckx emphasizes that in order to fully understand the importance of Mary in the history of salvation and revelation, it is necessary to take into account in such research those events of her life which played a decisive role in redemption.[93] The epiphanic character of Mary finds its confirmation in the fact that it was in her person that God's universal will to save humankind was revealed and realized by means of human actions and events that took place in the history of the world.

In Schillebeeckx's theology, the category of history plays a particularly important role in the explication of the reality of revelation.[94] Human history has become the environment for God's salvific activity and the place where human response to

---

92 "De Maagd uit Nazaret is na Christus de hoofdpersoon in dit historisch gebeuren. Het gaat in de Mariologie derhalve om *het leven van een mens,* om een bepaalde persoon uit de wereldgeschiedenis: om de moeder van een bepaald mens, Jesus uit Nazaret. Maria is het mysterie van een moeder die een kindje kreeg! Doch dit historisch geconditioneerde leven is de *openbaring* van de verlossende Godsdaad die in het Maria-kind tot een ook historische werkelijkheid wordt." MMV, 20.

93 "Haar eigenlijke betekenis wint slechts begrip vanuit de bezinning op haar *beslissende* menselijke dade. Zij zijn op een eminente wijze de polen waartussen de verlossende daad van God in onze mensengeschiedenis doorbreekt." MMV, 21.

94 Cf. Edward Schillebeeckx, "Die Rolle der Geschichte in dem, was das neue Paradigma genannt wird," in *Das neue Paradigma von Theologie, Strukturen und Dimensionen,* eds., Hans Küng and David Tracy (Zürich: Benziger, 1986), 75–86.

the gift of divine grace takes place. History is essentially realized through human freedom, and therefore, depending on the positive or negative attitude of man towards God's salvific will, it can take the form of a history of salvation or non-salvation. Man can recognize God in the world not only as the Creator of earthly reality, but, above all, as the God of salvation, i. e. the Savior. Due to the universal salvific will of God, the world as creation and the world as human history as well as the encounter of God with man take on a new meaning which they do not possess by themselves. All reality appears in this light as a gift of the internal call which is full of divine grace, and at the same time as a *medium* through which man recognizes this internal invitation of divine grace; and finally, as a space in which man gives a positive or negative response.[95]

In this way, the history of salvation and non-salvation extends into all reality. Jesus Christ is the perfect presence and expression of God's universal salvific will, which is the heart of Christian Revelation. Although one can legitimately speak of anonymous Christian Revelation which extends onto the whole of human history, the specific historical Revelation recognized in Jesus Christ gains absolute primacy. Divine Revelation in the Person of Jesus Christ did not take place in isolation from other people, events, encounters, and worldly reality. As a result, Revelation engages other people who enter into a real relationship and play their respective roles in the Jesus event.[96]

The person of Mary, therefore, is not some irrelevant element, or an addition to the reality of God revealing Himself, but, on the contrary, her life is a specific history planned by God, in which His salvific intention is gradually manifested.[97] An important consequence of Mary's epiphanic dimension is her active participation in the dialogue between God and humankind which takes place through the historically conditioned humanity of Jesus Christ. Jesus is the Son of God Who speaks to people through His humanity. Jesus' humanity is the *medium* of Divine Revelation, and Mary has her maternal part in this humanity. In the mystery of Divine Revelation, she is a real Participant (*deelgenoot*) in the dialogue of salvation. Schillebeeckx emphasizes that "religion is essentially a personal relationship of man to God; it is a relationship of person to person. It is a personal meeting or a personal

---

95 OTh, 14.

96 "Op dit plan gaat het om *heilsfeiten:* gebeurtenissen, voorvallen, mensen en gemeenschappen, die *beslissend* zijn voor de heilsbestemming van het hele mensdom. Het centrum van die heilsgeschiedenis ligt in de *mens* Jesus: de levende, handelende God zelf in een echt-menselijke, historische gestalte." MMV, 19–20.

97 "Doch deze levensgeschiedenis is tevens *openbaring.* Zij is het tastbare, zichtbare, historische aspect van een *bovenhistorische afmeting* die het heil van alle mensen betreft. Daarom noteerde de H. Schrift slechts die menselijke feiten in het leven van Maria, waarin precies de bovenhistorische heilsafmeting *beslissend* werd." MMV, 20.

union with God. This is truly what life concentrated upon God is. Because God in His love takes the initiative and descends to meet man in grace, man begins to live in a state of active and direct communication with the one who in this relationship becomes a living God. The very act of this meeting between God and man, which on earth can only take place in faith, is called salvation."[98]

Phenomenology of the word presented by G. Gusdorf in the book *La parole* is the philosophical foundation of the dialogic and dynamic concept of revelation. Schillebeeckx recalls a significant sentence from Gusdorf's work: "venir au monde, c'est prendre la parole."[99] The sentence means that the word and human speech are an important element in the realization of a person's humanity. The word is the way of human existence and one of the most typical forms of encounter. Man's religiosity is also realized in the dialogue with the living God.[100]

Based on Schillebeeckx's assumptions, it can be concluded that Mary is the personal medium of Divine Revelation, but in a slightly different sense than the Revelation which takes place in Jesus Christ. Divine Revelation which takes place in Mary and in the history of her life is always auxiliary, preparatory and, consequently, secondary to Christ's Revelation.

In conclusion, it should be emphasized that although Schillebeeckx does not perform an exegetical analysis of individual Marian pericopes in terms of showing detailed epiphanic features in the life of Mary, he draws a more general conclusion – on the basis of a holistic view on the image of Mary contained in the Gospels – about the existence of scriptural grounds for recognizing the epiphanic dimension of Mary. The basic theological assumption is that God desires to bring about salvation with the participation of man, which further leads to the conclusion that Mary represents a significant reference to a God Who participates in history. There is an appreciation of the reality created as part of the divine plan of salvation. Mary is not a silent witness to God's wonderful interventions, but she herself tell us something about God. Considering the dynamic concept of Revelation as inseparably connected with experience, one can legitimately consider Mary as a person whose life story became the stage for God's epiphany.

---

98 Schillebeeckx, *Christus sacrament van de Godsontmoeting*, 14.

99 Georges Gusdorf, *La parole* (Paris: Press universitaries de France, 1956), 8.

100 OTh, 36; cf. Edward Schillebeeckx, *Gott, Kirche, Welt* (Mainz: Matthias-Grünewald Verlag, 1970), 62–8.

3. The Mystery of Mary's Faith

The image of Mary contained in the Bible encourages us to undertake a theological reflection on the mystery of her faith.[101] Schillebeeckx strongly rejects the erroneous opinions, probably based on Stoic philosophy, which state that the life of the Nazareth family was a kind of fabulous existence, free from the burdens of everyday life. This false image is contrasted with a realistic vision of Mary's earthly fate, which takes into account the necessity of hardships and life struggles, including those regarding faith. The belief that Mary received some kind of vision during the Annunciation is based on medieval legends and has no biblical justification. The true greatness of Mary is revealed in the mystery of her life in faith which gradually grew thanks to meditation on the Word of God while in close contact with her Son.[102]

To highlight the dynamism and the development of faith in Mary's life, Schillebeeckx makes an exegetical analysis of the text of the Annunciation in comparison with the corresponding passages from the Old Testament. Thanks to this procedure, a significant similarity of the following passages has been found: Luke 1:28–31 and Zephaniah 3:14–17; Luke 1:32–33 and 2 Sam 7:12–13; Luke 1:42, 45 and Judith 13:23–24.

Particularly noteworthy is the verse: "The Holy Spirit will come upon you, and the power of the Most High will overshadow you; therefore the child to be born will be called holy, the Son of God" (Luke 1:35). It is impossible to find directly the right parallel to the above quote in the Old Testament. There is, however, a close connection between the term "the Son of God" and the Old Testament idea of "*shekinah*" which expresses the presence of God among His people on earth.[103]

Analysis of the above fragments leads, according to Schillebeeckx, to two conclusions. First of all, the texts from the Gospel of Luke completely conform to the Old Testament ideas about the Messiah. Secondly, the analysis of the relevant passages of the angel's message leads to the acknowledgment of the premises due to which Mary might have presumed that her Son was indeed God.[104] The exegesis of

---

101 The issue of Mary's faith is a fundamental Mariological theme of the Gospel of Luke, cf. Krzysztof Mielcarek, "Mary in the Apostolic Church in the Light of Lucan Writings," *Biblical Annals* 10, no. 4 (2020): 602–6; Bartnik, *Matka Boża*, 83–4; Andrzej Napiórkowski, *Maryja jest piękna. Zarys mariologii i maryjności* (Kraków: Wydawnictwo Naukowe UPJPII, 2016), 52.

102 MMV, 21–2; cf. Wojciech Życiński, *Matka, która pozostała Dziewicą* (Kraków: Scriptum, 2017), 129–130; Ortensio da Spinetoli, *Maryja w Biblii* (Niepokalanów: Wydawnictwo Ojców Franciszkanów, 1997), 83–6.

103 MMV, 26; Edward Schillebeeckx, "Het geloofsleven van de *dienstmaagd des Heren*," *Tijdschrift voor Geestelijk Leven* 10 (1954): 246.

104 MMV, 26–27. Schillebeeckx uses the research results of the famous Dominican exegete, Pierre Benoit (1906–1987).

the text, carried out by Schillebeeckx, seeks to answer the question of how Mary understood the words: "Therefore the child to be born will be called holy, the Son of God" (Luke 1:35).

Given the Old Testament tradition, which has repeatedly used the expressions "Son of the Most High" and "Son of God" with reference to the entire chosen people and to individuals (princes, judges, or kings), there is no reason to claim that Mary understood this title in a different way than according to the Old Testament tradition. Mary understood the term "Son of God" with reference to her future child as the long-awaited Messiah, as someone great sent from God, and particularly closely associated with God.[105] Therefore, the content of the angel's annunciation does not allow for a definite declaration of the divine nature of the Messiah to be born.

On the basis of the research conducted so far, the following questions arise: Was Mary aware of the divine nature of her Son, Jesus, from the very moment of Annunciation? What motivated her to give a positive response expressed by the word *fiat*? To what extent did Mary's awareness of her Son's mission develop and deepen throughout her life? Can one reasonably speak of Mary's gradual growth in her faith?

Mary's positive response in the mystery of Annunciation leads to a thesis that God enlightened Mary's spirit with a special grace – the light of faith which allowed her to accept the mystery of the unpredictable promise in complete obedience. On the basis of such an assumption, it can be acknowledged that everything *implicitly* expressed in the Marian *fiat* would gradually grow until it reached the state of full consciousness. The emphasis on the deeper meaning concerns not only the content of the Annunciation itself, but also the messianic trends contained in the Old Testament.[106] It follows that Mary did not have to have the *explicit* awareness of her Son's divine nature at the time of the Annunciation in order to express unconditional consent to the divine plan.

According to Schillebeeckx, a synthesis of two eschatological tendencies present in the Old Testament tradition took place in Mary. One was vertical and emphasized the truth that YHWH is the savior of Israel and He Himself would intervene at a specified time. The other tendency was horizontal and concerned the Messiah, i. e. a man who would be a tool in YHWH's hand. Both tendencies gradually became closer, focusing on the figure of Jesus Christ, the Son of God.[107]

Because of the supernatural gift of the light of faith, Mary displayed a sensitive readiness to accept and fulfill the messianic promises contained in the Old Testa-

---

105 MMV, 28.

106 MMV, 29.

107 "Bij de Boodschap is Maria de exponent van de oudtestamentische Gods- en Messiasverwachting, de synthese en het topverlangen van het joodse, messiaanse verlangen." MMV, 30.

ment. The Flemish theologian recognizes an important parallelism between the individual person of Mary and the collective people of Israel. Mary is an individual summary or a representation of Israel, which is clearly confirmed by the first part of the pericope on Annunciation. YHWH, Who comes to live among the people of Israel, becomes present in Mary's womb.[108] According to Schillebeeckx, Mary, aware of the messianic tradition and its importance, had a sense of the depth of the reality that was hidden in the person to be born of her, i. e. the Son of God. The allusion to "*shekinah*" contained in the description of the Annunciation even further emphasizes the special, immanent presence of God in Mary's life. As described in the Gospel of Luke, Mary, as the representative of all Israel, realized that her child would not only be an ordinary person with a specific religious mission to fulfill, but also a child whose nature would far exceed all human understanding.[109]

Taking into account the results of exegetical analyzes and attempts at psychological interpretation of Mary's reactions, Schillebeeckx draws an extremely important conclusion for realistic Mariology: Mary's faith as well as her religious life are not a static reality but are subject to the rules of development. This development, however, does not proceed from the state of positive ignorance towards a positive recognition or reaching the maximum state of knowledge, but rather from a blurred, though real consciousness, to reaching full awareness.[110] This internal growth in Mary's faith is sufficiently attested in the Bible. It is sufficient to consider Luke 2:33, 48, 50.[111]

The question arises about the period of time during which the significant development of faith took place and about determining the factors that caused this growth. Schillebeeckx gives a definite answer by seeing the decisive phase in the development of Mary's faith in the period between the Annunciation and the first

---

108 "Immers in het eerste deel van Boodschap wordt Maria vanwege het schriftuurlijk parallellisme gezien als het persoonlijk résumé van Israël. <Jahwe die in Israëls schoot komt als een heiland> (Sophonias) staat, zoals we zeiden, in parallellisme met Jesus, d. i. Jahwe-Heiland, die Maria in haar schoot ontvangt (Lucas). Levend in de lijn van het oudtestamentisch messianisme voorvoelde Maria de diepte van de werkelijkheid: Zoon Gods." MMV, 30–1.

109 MMV, 31; Edward Schillebeeckx, "Beata quae credidisti," *Biekorf* 36 (1954): 1–23.

110 "Heel de ontwikkeling van Maria's geloofsleven is dan ook niet een ontwikkeling van <positief niet-weten> tot <wèl kennen>, maar van onuitdrukkelijk doch reëel besef tot uitdrukkelijke bewustwording." MMV, 31; cf. Schillebeeckx, "Het geloofsleven van de *dienstmaagd des Heren*," 254–5.

111 MMV, 32. The gradual development of faith, which is a feature of all the redeemed, also takes place in Mary and is not diminishing for the Virgin of Nazareth, but rather it reveals her true destiny: cf. René Laurentin, *La Madonna. Questione di teologia* (Brescia: Morcelliana, 1964), 145; Franco Cecchin, *W poszukiwaniu Maryi. Komentarz egzystencjalny do encykliki "Redemptoris Mater"* (Warszawa: Wydawnictwo Księży Marianów, 1989), 35–37. M. Kluz, *Mary as a Model of Faith and Moral Life for the Contemporary Disciples of Christ*, "The Person and the Challenges" 8/1 (2018), 157–9.

miracle of Jesus in Cana of Galilee. The decisive factor in the development of Mary's faith was the so-called hidden life of Jesus, during which the mutual family closeness of the Mother and the Son became for Mary a perfect environment for the growth of her faith. For Mary, the years of the hidden life of Jesus were a gradual revelation of the mystery of Christ.[112]

Schillebeeckx particularly appreciates the stage of the hidden life of Jesus by perceiving it as a source of sanctification for Mary and a time of intense development of her faith. This stage played a significant role in Jesus' life and His revelation. While the apostles knew Jesus through His miracles and teaching, Mary knew her Son not so much through His public activities, but rather through the mystery of family intimacy in their home at Nazareth.[113]

Schillebeeckx uses the method of psychologization in the interpretation of family relations between mother and son. He emphasizes that dialogue, so important for the growth and the tightening of family ties, was not limited to a verbal conversation and did not concern the issues of future miracles or even paschal events, but took the form of an interpersonal exchange of spiritual gifts which took place at the deepest level of the religious life. However, a more precise definition of these mutual gifts is not possible and must remain a mystery.[114]

The central truth arising from the biblical image of the Mother of God is the fact of Mary's gradual growth in faith through everyday close contact with the humanity of Christ and with His Person. Despite the great privilege of the Immaculate Conception, Mary was not exempted from the universal law of gradual maturation in the spiritual life. Permanent contact with the reality of salvation realized in the atmosphere of hope and love is the factor which contributes to the growth of faith. At present, for the community of believers, this meeting takes place through the sacraments. In the case of Mary, the encounter with the reality of salvation took place in a unique way, i. e. through the motherly relationship with her Son. On the basis of the above, Schillebeeckx considers Mary as a prototype of the Church on pilgrimage on earth, and because of her Assumption also as a prototype of the eschatic Church.[115]

Considering the dynamic development of faith which takes place in the person of Mary, one can see in her an example of spiritual life for modern man. The realism with which Schillebeeckx presents Mary in the aspect of her faith makes the modern man perceive her as a sister who was perfect in her faith. The faith that

---

112 MMV, 32.

113 MMV, 34.

114 MMV, 34.

115 MMR, 32; cf. LG 69; RM 6, 47; LF 58–59; CCC 972; J. Salij, "Maryja eschatologiczną ikoną Kościoła. (Refleksja na marginesie KKK 972)," in Stanisław C. Napiórkowski, Bogusław Kochaniewicz, eds., *Maryja w Katechizmie Kościoła Katolickiego* (Kraków: Bratni Zew, 1996), 89–95.

grew gradually was present in every moment of Mary's life. It constituted a spiritual reality which Schillebeeckx calls a self-sacrificing faith and which was not subject to the pressure of human calculations concerning the unknown future events.[116]

The reality that Mary experienced seems to contradict the idea of the royal Messiah contained in the message of the Annunciation. The Bible clearly shows that Mary's faith developed in the face of growing contradictions whose apogee was the hour of the cross. Schillebeeckx sees in Mary's attitude a clear analogy to the sacrifice of Abraham. Mary, believing against all hope, persisted in faith even at the hour of her Son's death on the cross. In this act she rose even above the faith of Abraham, who ultimately did not have to sacrifice His own Son.[117]

This attitude of faith amid contradictions was shaped in Mary by Jesus also during His public activities. Jesus personally showed His mother the truth that, while being truly her Son, He also remained completely independent of her. Through the events in the Temple in Jerusalem and the wedding in Cana of Galilee, Christ gradually revealed Mary's proper role in the act of Redemption.[118] In response to the words of a woman: "Blessed is the womb that bore you, and the breasts that you sucked," Jesus said: "Blessed rather are those who hear the word of God and keep it!" (Luke 11:27–28). Schillebeeckx sees in Jesus' response the highest appreciation for His mother's faith. In this way, Mary became a prototype of the Christian life in faith.[119]

Mary's faith reached its maturity in the hardships of everyday existence. Schillebeeckx rejects the unrealistic, idyllic and static model of holiness, which would be a carefree and joyful experience of the closeness of God, devoid of suffering and burdens. Although through the privilege of the Immaculate Conception Mary never committed a sin, she was not isolated from human conflicts or sins, and thus she was exposed to the suffering caused by others. The theologian from Nijmegen emphasizes the realism of Mary's life and her full solidarity and participation in human fate. The uniqueness and greatness of the Virgin of Nazareth is not manifested in the absence of difficult, painful or dramatic situations, but in a strong, persistent

---

116 MMR, 33.

117 MMV, 34–35. The similarity between Abraham's and Mary's obedience to faith, as well as Mary's pilgrimage in faith were demonstrated by John Paul II in *Redemptoris Mater* 14–17; cf. Cecchin, *W poszukiwaniu Maryi*, 34; Bartnik, *Matka Boża*, 175; Wacław Siwak, *Fiat mihi secundum verbum. Maryja w Tajemnicy Wcielenia według Jana Pawła II* (Lublin: Redakcja Wydawnictw KUL, 2001), 57–8.

118 Ignace de la Potterie, *Mary in the Mystery of the Covenant* (New York: Alba House, 1992), 157–208; Adam Kubiś, *Jezus Oblubieniec. Metafora małżeńska w Ewangelii Janowej* (Rzeszów: Bonus Liber, 2023), 23–56.

119 "Maria is het prototype van het christelijk geloofsleven." MMV, 35; cf. MGVM, 49.

and constantly growing faith, which allowed her to survive even the death of the Messiah.[120]

Analyzing the relevant biblical texts, Schillebeeckx is looking for the key to discovering the secret of Mary's faith. This key is contained in the phrase "the handmaid of the Lord" (*dienstmaagd des Heren*). The term is closely related to Old Testament spirituality and contains several layers of meaning. It must be taken into account that the words uttered by Mary, "Behold, I am the handmaid of the Lord," derive from the Old Testament tradition and, in accordance with its semantics, they express complete dependence on God's will and readiness to totally put oneself at God's disposal. With reference to YHWH recognized as the sovereign ruler of Israel, the word "handmaid" denotes a deep conviction of belonging to God as His property.

In order to acquire a fuller understanding of the meaning of the term "handmaid," Schillebeeckx recalls the words of the *Magnificat* in which Mary describes herself as "*anawah*." "*Anawim*" are the poor of YHWH, i. e. God's servants who fear the Lord, unconditionally trust God, and seek refuge in him. They are humble and rejoice in God. The Old Testament books written after the Babylonian captivity are clearly marked by the spirituality of "*anawim*." The theme of "*anawim*" is discussed in the Sermon on the Mount by Christ, Who recognizes their unconditional readiness to accept the Kingdom of God. The revelation of the Kingdom of God to the poor and lowly is a confirmation of Christ's messianic mission. In addition, He reveals Himself as a real "*anawah*," quiet and humble (or gentle and lowly in heart).[121] The messianic prophecies contained in the Old Testament show the Messiah as a poor Servant of YHWH (cf. Isa 52:1). In the mystery of the Annunciation and the visitation to Elizabeth, Mary reveals the spirit of the "*anawim*," which manifests itself in total humility and readiness to receive the Son of God. Schillebeeckx sees in Mary the personification of Israel understood as the poor of YHWH.[122] The parallels: Christ-the servant of YHWH (*Servus Yahwe*) and Mary-the handmaid of YHWH (*Ancilla Yahwe*) seem to point to the christo-typical element in the Mariological reflection provided by the author in question.

The phrase "the servant/handmaid of the Lord" has yet another layer of meaning. This name is given to people who have a special role or mission to play in history. The complete openness and acceptance of God's plans is a distinctive feature here. Mary's words uttered at the Annunciation can be interpreted as an agreement to and the acceptance of the mission given by God – that of becoming the mother of the Messiah. Analyzing Mary's response carefully, "Behold, I am the handmaid

---

120 MMV, 35–6; cf. E. Schillebeeckx, "De zware strijd van Maria's geloof," *Thomas* 8, no. 2 (1954/55): 6–7; HK, 100, 194.

121 MMV, 38–9.

122 Schillebeeckx, "Het geloofsleven van de *dienstmaagd des Heren*," 226.

of the Lord; let it be to me according to your word," Schillebeeckx emphasizes her absolute openness, her unconditional readiness to accept God's plans and the complete freedom of her decision.[123]

According to Schillebeeckx, Christ revealed the essence of Mary's holiness in the Sermon on the Mount. The individual Beatitudes do not refer to an abstract ideal of a Christian, but are an expression of the reality that Christ experienced in the Nazareth house. As a result, Mary is an outstanding example of the realization of the spirit of the Beatitudes.[124] The positive development of Mary's faith is the result of a lasting and deep relationship with God, which was confirmed in the mystery of the Annunciation by the words, "The Lord is with you." The grace of the divine presence in Mary's life became for the Mother of the Lord a call to make a pilgrimage of faith.[125] Mary meets the forthcoming God half-way. The Incarnation event is the meeting of the living God with the person of Mary who represents all humanity that awaits the Messiah. The longing and waiting for the Son of God in the heart of the Virgin of Nazareth became an anticipation of the reality of the Incarnation in accordance with the Augustinian principle that Mary conceived first in her mind and then in her body (*prius mente quam corpore*). Mary's deep personal relationship with God created an optimal environment for the conception of Christ in love and faith. Participating in a divine-human dialogue of love, Mary became the real mother of the Incarnate Word through her pure love in faith.[126]

---

123 Schillebeeckx, "Het geloofsleven van de *dienstmaagd des Heren*," 227; MMV, 40.

124 "Wanneer Christus immers in de bergrede het heil van de <acht zaligheden> verkondigt, d. i. ten slotte de steeds herhaalde zaligprijzing van de *anaw* (de arme), dan had Hij niet een abstract-christelijk ideaal voor ogen, maar wist Hij dit ideaal reeds concreet verwezenlijkt: in huize Nazaret bij Maria en Jozef. Die <acht> zaligheden, vrucht van de H. Geest, zijn geen onbereikbare chris-telijke utopie, maar Christus' *heiligverklaring* van moeder Maria en van al wie leeft naar haar voorbeeld." MMV, 40. The idea of a Mariological interpretation of the Sermon on the Mount, previously suggested by Lagrange, was taken up and further developed by a Protestant theologian, H. Asmussen, in the book *Maria, die Mutter Gottes,* Stuttgart 1950. For more information on Asmussen's Mariological views, see: Stanisław C. Napiórkowski, *Spór o Matkę. Mariologia jako problem ekumeniczny* (Lublin: Wydawnictwo KUL, 2011).

125 MMV, 42.

126 "In Maria was alles *verwachting* en verlangen naar de komende God. Daarom ontving Zij ook God toen Hij metterdaad kwam. Haar verlangen was vooruit op de werkelijkheid van de zo tere ontmoeting in haar hart en in haar schoot, precies omdat God van het eerste ogenblik van haar bestaan met Haar was. De intimiteit van de mens Maria met haar God was zo innig dat God in zijn intimiteit met Haar, in haar nabijheid, als vlees van eigen vlees, tot mens kon en wou worden. Maria's moederschap kwam door louter gelovende *liefde tot* stand: gevende liefde vanwege God, wederliefde schenkende liefde van de Maagd die door geloof en liefde moeder werd van de Godmens." MMV, 42.

***

Summing up the analysis carried out in this section, it should be emphasized that in the image of the Mother of the Lord conveyed by the Gospels, the issue of Mary's faith, associated with her consciousness of Christ's divinity, comes first. The Gospel of Luke in particular exposes the dynamic and realistic concept of Mary's faith, which is subject to the rules of development and the challenges of life. According to Schillebeeckx, a gradual maturation of faith takes place in the person of Mary through the personal maternal love for her Son. The maternal-filial dialogue of love results in a mutual exchange of spiritual gifts. Biblical evidence undoubtedly indicates that Mary's faith grows out of the Old Testament spirituality of the poor of YHWH and is exemplary for all humanity. A particularly important thesis here is that Mary remains the prototype of the Christian life of faith (*prototype van christelijk geloofsleven*).

II. A Historical-Salvific Icon of Mary

Observing the development of Catholic theology from a diachronic perspective, one can easily see the pluralism of types and methods. Social and cultural changes constantly shape new theories of practicing theology as a science. In principle, every type of theology is subject to the law of aging as a venerable anachronism gives way to new substantive and formal propositions. The speculative method, commonly used before the Second Vatican Council, is slowly being replaced by the historical-salvific approach. Nowadays, the entirety of Catholic theology is undergoing a gradual transformation towards the historical-salvific approach.

Edward Schillebeeckx is undoubtedly one of the thinkers who promoted the historical-salvific theology recommended by the Second Vatican Council (*Optatam totius* 16), which is a natural consequence of emphasizing the biblical aspect in his scientific research. The application of the history of salvation to Mariology leads Schillebeeckx to attempt constructing a new type of Mariological reflection whose primary subject and source are no longer texts of the Magisterium's rulings, but a real, existential and historically conditioned accounts of human dialogue with God. Placing Mary at the center of the history of salvation results in building a realistic concept of her specific bodily and spiritual motherhood as the basic Mariological category. Through the realization of her maternal mission, Mary participates in the reality of both objective and subjective redemption.

1. Towards a Historical-Salvific Mariology

The crisis of speculative theology, which has been affecting almost all major academic centers for several decades now, postulates the development of a new type of theology: not an *a priori* speculation, but a thought construct based on the events from the history of salvation. According to Schillebeeckx, the deep split between textbook theology and kerygmatic theology is an anomaly that must be overcome as soon as possible. Using technical terms, Schillebeeckx emphasizes that theology which perceives reality only from the perspective of God's transcendent being (*sub ratione Deitatis*) must be complemented with a Christological approach (*sub ratione Christi*). As a result, the entirety of theology will become less abstract and metaphysical, and more specific and historical-salvific. What is meant here is the need to find and emphasize the meaning of salvation in real, human life.[127]

---

127 OTh, 265–6; 303–4.

For Schillebeeckx, the inspiration to develop a new type of theology can be found in the concept formulated by a Protestant theologian, Oscar Cullmann (1902–1999). According to the latter, history is understood in a linear way – as a sequence of interrelated divine interventions called *kairoi*. The fundamental *kairos* consists in the Incarnation of the Word and the redemptive work of Jesus, through which both the past and the future become understandable in the present.[128]

The interest in historical-salvific thinking has its source in contemporary philosophical trends, especially in existentialism, in which an attempt was made to combine philosophical concepts with the real experience of human existence. Purely conceptual thinking in relation to reality raises serious doubts here, and it is natural to seek supplementation. Anti-speculative attitude in theology is a symptom of the insufficiency of the solutions proposed so far.[129]

Schillebeeckx notes that, throughout history, the Church has reacted differently, and not always consistently, to the attempts of introducing philosophical concepts to theology. In the thirteenth century, Pope Gregory IX opposed the so-called philosophism in theology, while seven centuries later the encyclical of Pope Pius XII, *Humani generis*, opposed theologians who were in favor of experience and existential trends and who wanted to reduce the excessive amount of speculation. According to the Flemish theologian, the conclusion is that not every speculation must be assessed as wrong. There is a type of reflection that does not lead to a pure rationalization of supernatural reality, but allows a mystery to remain a mystery. Speculation can even help discover the practical meaning of dogmas for Christian life, as exemplified by the theology of Saint Thomas Aquinas. The adoption of the Aristotelian way of thinking by the Middle Ages resulted in the creation of an integral theological system. Without the support of philosophy, theology would fall into fideism or illuminism and would not manage the challenges of time. However, in this combination of philosophy and theology, there is a real danger of reducing or even negating the mystery dimension of Revelation itself. Another danger to the proper development of theology is an insufficient specification of concepts, which leads to the disappearance of a clear definition of dogma, its content and its development.[130]

Schillebeeckx recognizes the historical rule regarding the emergence of new theological trends in the heat of polemics and anathematism, when there is an intensified intellectual effort made. Any crisis leads ultimately to some sort of growth. From the historical point of view, the continual development of the secular culture,

---

128 Oscar Cullmann, *Christus und die Zeit* (Zürich: Evangelischer Verlag A.G., 1948), 17; cf. Krzysztof Góźdź, *Teologia historii zbawienia według Oscara Cullmanna* (Lublin: Redakcja Wydawnictw KUL, 1996).

129 OTh, 286–291.

130 OTh, 267–9.

i. e. the rise in human consciousness, has been reflected adequately in theology. The discovery of the dialectical method prompted its application to ordering the content of faith. The gradual introduction of Aristotelianism into the world of Western culture resulted in the emergence of speculative and philosophical theology. On the other hand, positive theology was a response to the application of the historical method in secular sciences. The history of theology confirms the fact that, along with the search for new types of theology, there has always emerged a temporary critical period of pilot study before proper balance is reached. From the sociological point of view, each epoch has an *a priori* right to hear God's voice, which helps accept or reject new theological trends.[131]

Bearing in mind the crisis of speculative theology, Schillebeeckx asks the following questions: What kind of theology does modernity expect, one based on abstract, metaphysical truths or one based on events from the history of salvation? Should theological explanations follow the method of *sub ratione Deitatis* or *sub ratione Christi*? Is the conceptual formulation of the mystery of faith a thing of the past or does it lead to a more reasonable theology?

According to the Dominican theologian, the answer to the above questions originates from the objective structure and depth of Revelation. If theology can be defined as the scientific status of the faith, and faith is a reality that lives in a reflective human subject, then the structure of Revelation itself will have to indicate objectively which path should be followed by modern theology: metaphysical and theocentric or historical-salvific and Christocentric.

Divine Revelation directed toward man is a fact that requires a more comprehensive definition of the way it is communicated. The following question arises: is Revelation a simple communication of knowledge and of divine truths, or is it concerned with the sacramental dimension of Revelation which takes place in human and historical form? According to Schillebeeckx, one cannot separate God's redemptive work from specific human (hi)story. God, through grace, becomes one of us (*Theos pros hemas, Deus propter nos*).[132]

It is true that we can actually affirm God as a personal being already in the act of creation, but the mystery of His internal personal life remains hidden at this stage. The work of divine grace is a totally free intervention into human history on God's part. God's work has a historical dimension in the sense that God Himself enters into personal relationships with people as part of an already constituted history, revealing His inner life in a partner-like dialogue with humanity, a dialogue which constantly evolves. Hence, it is only at the level of the history of salvation,

---

131 OTh, 269–270.

132 OTh, 270–1; cf. Schillebeeckx, *Gerechtigheid en Liefde. Genade en bevrijding*, 54; D'hert, *Een spoor voor ons getrokken. De Jezustrilogie van Edward Schillebeeckx*, 36–9; Wiel Logister, "De passie van en voor Jezus Christus," *Tijdschrift voor Geestelijk Leven* 1 (2009): 48–51.

which begins with the act of creation, that we can discover God revealing Himself to us as God in Trinitarian mystery. Divine Revelation *propter nos* culminates in the event of Christ, Who is the only Mediator of grace that comes through Him in a historical way, as clearly confirmed by St. Paul (Romans 8:39). The historical nature of grace, visible in the economy of salvation, results from the free initiative of God, Who engages in a dialogue with human freedom. Schillebeeckx emphasizes the personalistic and historical dimension of Divine Revelation, which is not a mere share of superhuman knowledge transmitted by the prophets and Christ. Revelation is a dynamic reality in which God's redemptive initiative has primacy in the structure of human history. Divine Revelation is realized in the deeds and words of God which are internally related to one another. According to Schillebeeckx, Christian Revelation presents God both as the philosophically expressed "first cause" of existing reality, and as a Savior acting truly within the history of the world He created, which, according to the Augustinian message, is the realization of Divine Providence in time (*historia dispensationis temporalis divinae providentiae*).[133]

The historical structure of Revelation, which is part of the divine salvific plan, has important implications for the theological method. Since, according to Schillebeeckx, the objective content of faith is given to us in the form of historical-salvific theophany, then theology cannot create thought structures detached from earthly realities, including history. Theology proper is contained in the economy of salvation.[134] This does not indicate, however, extreme historicism, which deprives human history of its mystery dimension. In principle, there are no contradictions between historical-salvific and speculative theology. God in His inner mystery is the real object of theology. He reveals Himself in the historically conditioned economy of salvation, that is, in Jesus Christ. According to Schillebeeckx, Aquinas's thought expressed in the words: "Christ as man is for us the path leading us to God" is *ipso facto* an acceptance of a theological method in which there is no room for a gap between life and the reflection on the content of life.[135]

Summarizing his reasoning, Schillebeeckx states that theology is essentially Christological in terms of its method, that is, its basis is always the history of salvation which culminates in the event of Christ. The theocentric and Trinitarian nature of theology, in turn, results from the fact that theology is a reflection about God Who addresses man in the economy of salvation (*Theocentrische <trinitarische> theologie met christologische methodiek*).[136]

The analysis presented above create a relevant context for addressing the problem of determining the relationship between historical-salvific theology and theological

---

133 OTh, 271–3.

134 St. Augustine, *De vera religione*, c. 7, PL 34, 128; OTh, 273.

135 OTh, 276.

136 OTh, 95.

concepts. According to Schillebeeckx, it is a grave mistake to separate the definition of the content of faith from the salvific value of that content or omit the definition itself. The content of faith is not some theological concept, but the God of Salvation Himself, in concord with Thomas Aquinas's statement that "the act of the believer does not terminate in a proposition, but in a thing" itself.[137] There is no faith without some degree of understanding. The structure of human consciousness is by its nature adapted to grasping reality only through the meaning of concepts. Hence, any intelligibility of the content of faith can only be expressed by means of concepts and their meanings. Therefore, if theology wishes to maintain the status as a science, it must accept the logical discipline imposed by the set of specific concepts it uses. In theology, there must be a conceptual definition of faith (*determinatio fidei*).[138]

According to Schillebeeckx, the speculative method should not lead to an extreme conceptualization of mystery, but protect the objective perspective of the mystery from misunderstandings. Ultimately, then, even in historical-salvific theology, metaphysics plays an irreplaceable role, although always a subordinate one. There is a close relationship between theology and philosophy because they both refer to the same reality, despite following different paths. The historical-salvific approach in theology leads to the discovery of a personal and dialogic relationship between God and man. On the one hand, an extremely conceptual theology results in a discord between faith and theology; on the other, anti-philosophical tendencies blur the specific content of Revelation. Hence, the ultimate postulate formulated by Schillebeeckx back in the 1960s was the need for complementarity of philosophical and historical-salvific approaches in theology.[139] The argument for applying philosophy to theology was constituted by the thesis on the existential unity between the order of creation and the order of salvation, strongly propagated by Schillebeeckx. In later years, the Flemish theologian gradually departed from these views, giving up theological thought based on a specific philosophical system.

In the light of the general assumptions of historical-salvific theology formulated by Schillebeeckx, his Mariological output will be assessed in order to determine how and to what extent the postulates of historical-salvific theology have been implemented in Mariology. Schillebeeckx resigned from the static, scholastic and purely speculative way of presenting Mariological truths, which was characteristic of many pre-conciliar textbooks. These textbooks treated Thomistic philosophy as the principle which explains and orders revealed truths. The professor from Nijmegen attempts to present Mariological issues from the historical-salvific perspective, emphasizing, already in the introduction to his basic Mariological work,

---

137 "Actus credentis non terminatur ad enuntiabile, sed ad rem." Sth II-II, q. 1, a. 2, ad 2.
138 OTh, 277–9.
139 OTh, 280–1.

the necessity for the contextual practice of Mariology, which would be connected with Christology and ecclesiology, and later with pneumatology.[140] The history of salvation as a concept is raised here to the rank of a prime category that shapes Mariological thought. The emphasis on the historical-salvific perspective is reflected in the analysis of the biblical image of the Mother of God which includes the latest exegesis. The theological vision of Mary is not constructed on the basis of metaphysical assumptions, but is the result of applying the historical-salvific method (*sub ratione Christi*) to the analysis.[141]

Mary's participation in the mystery of Christ and her role in the history of salvation are determined on the basis of a thorough analysis of the dialogic nature of the historically conditioned Divine Revelation which involves the human subject. The historical-salvific nature of the Revelation, which culminates in the Person of Jesus Christ, allows us to appreciate and emphasize Mary's personal activity in the realization of the historical acts of redemption.[142]

Schillebeeckx's attempt to present the *mysterium Mariae* in a historical-salvific manner leads to a realistic interpretation of the person of Christ's Mother. Mary's personal story, devoid of fictional embellishments typical of medieval legends, intertwines with the history of salvation. The individual, particular and unique story of Mary has an important, real and universal reference to the history of salvation of the whole world. In his Mariology, Schillebeeckx avoids arguments from authority. He does not analyze the texts issued by the councils or papal statements, but the actual redemptive meeting of man and God within the framework of human history. The historical-salvific approach does not exclude theological speculation or the use of metaphysical categories. Instead, the historical method complements classical theology. Emphasizing personalistic and existential aspects, it strengthens the realism of theological knowledge, while defending against the dangers of idealism and mythology.

Despite the emphasis on the economy of salvation, which is evidently innovative for his times, Schillebeeckx does not resign from using traditional theological concepts that organize and theoretically support the entire Mariological project. These concepts include "grace," "nature," "relationship," "revelation," "objective redemption," "subjective revelation," "sacrament," "Church," "charism," "office," and many others. His historical-salvific Mariology is influenced by important philosophical ideas derived mainly from the phenomenological interpretation of Thomism pro-

---

140 MMV, 13–15; MGVM, 39.

141 MMV, 43.

142 Schillebeeckx, "Verschillend standpunt van exegese en dogmatiek," 55–6; cf. Marinus Houdijk, "Edward Schillebeeckx," in *Modern Theologians. Christians and Jewis*, ed. Thomas E. Bird (Notre Dame, Indiana: University of Notre Dame Press, 1967), 92.

posed by Dominique-Marie De Petter, a professor from Leuven, and from the basic assumptions of the philosophy of dialogue.[143]

2. Mary's Redemption

Defining Mary's role in the history of salvation requires, first and foremost, a theological consideration of the unique nature of her personal redemption. Schille-beeckx, even before he begins any complex dogmatic analysis, clearly states that Mary, like any other human being, is a redeemed human being. Any false concept of Mary's "autonomous" holiness, understood without connection to the act of Christ's objective redemption, is thus excluded.

a) Mary's Immaculate Conception
The dogma of the Immaculate Conception implicitly confirms the fact that Mary is truly redeemed, but in a unique and different way than the rest of humanity. In Schillebeeckx's theological research, the problem of Mary's relation to original sin is fundamental. The universal solidarity of the human race in sin is not based only on the biological unity of the human community, but concerns its supernatural dimension. In the case of personal beings, *communio personarum* is established on the basis of a community of spiritual values in the unity of purpose, fate and calling. Biblical Adam as the progenitor of mankind is not a head in a biological or juridical sense, but in a religious and salvific one.[144]

Schillebeeckx emphasizes that the mystery of original sin can be properly under-stood only in the context of Adam's representative function, which is connected with the universal call of humanity to unity. As the father of humankind, Adam personally received from God a gift of grace for the whole of humanity. As part of the divine plan, Adam must be interpreted as a universal mediator of grace (*caput gratiae*). Due to Adam's sinful act, all humanity is deprived of God's gift and is faced with the situation of non-salvation, i. e. the lack of grace. The biblical confirmation of this reasoning can be found in Romans 5:12. There is, therefore, a causal rela-tionship between Adam's sin and the sinful condition of every human being, even

---

143 Jan Ambaum, *Glaubenszeichen. Schillebeeckx' Auffassung von den Sakramenten* (Regensburg: Pustet, 1980), 72; cf. Dominicus M. De Petter, *Begrip en werkelijkheid. Aan de overzijde van het conceptua-lisme* (Antwerpen: Paul Brand, 1964); Dominicus M. De Petter, "Een geamendeerde phenomenolo-gie," *Tijdschrift voor Philosophie* 22 (1960): 286–306.

144 "De eenheid van een mensengemeenschap is formeel dan ook een eenheid van een gemeenschap van *personen*; de biologische eenheid is hiervan slechts de onderbouw. De eenheid nu van een personengemeenschap kan *eigenlijk* alleen gelegen zijn in wat men noemt *l'appel des valeurs*, kortom: in de eenheid van roeping en bestemming." MThS, col. 3126; MMV, 48–9.

before his or her individual conscious consent or commission of sin. However, the universal reach of original sin did not overturn God's universal salvific will.[145]

God mysteriously allows Adam to fall in order to realize His salvific plan in and through Christ. Original sin and redemption are like two sides of the same reality, but solely on the condition that only man is responsible for the sin committed. In this sense, the first Adam is a pre-revelation of Christ, the second Adam. With reference to God's salvific will, original sin does not have to be perceived as a mystery of the absurd, but as a reality that requires Christ's redemption. According to Schillebeeckx, each person participates in the fate of the first Adam, who brings humanity into the fallen, sinful state, and of the second Adam, who introduces man to his destiny of salvation. In other words, human union with God is made possible due to the grace derived from redemption. Because of the occurrence of original sin, the sanctification of everyone without exception always takes place due to Christ's redemption. Therefore, one should accept Thomas's thesis that Christ's humanity was justified so that it could become the source of our sanctification. Christ as God was without sin, but as a man He accepted the sinfulness of human nature.[146] Christ assumes His representative function of humanity that has fallen because of sin, and in this aspect is redeemed in the mystery of resurrection. Hence, Christ is the representative of the fallen and the redeemed mankind. He is the principle of redemption *par excellence* and at the same time its first representative Recipient (*Receptor redemptionis*). Since the redemption of Christ is representative by nature, all people are already substantially redeemed in His Person. Christ representatively redeemed is called by Schillebeeckx an objective redemption (*objectieve verlossing*).[147]

The need to redeem Mary seems obvious because of the universal redemption of humanity in Jesus as the Head. Belonging to a specific community of people, Mary found herself in a situation of inability to attain salvation outside Christ. However, there is a significant element that distinguishes Mary from other people. It is the undeniable fact of her being chosen by God. The fact that Mary was conceived without original sin does not result directly from her nature, as is the case with Christ, but is the result of God's redemptive work. Sin is the internal reality of a human person. Therefore, the fact of Mary's freedom from sin must have its cause externally to her person, that is, in Christ.[148] The tension that arises between

---

145 MMV, 50–1; MThS, col. 327.

146 MMV, 53.

147 "Jezus is de *gevende* maar ook de in onze naam *aanvaardende* verlossing." MThS, col. 3128; MMV, 54.

148 "In het geschetste perspektief wordt het onmiddelijk duidelijk dat Maria's vrijdom van de erfzonde haar niet onttrekt uit verlossing. Het feit dat zij geen erfzonde beliep is in tegenstelling tot Christus niet in haarzelf gefundeerd, maar in Christus." MThS, col. 3128.

the inner nature of original sin and the external principle of Mary's redemption prompts us to interpret Mary's immaculate condition as the fruit of redemption accomplished through a unique preservation from the effects of the original sin. Original sin is a reality which, by virtue of its universal necessity, also concerns Mary in her inner dimension, although in reality, due to the external intervention of redemptive grace, she is preserved from it.[149]

The Immaculate Conception of Mary is understood by Schillebeeckx as her participation in the redemptive grace of the representatively redeemed Christ by virtue of her being chosen as the Mother of God. The unique redemption of Mary by delivering her from original sin and every other sin (*verlossing door vrijwaring*) has significant consequences. Mary's absolute freedom from sin is the result of the sanctifying power of Christ's sacrifice on the Cross. For Mary, redemption is only a pure gift of mercy, without the necessity for the grace of forgiveness, as is the case with other people. Mary's maternal holiness was the fruit of the blood shed by Christ. Schillebeeckx does not hesitate to make a rather surprising statement that Christ's salvific suffering came first and foremost for Mary, who, thanks to this, can be called the most beautiful creation of Christ's redemptive death (*mooiste wonderschepping van Christus' verlossingsdood*).[150]

The difference between the redemption of Mary and the redemption of other people seems to be very clear. There has never been any evil or sin in the Mother of God. Although deliverance from committing a sin and forgiveness of already committed sins are the fruits of one and the same redemptive grace, the unique nature of Mary's redemption lies in the identity of her creation and redemption. Mary's deliverance from original sin and, consequently, from any actual sin committed by means of her participation in the paschal mystery, does not violate the logic and structure of the entire salvific plan. It does not question the biblical truth about the necessity to redeem everyone without exception. Although the assertion of Christ's redemptive suffering first and foremost for Mary may cause theological anxiety, the recognition of Mary's holiness and sinlessness as the fruit of her Son's sacrificial love enables the affirmation of the basic truth that Mary, like any other human being, needed redemption. She was truly redeemed in a unique way, and by the privilege of the Immaculate Conception, she was not separated from the rest of the humankind which finds salvation only in Christ.[151]

---

149 MThS, col. 3129; MMV, 55–6.

150 MMV, 56.

151 "Zo staat Maria niet als een *buiten-christelijk* paradijskind buiten de verlossingsorde, maar zij treedt als begenadigde dit onverloste mensdom binnen: zij brengt het paradijs in het zondige mensdom. Als één der onzen, en daarom, wijl onbevlekt ontvangen, als bij voorbaat verlost is zij het kanaal langswaar de verlossing van Christus doorbreekt in de mensheid." MThS, col. 3130; MMV, 57.

The objective fact of Mary's redemption at the moment of her conception does not exclude or prevent the gradual subjective appropriation of the grace of redemption throughout her life.[152] According to Schillebeeckx, there are no reliable grounds for formulating views about Mary's alleged omniscience or super-consciousness, which would miraculously facilitate Mary's reception of the grace of redemption already in the prenatal life. According to the Flemish theologian, points of such specific culmination can be identified in Mary's subjective reception of the gift of objective redemption. These points include: her decision to remain a virgin, her conscious *fiat* expressed in the Nazareth event, her union with the suffering Christ and her participation in the mystery of Pentecost.

b) Mary's Virginity

A full understanding of Mary's decision to live in chastity and remain a virgin first requires recalling the fact that Mary is a personal expression and representative of the Old Testament messianic expectations. Mary's holiness, attained even before the Annunciation, was of a preparatory, ancillary and empowering nature. It allowed her to consent to the work of the Incarnation. Like all holiness realized under the Old Covenant, it was the fruit of redemption based on the anticipatory grace.[153] Due to the grace of being elected (*electio*), Mary realized in her person a fundamental openness and developed the ability to receive (*receptivitas*) the Old Testament messianic expectations with different developmental lines, which gradually moved towards a single point of ultimate readiness for the Incarnation. Schillebeeckx emphasizes that Mary's holiness in the pre-Annunciation period was a pure receptivity and openness to the potential gifts of God. Mary was a mystery to herself, like an open question awaiting an answer. Mary's attitude towards the decision to preserve virginity developed gradually, moving from the Old Testament understanding of the value of virginity to the discovery of its specifically Christian meaning. The biblical basis for the above conclusion is expressed by Mary's words: "How can this be, since I am a virgin?" (Luke 1:34).

Regarding Mary's virginity, Schillebeeckx provides three interpretations:

1) Traditional interpretation emphasizes the fact that Mary, even before the Annunciation, decided to remain a virgin in her married life with Joseph, which does not find unanimous recognition among biblical scholars. Schillebeeckx emphasizes that, according to many exegetes, a woman's intention to lead a virginal life in marriage did not correspond to the religious mentality of the Jewish communities of that time and would not find understanding in the context of the religious and social conditions of that era. However, taking into account the Immaculate

---

152 MMV, 58–9.
153 MMV, 59–60.

Conception of Mary and her being chosen by God, it cannot be ruled out *a priori* that Mary made a decision which was contrary to Old Testament beliefs, but which was a harbinger of a new way of thinking and living that came along with Christ.

2) The second interpretation assumes that Mary did not promise to lead a virgin life in marriage to Joseph before the Annunciation. In modern language, Mary, as a person who was only engaged to Joseph before they officially moved in together, remained a virgin, intending live normal marital relations after the wedding. Not until the Annunciation did she make her decision to remain a virgin permanently for the sake of Christ. The promise of divine motherhood contained in the angel's message, although expressed in the future tense, concerns, in accordance with the biblical way of presenting similar messages, a reality that had already begun.

3) The third interpretation, like the previous one, assumes that the decision about leading a virginal life was made by Mary at the time of the Annunciation. The words, "I do not know man," have a strong connection with the prophecy of Isaiah (Isa. 7:12). The word "*almah*" means a young girl capable of marriage. According to this interpretation, Mary knew the prophecy of Isaiah and meditated on it at the time of the Annunciation. There is, therefore, a reasonable basis for believing that Mary as a virgin could relate Isaiah's text to herself, asking the angel if she may or must remain a virgin, and what conditions she must meet in order to fulfill Isaiah's prophecy. The angel's response indicated to Mary the path of complete trust in the divine plans. In view of the above interpretation, it can be argued that Isaiah's prophecy did not play a primary role in the rabbinical tradition and its deeper meaning was not widely known at the time of the Annunciation. However, it cannot be ruled out that Mary might have been more sensitive to the depth of the Scriptures than the rabbis. Still, it is difficult to assess to what extent the knowledge of the Messiah's virgin birth was spread among the people of Israel. It would be a mistake to attribute to Mary some secret knowledge and an extraordinarily deep understanding of the meaning of the Old Testament texts.[154]

Schillebeeckx recognizes the weaknesses of each interpretation presented above, but he strongly supports the middle option, which, in a realistic way, portrays Mary as a virgin who wants to marry Joseph and lead a normal married life with him. Mary's holiness, which is the fruit of divine grace, turned her into a person who is completely open to the signs of God's intentions and ready for a radical, unconditional change in her own life in favor of the fulfillment of God's promises. According to the Flemish theologian, one should always take into account the fact that the privilege of the Immaculate Conception had a real impact on the

---

154 MMV, 61–6.

development of Mary's religious awareness. Her marriage with Joseph had a deep dimension of mystery.[155]

c) Mary's Fiat

In the process of Mary's subjective redemption, an important role is played by her trustful *fiat*, which is the first explicit consent for the realization of the redemptive plan in Christ. Schillebeeckx interprets the *fiat* as a meeting between the divine gift of redemptive love in a descending dimension and the human longing for the coming of the Savior, expressed in particular in Mary's positive and free response. Her subjective redemption was accomplished through a completely free act of accepting her divine motherhood.[156] In this way, a synthesis of the objective gift of the Immaculate Conception and the subjective holiness consisting in a pristine state of full openness to divine grace was realized in the figure of Mary. Through her active receptivity, Mary became a collaborator in the work of her own redemption as a partner *ex parte recipientis*.[157] In the mystery of her *fiat*, Mary agreed that the Redeemer could first offer Himself to His mother and redeem her in a sublime way. Mary became the first fruit of redemption because, as a mother, she consciously, voluntarily and in the obedience of faith, conceived and received Jesus the Redeemer, Who was the fulfillment of the messianic promises. Mary's participation in the work of her own subjective redemption consists in the active bodily and spiritual conception of the God-Man (*aktieve lichamelijk-geestelijke ontvangenis*).[158] For Schillebeeckx, the act of Mary's subjective redemption took place in the mystery of the historical conception and birth of her Son, which was expressed in the brief phrase: "Mary had a child whose name was Jesus."[159]

d) Communion with the Suffering Christ

Mary's personal union with Christ suffering on the cross is the crucial stage in the process of her subjective redemption. Mary is a participant in the sufferings of her Son in the literal sense because of her maternal communion with Christ. Schillebeeckx describes Mary's love for her Son as a sacrificial love, which at the foot of the cross became the culmination point for the subjective reception of redemption, as evidenced by the title "Queen of Martyrs." The suffering experienced by Mary encourages us to raise the issue of the physical death of the Mother of God. The dogma of the Assumption announced by Pope Pius XII does not propose any unequivocal solution as to Mary's physical death. According to Schillebeeckx,

---

155 MMV, 67.
156 MMV, 71.
157 MMV, 72.
158 MThS, col. 3132.
159 MMV, 71.

the arguments that deny her real death do not stand the pressure of criticism. The dogma of the Immaculate Conception does not exclude the possibility of a natural death of the Mother of God, who, although saved from original and actual sin, lived in an environment filled with the consequences of sin. If Christ, being without sin, accepted the consequences of sin (i. e. suffering and death), then there is a justified belief that Mary *sublimiori modo redempta* on account of Christ's salvific death, also participated in death understood in a specifically Christian way.[160]

Therefore, according to Schillebeeckx, Mary's actual physical death cannot be interpreted as a punishment for sins, but as the fruit of Christ's sacrificial death, which is completed in the eschaton of the history of salvation. The affirmation of the Mother of God's actual death expressed by the specific phrase of "falling asleep" (*dormitio*) is the finest example of the Christian understanding of death which contains a promise of resurrection. There is no reason to artificially exclude Mary from the universal law of biological death, but the specific Christian sense of her death should be clarified.[161]

e) Mary in the Mystery of the Pentecost and the Assumption

Mary's presence in the Upper Room, as recorded in the Acts of the Apostles, was an expression of her anticipation for the Holy Spirit, Who is an extension and a complement to the Old Testament prophecies about the coming of the Messiah. The event of the Pentecost was for Mary a continuation of her participation in the drama of salvation and the beginning of the last stage in the mystery of her spiritual life on earth. The presence of the Mother of God at the heart of the young Church of the apostolic times was not accidental, but was a confirmation of a significant increase, through faith, in her understanding of the whole salvific plan. Schillebeeckx notices that in the experience of the Pentecost, Mary reached the state of complete understanding of her place at the center of the early Church.[162]

The mystery of Mary's glorious Assumption is the last lofty act in the process of subjective redemption. Christ's redemptive work is not limited only to His sacrificial death, but is completed in the event of the resurrection, which can be seen as God's acceptance of His atoning sacrifice. His sacrificial death and resurrection constitute an inseparable twofold whole. On account of the resurrection, the objective redemption, i. e. the sacrifice of the cross, becomes a perfect reality.[163] Schillebeeckx perceives Mary's fate as an analogy to Christ's resurrection: the sacrifice of her life

---

160 MMV, 74.

161 MMV, 74–5.

162 MThS, col. 31–9; Edward Schillebeeckx, "De bruid van de Heilige Geest," *Thomas* 8, no. 3 (1954/55): 3–5; cf. HK, 225: "Die christliche Kunst hat in den Pfingstdarstellungen gerne Maria in die Mitte gestellt. Da steht sie mit der Flamme über ihrem Haupt: ein Bild der Kirche, erfüllt von Jesu Geist."

163 MMV, 75.

is also fully accepted by God. On the basis of the parallelism between the sacrifice of the Mother and the Son, the Assumption of Mary should be considered as the final closing of the process of her subjective redemption through a perfect, lasting, bodily, spiritual, and personal union with Christ, and in Christ also with the whole Trinity. Through the Assumption, Mary has achieved a qualitatively higher state of glory which involves the whole of her personal being. In comparison with other saints, who are still in a state of waiting, she is already saved.[164]

The stages of gradual active reception of Christ's redemption presented above allow for the final conclusion that Mary has been redeemed both objectively and subjectively. As the Mother of God, she was redeemed in a unique way while actively cooperating in the process of subjective redemption. In the mystery of Mary's redemption, her spiritual and bodily motherhood is at the center. This motherhood justifies her unique character from a theological point of view.[165]

3. Mother of Redemption

The analysis carried out in the previous section showed that Mary was the first fruit of Christ's redemption. She actively, consciously and freely cooperated in the process of personally receiving it. During the identification of particular peak moments of Mary's collaboration in the work of her own redemption, some intuitions emerged as to the universal meaning of her subjective redemption. They provide a convenient basis for formulating an extremely important problem in Mariology. The problem concerns the relationship of Mary's subjective redemption with the work of objective redemption carried out by Jesus Christ.

Edward Schillebeeckx notices a particular tension between the truth that presents Mary as a member of humanity redeemed by Christ and the thesis concerning her sublime place among the redeemed.[166] In order to show the non-contradiction of these two views, it is necessary, according to the Flemish theologian, to bear in mind that Mary's activity within the divine plan is the result of her unique redemption

---

164 "De tenhemelopneming van Maria is niet zomaar een losstaand voorrecht zonder verband met de diepste kern van het Maria mysterie. Zij is vooreerst de top van Maria's uitzonderlijke verlossing. Het heil of de verlossing belangt de gehele mens aan. Het definitief, geestelijk en lichamelijk samenzijn van de mens met de verheerlijkte mens Jesus en in Hem met de Drieëenheid is de nooit ophoudende eindfase van de verlossing: dit pas is *voltooide* verlossing." MThS, col. 3140; MMV 101; cf. E. Schillebeeckx, "Het mensdom is reeds verheerlijkt in Christus en Maria," *De Rozenkrans* 88 (1961/1962): 136–7; cf. HK, 527.

165 "Maria is *verlost tot* moeder van de Verlosser en van de verlossing." MThS, col. 3151; cf. Edward Schillebeeckx, "Maria, meest-verloste moeder," *De Linie* 641 (1958): 2.

166 MMV, 77.

and always remains totally subordinated to the salvific activities of Christ, the only Mediator. Determining Mary's participation in the work of objective redemption will help us understand the role that the Mother of God plays in our subjective redemption.

a) Mary's Virginal Motherhood and the Universal Meaning of Her "Fiat"
In Schillebeeckx's understanding, the Incarnation is a specific salvific event of universal significance and scope in regard to all humanity. In this context, Mary's *fiat* was a completely free act of consent to become the mother of Christ Who represents all humanity. As the Mother of the incarnate God, Mary became, at the same time, the spiritual mother of all the redeemed (*de geestelijke moeder van alle verlosten*).[167] Through the prism of motherhood, one can notice an even deeper meaning of her virginity. Being both a virgin and a mother, Mary belonged exclusively to the Savior. Virginity assumed for the sake of the kingdom of heaven (*propter regnum coelorum*) gave her motherhood an apostolic significance. The conception of Christ was not an ordinary, natural act of procreation that takes place in marriage, but was directed universally: for the benefit of all humanity. That is why Mary's virginal motherhood is indeed a religious and apostolic event.[168]

The *fiat* expressed by Mary should be seen as her fulfilling the condition for the realization of redemption. In this sense, a conscious and free act of faith expressed in Mary's *fiat* became a constitutive part of the objective redemption realized in its historical dimension.[169] That is why Mary can be recognized as a partner in the work of Christ's redemption. The phrase "giving a direct cooperation in the work of objective redemption" (*ontvangende onmiddelijke medewerking in het objectieve verlossingsgebeuren*) used by Schillebeeckx should be understood in close connection with Mary's active conception and acceptance of the Savior.[170]

---

167 "Als Moeder van Christus, de tastbaar verschenen roeping van heel het mensdom, is Zij dan ook de Moeder van de personengemeenschap der mensen bij de verwezenlijking van hun levensbestemming. Zo is Maria, vanwege de inhoud van haar *concreet* moederschap, *fundamenteel* reeds de geestelijke moeder van alle verlosten." MMV, 79.

168 "In het moeder-van-een-kind-worden behoort Maria volstrekt en maagdelijk God toe. Het maagdelijke moederschap is dan ook wezenlijk een religieus en apostolisch gebeuren." MMV, 80.

169 "Bij de Annuntiatie heeft Maria bewust haar *fiat* op de *Messias*, dat is de Redder van het volk, gegeven. Zij heeft derhalve gelovend en lichamelijk *ten voordele van alle mensen* de voltrekking van het objektief verlossingsgebeuren aanvaard en in die zin ook op het historisch plan geconditionneerd. Fundamenteel is Zij aldus reeds deelgenote in de door Christus zelf gebrachte verlossing. [...] Haar *geloofsfiat* op de Boodschap van de verlossende Menswording is, als bewuste en vrije toeëigening van haar eigen verlossing, meteen een mede-constitutief element van onze objectieve verlossing door Christus." MCMW, 40-1.

170 MCMW, 39; MMV, 81.

One should always take into account the fact that all the merits of Mary must be considered in a significant causal relationship with the merits of Christ. Therefore, it is unacceptable to treat Mary as a second, equal and parallel principle of redemption. However, her active bodily and spiritual conception as well as her acceptance of the Savior require her real cooperation not only in her particular subjective redemption, but also in the objective redemption for the good of humanity.[171] According to Schillebeeckx, humanity was actually reconciled with the Father both in the Person of Christ, the Redeemer, and in the person of Mary who was the first fruit of redemption and the first among the believers. Therefore, Mary is also a co-principle (co-participant) of our subjective redemption on the basis of a purely receptive cooperation in the work of objective redemption.[172] Her spiritual reception (*fide concepit*) and bodily conception of Christ should be seen as a gift for humanity. It is the gift of conception and birth of the only Mediator, Jesus Christ, Who is grace incarnate, the primordial sacrament (*oersacrament*) and the sole source of salvation.[173]

b) Mary's Participation in the Sacrifice of the Cross

Considering the salvific dimension of the Incarnation, it can be said easily that Jesus' entire life, marked by the sacrificial stigma, was heading towards the culmination point of a consciously accepted death on the Cross. Schillebeeckx recognizes the sacrificial character of Jesus' entire life. Mary did not have full, detailed or clear knowledge of her Son's future fate. However, during the Annunciation, she expressly gave unconditional consent to all the possibilities related to the fulfillment of Christ's messianic mission.[174]

According to the Dominican theologian, throughout her life Mary gradually learned the meaning of previously unpredictable events related to the divine plan of salvation. Her consent to the gift of motherhood, expressed consciously in the spirit of faith, was at the same time an implicit acceptance of Christ's sacrifice and suffering.[175] On account of this, Mary became the spiritual Mother of redeemed humanity already at the time of the Annunciation.[176] The acceptance of Christ's

---

171 MMV, 81.

172 MMV, 82.

173 "Zij [Maria] ontving in geloof het oersacrament, de mens Jesus, de in haar schoot menswordende God, de unieke heilsoorzaak." MCMW, 41.

174 MThS, col. 3136.

175 MMV, 83-4.

176 "Op grond van deze fundamentele openheid van Haar *geloofsfiat* op het aanbod van Moederschap, ligt er in het Moederschap ten aanzien van alle mensen, dat daarin reeds fundamenteel geïmpliceerd ligt, een grondige oriëntering op haar later uitdrukkelijk *geloofsfiat* op het Kruisoffer: *fundamenteel* is Zij daarom reeds bij de Annuntiatie de geestelijke Moeder van het *door het Kruis* verloste mensdom." MCMW, 43-4.

sacrifice in the mystery of the Annunciation was confirmed and highlighted at the foot of the Cross. Mary's suffering took place in communion with the suffering of Christ. As the Mother of Jesus, Mary experienced the Savior's suffering in a unique way, at the deepest level of her maternal love. She alone was directly involved in Christ's redemptive work.[177] Mary's sacrificial love was a conscious extension of the bodily conception and the spiritual acceptance of the Savior for the good of all people. Communion with the suffering Christ revealed a new dimension of Mary's motherhood, both in relation to the crucified Christ and to the Church, the Mystical Body of Christ, born of the mutual, sacrificial, suffering love of the Son and the Mother.[178]

c) Mary's Participation in Glory

The central moment of the paschal mystery is constituted by the events of Christ's resurrection, His ascension and reign at the right hand of the Father. According to Schillebeeckx, the salvific function of Christ as the Messiah was a dynamic reality, which developed and grew towards the fullness of His messiahship and His glorified state as *Kyrios*. It was only in the resurrection that the kenotic dimension of the Son of God was raised to the level of exaltation. Relevant passages in the Bible clearly indicate that the full power and efficacy of Christ's sacrifice were only achieved in the resurrection (Rom 1:4; Acts 2:33; Heb 5:10). On account of her privilege of the Assumption, Mary as a mother and partner in Christ's redemptive work, also participated in the glory of her Son, the Lord.[179]

For Schillebeeckx, the Assumption of Mary anticipates participation in the future universal resurrection and is the act of establishing a universal maternal relationship with all people.[180] Schillebeeckx calls Mary's reign in glory the ultimate fruit and the crowning of her state of redemption as well as the reward for her role in the redemption of the world. Mary's maternal function is not limited only to the earthly dimension, but finds its effective continuation within the mysterious relationship between the Mother, glorified Mary, and the Son, the exalted *Kyrios*.[181]

On the basis of the multifaceted analysis presented above, it can be concluded that in Schillebeeckx's view, Mary's role in the work of objective redemption consists in a direct, purely receptive and universal participation. The expression "pure receptivity" (*loutere ontvangenis*), used by the Flemish theologian, allows us to

---

177 MMV, 84.

178 MCMW, 45; MMV, 85.

179 "Als moederlijke deelgenote in de objektieve verlossing van Christus deelt door haar tenhemelopneming Maria als moeder in de kyriale macht van Christus. Haar tenhemelopneming is *het in kracht gesteld worden* van haar goddelijk en geestelijk moederschap." MThS, col. 3141.

180 MMV, 86.

181 MMV, 86; MThS, col. 3142.

determine Mary's cooperation in the work of objective redemption, while maintaining the central position of Jesus' unique, irreplaceable and effective work. Mary's cooperation in the work of redemption (*Maria's medewerking in de verlossing*) has a real, significant value in itself, as well as its own efficacy. However, it cannot be considered as an external addition to Christ's redemptive work. Mary's receptivity and her subjective redemption have the features of universality and are a way of her participation in the reality of our redemption. Specifying the problem in question, Schillebeeckx emphasizes that Mary's cooperation should be understood as a close communion with Christ, the only Redeemer. Mary's receptivity does not have a passive, static character, but takes the form of an active, sacrificial attitude in spiritual and physical dimensions. It gives Mary's actions a universal meaning, which is the highest fruit of redemption.[182] Consequently, the universal nature of *fiat* is manifested in Mary's acceptance of all the gifts from Christ for the good of all people. Schillebeeckx notices here an even more profound consequence. Humankind owes its redemption to both Christ and Mary, though their activity within this work were carried out at completely different levels. Mary's activity, actual and irreplaceable in its value, does not depreciate and does not replace the salvific efficacy of Christ. It should be remembered that Mary, as the subject of her individual actions, made it possible for God to enter the world and implement the plan of salvation through a fully free and personal decision. According to Schillebeeckx, the act of consent on Mary's part is an important element of her participation in both objective and subjective redemption.[183]

d) Mary's Mediation

Affirmation of Mary's maternal participation in objective redemption leads to the reflection on the problem of Mary's mediation. Like her motherhood, Mary's mediation is also universal. Following Saint Augustine, Schillebeeckx states that the mediation provided by Mary, the mother of Christ and the mother of all people, is not a mediation of the Head in relation to the members, but a mediation of a member to and among other members. It should be remembered that Mary is a privileged member of the Mystical Body because of the mission entrusted to her by God and due to the gift of her exceptional redemption associated with it (*sublimiori modo redempta*). One can rightly speak of a certain exaltation of Mary in relation to other co-redeemed members of the Church. Schillebeeckx even recalls a traditional and very vivid description of Mary as the neck connecting Christ, the Head, with the rest of those redeemed in the Church. Redeemed by God in a unique way, Mary has become a prototype of the community of saints and a universal womb that gives

---

182 MMV, 87–8.
183 MMV, 87.

life to the Christian community of faith. She is a figure of the Church and at the same time an intermediary for grace in relation to all people, which results from the fact of her spiritual and bodily motherhood.[184]

If the Mariological writings of the Dominican theologian are not read very thoroughly, the impression is that the classic concept of a tiered mediation comes to the fore: Christ is the mediator between the Father and people, and Mary is the mediator between Christ and us. Although formally Schillebeeckx seems to support the traditional understanding of Mary's mediation expressed in the Latin formula *per Mariam ad Iesum* (through Mary to Jesus), further subtle theological analysis effectively lead to discoveries of innovative, substantial implications. The theory of mediation constructed by the Flemish theologian consistently avoids the "ladder of mediation" and does not depreciate the possibility of meeting Christ directly, i. e. without mediation on the part of other people. Instead, Schillebeeckx emphasizes the truth that all human cooperation with the saving grace of Christ is internally connected with Mary's priority in her vocation and reception of the Redeemer Who is grace incarnate. There is, therefore, an objective personal relationship between Mary's motherhood and our Christian life.[185]

Edward Schillebeeckx does not treat Mary's mediation as an additional, indirect path to Christ or as a humanly understood search for protection in order to gain the possibility of a personal and direct contact with the Savior. Mary's mediation is a constitutive element, though not always a conscious one, in the structure of every direct encounter of a human person with Christ. According to the Flemish theologian, Mary's mediation can be better understood by considering St. Thomas Aquinas's commentary on the *Ave Maria*: "It is wonderful when one saint has so much grace that it is enough for the salvation of many. But there is nothing more wonderful than the fact that someone has so much grace that it is enough for the salvation of all people in the world, which is the case of Christ and the Blessed Virgin."[186] The excess of grace that Mary possesses is the source of grace for others, in accordance with the principle that grace does not only have an individual dimension, but is always intended for the good of the community of people (*quia quilibet de gratia sibi collata debet proximo inservire*). However, there is a fundamental difference between the excess of grace in Christ and the grace flowing from the

---

184 "In haar verlost-zijn en in haar daarin vervatte universele heilsfunctie ten aanzien van alle medeverlosten is Zij [Maria] het actieve oerbeeld van door Christus verloste <gemeenschap der heiligen>, waarvan Zij de universeel-ontvangende, levenbarende schoot is: typus van de Kerk." MMV, 89.

185 MMV, 91.

186 St. Thomas, *In Salutationem Angelicam,* Opusc. Theol. II, 240 No. 1118: "Magnum est in quolibet sancto quando habet tantum de gratia quod sufficit ad salutem multorum. Sed quando haberet tantum quod suffiret ad salutem omnium hominum de mundo, hoc esset maximum; et hoc est in Christo et in Beata Virgine."

fullness of Mary. Christ, *ex definitione*, is a man of grace: as God incarnate, He is grace by His very nature. Mary enjoys the fullness of grace thanks to Christ. Christ as the only Mediator and Redeemer is enough for Himself. The abundance of grace in Mary is the result of her objective and subjective redemption. The fullness of grace in Mary is the fruit of her full participation in the divine life of Christ. Grace that, due to Mary's mediation, flows onto other people is the result of the universal nature of her redemption, which was accomplished through the privilege of her divine motherhood.[187]

According to Schillebeeckx, the title "Suppliant Omnipotence" (*de smekende Almacht, omnipotentia supplex*), bestowed on Mary by Pope Pius XII, can be easily justified. Seemingly shocking with its maximalism, the title is a summary of the whole mystery of Mary's mediation. The word "suppliant" (*smekende*) points to Mary's active receptivity to the gift of Christ's Redemption. Mary's work does not go beyond the framework set by the history of salvation and is strictly subordinated to the divine plan. The reference to Mary as "omnipotence" (*Almacht*) cannot be understood as granting this divine attribute to Mary, a human being. Instead, it indicates Mary's *a priori* consent to the realization of God's salvific omnipotence in the Person of Christ.[188]

According to the Flemish theologian, the very term "mediator" (*middelares, mediatrix*) used with reference to Mary has three layers of meaning.

Firstly, it points to the spiritual acceptance and bodily conception of Christ, through which Mary manifested complete obedience to the universal salvific will of the Father, a will that was gradually revealed in the subsequent stages of her life.

Secondly, the term expresses a gradual increase in Mary's awareness of her maternal function with reference to the entire Church and all people, which reached its apogee at the hour of the Cross and in the event of the Pentecost. Mary's maternal task realized in the community of the Church in the power of the exalted Christ-Kyrios has been effective since the day of the Pentecost.[189]

Thirdly, the term "mediator" (*middelares*) underlines the fact that, in the mystery of her glorious Assumption, Mary became definitely aware of her maternal function within the salvific plan and achieved a perfect union of her will with the intentions of the salvific will of the sole Mediator and Redeemer, Jesus Christ.[190]

According to the Flemish theologian, Mary's universal maternal mediation (*universele moederlijke bemiddeling*) points, above all, to the fact that she occupies a privileged position among the redeemed by virtue of her most personal, human

---

187 MMV, 92.

188 MMV, 92.

189 "In kracht van de kyriale verheffing van Christus werd sinds het pinksterfeest de moederlijke taak van Maria effektief in de kerk." MThS, col. 3142.

190 MMV, 92–3.

and maternal relationship with the only Mediator, Jesus Christ.[191] Schillebeeckx opposes erroneous concepts of mediation based on theologically incorrect image of Mary as a co-redeemer (*coredemptrix, medeverlosseres*), i. e. a principle of salvation equal with Christ and artificially connected with the Redeemer. One must not make the mistake of reductionism that consists in diminishing Christ's full humanity (Christological monophysitism). Although traditional Chalcedonian Christology does not accept the existence of a human person in Christ, the human nature of Christ has no defects: it is real and complete. That is why Christ does not need the help of any man, including Mary, to reconcile humanity with God. He is the atonement in Himself. Mary's active cooperation with Christ, Who is true God and true man, cannot be understood as attributing to her salvific functions that belong to Christ's prerogatives. An unjustified transfer of Christ's functions to Mary leads to harmful effects in the understanding of the sacramental life of Christian community. Schillebeeckx reminds us that Christ (Redeemer and Mediator) was first to express, on behalf of all people, His perfect *fiat* for the realization of the divine salvific plan. That is why Mary's *fiat* must be always understood as secondary and dependent on Christ's act of obedience to the Father Who wants to save the world. The recognition of the absolute priority of Christ's *fiat* makes it easier for us to understand the essential truth that Christ is the concrete, visible realization of this gift of love and, at the same time, the absolute response of humanity to the love of God. That is why, according to Schillebeeckx, wrong attribution to Mary of the functions proper to Christ is a depreciation of the very fact of the Incarnation.[192]

Schillebeeckx's stance on the issue of Mary's mediation is based on the adopted *pisteological* interpretation (through the prism of faith) of all actions of the Mother of God, Who, because of her priority in faith and on the basis of her merits gained during her earthly life, works, in a maternal way, as a mediator (*middelares*) and advocate (*voorspreekster*) for all people.

According to the Flemish theologian, the basis of Mary's mediation is constituted by her maternal love, which, due to her perfect union with God in heaven and due to the state of bodily exultation, has achieved such a high degree of intuitive sensitivity that she is able to know in detail the need of each of her spiritual children. That is why Mary's function can be rightly described as a universal maternal

---

191 MMV, 93.

192 "Niet Maria vertegenwoordigt ons *bij de Vader*, maar alleen Christus. De mens Jezus is niet alleen de concrete realisering en zichtbaarwording van het *goddelijk liefde-aanbod* aan de mensen, maar tevens de zuiverste en absolute realisering van het *menselijk liefde-antwoord* op Gods aanbod. [...] Deze diepe realiteit mogen we aan Christus niet ontnemen om ze dan aan Maria toe te schrijven. Dit ware een miskenning van een dieptedimensie van de Incarnatie zelf." MMV, 90.

mediation (*universele moederlijke bemiddeling*).[193] Schillebeeckx emphasizes, above all, the personalistic dimension in the effective mediation of Mary as mother. The effectiveness of Mary's mediation arises primarily from the personal community of love (*liefdevolle persoonsgemeenschap*) created by Mary, the Mother, and Jesus, the Son. An internal exchange of grace takes place between Jesus and Mary within the community of people, with the absolute priority of the Redeemer. However, this does not mean that Mary's personal dynamics is disappearing. In her ontic union with Christ, she can realistically undertake initiatives related to the mystery of redemption. Mary's interpersonal relationship with Christ in heaven is unique and irreducible to the eschatic situation of other saints. Because of the mother's relationship with her Son based on the incarnation, Mary participates in a permanent dialogue with the exalted Christ directly and universally for all people. Due to the privilege of the Assumption of her soul and body, Mary is characterized by an integral, eschatic, bodily, spiritual and direct openness to every human being.[194]

For Schillebeeckx, the basic category that explains the phenomenon of Mary's mediation is the reality of Mary's eschatic encounter with Christ (*verheerlijkt-lichamelijke ontmoeting*), which definitely increases her awareness and perfects her in her being. "Intuitively conscious maternal mediation in a glorified bodily openness" (*intuitief-bewuste moederlijke bemiddeling in verheerlijkt-lichamelijke openheid*) is the effect of the full union of the Mother and the Son.[195]

The theologian from Nijmegen notices, however, a particular awkwardness of the word "mediator" (*mediatrix, middelares*), due to the risk of theological misunderstandings which might suggest an equal meaning of Mary's and Christ's work in the realization of the salvific plan. Therefore, he suggests using the term "Mary's intercession" (*voorspraak van Maria*), which allows for the avoidance of theological ambiguities. "Mary's intercession" indicates, above all, Mary's maternal concern for the salvation of the whole world and derives from the mystery of her being chosen as the Mother of God, thanks to which she could participate, in a maternal way, in the redemption of the world by Jesus Christ. Her universal intercession to God for the salvation of all people is an extension of the unconditional consent expressed during the Annunciation, through which she co-merited salvation for the world. That is why human prayers, good deeds, noble intentions and all human

---

193 The idea of Mary's maternal mediation was portrayed by John Paul II in his encyclical *Redemptoris Mater* (chapter III). Cf. Joseph Ratzinger, "The Sign of the Woman: An Introductory Essay on the Encyclical *Redemptoris Mater*," in Joseph Ratzinger and Hans Urs von Balthasar, *Mary. The Church at the Source* (San Francisco: Ignatius Press, 2005), 53–8; Daniel Lázaro Ilzo, *La mediazione materna di Maria in Cristo negli insegnamenti di Giovanni Paolo II* (Collana di Mariologia 9, Lugano – Gavirate: Eupress-FTL, 2011), 3–13.

194 MThS, col. 3143.

195 MThS, col. 3142.

holiness, which are a free response to divine grace, are included in the wonderful *fiat* of the virgin Mother of Christ. Mary, as the prototype of every instance of the human acceptance of faith, hope, love, grace and religious life, rightly deserves the titles: "Help of Christians" (*auxilium christianorum*), "Refuge of Sinners" (*refugium peccatorum*) and "Suppliant Omnipotence" (*omnipotentia supplex*).[196]

It should be mentioned that Schillebeeckx does not totally eliminate Mary's titles, such as: "co-redeemer" (*medeverlosseres*), "mediator" (*middelares*), "dispenser of grace" (*uitdeelster der genade*), or "universal advocate" (*algemene voorspreekster*), from theological language. Considering the pre-Vatican II context of Schillebeeckx's work which was conditioned by the flourishing of maximalist Mariology, it is easy to understand the Flemish theologian's fear of a radical removal of these widely accepted, though not always theologically precise, terms. Despite the evident tendency to construct theological neologisms, Schillebeeckx is more in favor of a historical-salvific and personalistic reinterpretation of the existing Mariological terms than of their too rapid elimination or substitution. According to the Flemish professor, the above-mentioned titles emphasize, above all, the fact that Mary exalted by God is the Mother of Redemption (*Moeder van de Verlossing*).[197] This redemption is realized only by Christ. Mary's participation in the reality of objective redemption consists in the unequivocal maternal and loving identification with the redemptive work of her Child, the Redeemer, which, in turn, leads to the exposure of Mary's deep maternal relationship with the mystery of redemption.[198]

***

In conclusion, it should be emphasized that Schillebeeckx's theory of Mary's participation in the reality of objective redemption is based on appreciation for Mary's maternal activity. The Flemish theologian rejects J. Lebon's thesis of Mary's co-redemption due to the *de condigno* merit of voluntarily giving up her natural maternal rights for the salvific sacrifice of her Son-Redeemer. Schillebeeckx also opposes H. Köster's theory based on the biblical category of "a covenant," which shows Mary as a representative of all humanity accepting in a passive way the gift of Christ's redemption (*pura receptivitas*). In view of the above concepts, the Flemish

---

196 MMV, 93; cf. Edward Schillebeeckx, "Maria onze hoop," *Thomas* 8, no. 1 (1954/55): 4–6; Edward Schillebeeckx, "Het wonder dat Maria heet," *Thomas* 7, no. 7 (1953/54): 5–7.

197 Schillebeeckx borrowed the term "Mother of redemption" (*Moeder van de verlossing, Mater redemptionis nostrae*) from the medieval theologian, Aelred Rievaulx (1100–1167), cf. Rievaulx, *Sermones ex tempore, XX, In nativitate BMV,* PL 159, 223; MGVM, 29. See also: L. Gambero, *Mary in the Middle Ages. The Blessed Virgin Mary in the Thought of Medieval Latin Theologians* (San Francisco: Ignatius Press, 2005), 162–9.

198 MThS, col. 3143.

theologian challenges Christological monophysitism and the depreciation of Mary's maternal mission.[199]

In his own work, Schillebeeckx does not focus on demonstrating some specific co-redemptive work of Mary, but refers to the Annunciation and the Incarnation, in which the Virgin married to Joseph gives her informed consent to cooperate in the redemption of the world. Schillebeeckx, like M. D. Koster, does not narrow the reality of redemption only to the paschal events, but treats the entire event of the Incarnation as a salvific reality. Hence, Mary's act of faith expressed during the Annunciation has a universal character and objectively allows for the salvation of all people. In this way, it is a constitutive element of objective salvation based on active reception (*aktieve ontvangenis*). Schillebeeckx, like K. Rahner, notices the awkwardness of the term "co-redemptrix" (*medeverlosseres*), emphasizing the central idea of Mary's motherhood in the explication of the mystery of Mary's cooperation in the work of redemption.[200]

Regarding Mary's mediation, Schillebeeckx rejects a static, tiered, schematic model. However, he puts special emphasis, in an extremely original way, on the loving community of persons – Mary and Jesus – established in an eschatic reality. The interpersonal, dialogic relationship between Mary and Jesus creates a perfect foundation for a personalistic interpretation of Mary's mediation, without violating the absolute, unique mediation of the Redeemer.

---

199 Cf. MThS, col. 3138. For more on the views of J. Lebon and M. D. Koster, see: Stanisław C. Napiórkowski, "Natura współodkupieńczej zasługi Maryi," *Roczniki Teologiczno-Kanoniczne* 12, no. 2 (1965): 69–83.

200 Cf. MThS, cols. 3137–8.

III. Ecclesial Icon of Mary

Contemporary Mariology cannot be developed in isolation from other branches of theology. A Mariology divorced from other branches of theology leads to one-sided approaches and is the cause of serious abnormalities in shaping the theological image of the Mother of God. The postulation of an interdisciplinary approach to Mariological issues based on interrelating them with both theological and non-theological disciplines comes to the fore more and more frequently.[201]

Ecclesiology, understood as a theological reflection on the reality of the Church, is widely regarded today as an inseparable context in constructing a realistic Mariology based in salvation history. Along with Christology, pneumatology and (more and more often) Trinitarian theology, ecclesiology forms the substantive basis for Mariology and its methodologically optimal protection against falling into the trap of alleged self-sufficiency.

The universal meaning of Mary is revealed in her relationship with the Church and, consequently, with humanity and the existential experience of man. In the theological reflection of Edward Schillebeeckx, Mary acquires the status of an ecclesiological category, by which it is possible to overcome the antinomy of Mariological minimalism and maximalism. From the second half of the twentieth century onward, the interest in the ancient parallelism between Mary and the Church has been growing in theology.[202] As far as the problem in question is concerned, Schillebeeckx rightly strives for a synthesis of Christotypical and ecclesiotypical tendencies. Both approaches condition and complement each other.

The Flemish theologian emphasizes the significant influence of the dialogical concept of the Church on the shape of the theological image of Mary. There is a real ontic relationship between her and the reality of the Church, and a kind of feedback in the cognitive aspect, thanks to which it is possible to recognize ecclesial features in Mary, and Marian features in the Church. The appreciation of the ecclesiotypical tendency was reflected in the following formulation proposed by Schillebeeckx: "Mary, mother of all believers" (*Maria moeder van alle gelovigen*).

---

201 Damian Wąsek, "Interdisciplinarity in theology," in *Perspectives on Interdisciplinarity*, eds. Bartosz Brożek, Marek Jakubiec and Piotr Urbańczyk, 155–173 (Kraków: Copernicus Center Press, 2020), 158–162.

202 Cf. Hans Urs von Balthasar, "The Marian Mold of the Church," in Joseph Ratzinger, Hans Urs von Balthasar, *Mary. The Church at the Source* (San Francisco: Ignatius Press, 2005), 125–144.

1. The Ecclesiotypical Shift in Mariology

Methodological sensitivity has resulted in the distinction between Christotypical Mariology and Ecclesiotypical Mariology, a distinction which is already widely recognized today in theological circles.[203] The genesis of this division can be traced back to the Mariological Congress which took place in Lourdes in 1958. The bold speech given by Heinrich Maria Köster has gone down in history. This German Pallottine introduced two neologisms in adjective form into theological language: Christotypical and ecclesiotypical Mariology. Christotypical Mariology is most frequently understood as interpreting the person of Mary in the way that indicates the greatest resemblance to Christ the Redeemer. According to the ecclesiotypical concept, Mary is very similar to the Church, the latter understood as the community of the redeemed. The fundamental differences between the Christotypical and the ecclesiotypical approach do not concern the historical facts that determine Mary's active participation in the work of redemption, such as the calling of Mary by God and her role in the incarnation, but rather lie in their interpretation and in the recognition of their importance. For Christotypists, Mary is a co-redemptrix whose actions must be interpreted as indicating a particular likeness to the redemptive acts of Christ Himself. As proclaimed by Gabriele Roschini, a leading representative of the Christotypical movement, Mary is a co-principle of redemption.[204]

The basic features of Christotypical Mariology include:

a) excessive exposition of Eve's participation in Adam's sinful fall as opposed to Mary's participation in the work of redemption accomplished by Christ, the New Adam,

b) presenting Mary as a subject who co-creates the reality of redemption from within,

c) systematic use of the analogy between Eve and Mary,

d) tendencies to treat the personal acts of Mary and Jesus equally,

e) recognition of one, though two-person, principle of redemption,

f) emphasizing the spousal unity of Christ and Mary by the cross, Mary's co-agency which is parallel to the effectiveness of Christ's work, and a biased use of Christotypical motifs in papal statements while omitting ecclesiotypical elements.

---

203 Stanisław C. Napiórkowski, "O mariologii eklezjotypicznej." In *Matka Jezusa pośród pielgrzymującego Kościoła*, eds. Sergiusz J. Gajek and Kazimierz Pek (Warszawa: Wydawnictwo Księży Marianów, 1993), 19–36; cf. Stanisław Budzik, *Maryja w Tajemnicy Chrystusa i Kościoła* (Tarnów: Biblos, 1997), 146–151; Bruno Forte, *Maryja Ikona Tajemnicy. Zarys mariologii symboliczno-narracyjnej* (Warszawa: Wydawnictwo Księży Marianów, 1999), 33–43.

204 Napiórkowski, *Matka naszego Pana*, 146.

On the other hand, the fundamental ideas of ecclesiotypical Mariology are:

a) the sovereign power of God over the history of salvation which is carried out by means of a spousal covenant,

b) the dialogic structure of the relationship between God and humanity, the primacy of God's initiative,

c) humanity as God's partner in the spousal covenant of love,

d) incarnation understood as a dialogic event that requires a response from humanity in the form of acceptance, dedication and respect for God's promises,

e) Mary as a representative of humanity and a type of the Church, making a gesture of self-offering and accepting God's initiative,

f) Mary's cooperation in the redemptive incarnation, understood as a gift of human nature to the eternal Word,

g) the representative nature of Mary's presence by the cross as a continuation of the representative character of her *fiat* uttered during the Annunciation,

h) Mary as the type and the model of reception of the fruits of objective redemption understood as a great sacrament,

i) Calvary as the site of the solemn covenant between Mary and Christ.[205]

Looking at the discussed problem schematically, it should be noted that, according to Christotypists, Mary, who was united in the most perfect way with Christ the Redeemer, stood between the angry God, the Father expecting compensation, and humanity. On the other hand, in ecclesiotypical terms, Mary represented humanity before Christ and stood on the side of the Church.[206]

The idea of ecclesiotypical Mariology was taken up and accepted by the Second Vatican Council and today is one of the basic norms for confirming the correctness of the Marian doctrine.[207] Despite the buzz of sharp polemics, Schillebeeckx perfectly grasped the important message of the Council, which, in an attempt to reflect on the co-responsibility of all believers for good and evil in the Church, at the same time drew attention to the need for theological clarification of the relationship between the Church and the world, as well as faith and science, and put forward

---

205 Napiórkowski, *Matka naszego Pana*, 143–8; Henri de Lubac, *The Splendor of the Church* (San Francisco: Ignatius Press, 1999), 314–79; Raniero Cantalamessa, *Mary: Mirror of the Church* (Collegeville: The Liturgical Press, 1992), 94–116.

206 Napiórkowski, *Matka naszego Pana*, 149. See Jan Krzysztof Miczyński, ed., *Maryja i Kościół* (Lublin: Wydawnictwo KUL, 2018).

207 Cf. Stanisław C. Napiórkowski, "Trudne dojrzewanie mariologii soborowej," in *Matka i Nauczycielka. Mariologia Soboru Watykańskiego II*, Stanisław C. Napiórkowski and Jan Usiądek (Niepokalanów: Wydawnictwo Ojców Franciszkanów, 1991), 13–159. See also: John C. Cavadini and Danielle M. Peters, eds., *Mary on the Eve of the Second Vatican Council* (Notre Dame: University of Notre Dame Press, 2017).

the postulate of developing a salvation history theology adapted to the mentality of modern societies.[208]

The evidently ecclesiological inclination of the Second Vatican Council provided an opportunity for the intellectual confrontation between the two tendencies in Mariology. During the deliberations, the ecclesiotypical interpretation of Mariology clearly came to the fore. Mary was presented as our Sister, the greatest member of the Church and a type of the ecclesial community of faith.[209] There were also supporters of Christotypical Mariology, according to which, Mary stands by Jesus Christ's side and, as the Mother of the Head of the redeemed Church, she can rightly be called the Mother of the Church. At the Second Vatican Council, the vast majority of participants, including Schillebeeckx who acted as a theological adviser to the Dutch Episcopate, opted for the ecclesiotypical version of Mariology.[210] Already before the Council, i. e. in the 1950s, Schillebeeckx focused his interests on ecclesiotypical Mariology. His ecclesiotypical vision was outlined in the fundamental Mariological work: "Maria, moeder van de verlosing" ("Mary, Mother of the Redemption").[211]

In the early 1990s, Schillebeeckx carried out a critical retrospective of his Mariological legacy. He noted the existence of two conflicting Mariological concepts which, a few years later, would reverberate in the polemics about the Council. The result of the intellectual effort of that period is a booklet entitled "Mariologie: gisteren, vandaag, morgen" ("Mariology: Yesterday, Today, Tomorrow").[212] The pre-conciliar work "Maria moeder van de verlossing" combines the two different visions and, by necessity, is frequently incoherent, as if constantly searching for the ultimate synthesis of the Christotypical and the ecclesiotypical appoach. In this sense, Schillebeeckx's Mariology of the 1950s and earlier might be regarded as the preliminary of the Conciliar disputes concerning Mariology. Nevertheless, the ecclesiotypical line is clearly present in Schillebeeckx's Mariology of both the

---

208 Edward Schillebeeckx, *Een democratische Kerk* (Utrecht: Impress, 1989), 5; Schillebeeckx, *Het Tweede Vaticaans Concilie, II*, 59.

209 See: Elizabeth Johnson, *Truly Our Sister: A Theology of Mary in the Communion of Saints* (New York – London: Continuum, 2006), 123–134; Bogdan Ferdek, *Nasza Siostra – Córą i Matką Pana. Mariologia jako przestrzeń syntezy dogmatyki* (Świdnica: Świdnicka Kuria Biskupia, 2007), 133–148: Elżbieta Adamiak, *Błogosławiona między niewiastami. Maryja w feministycznej teologii Cathariny Halkes* (Lublin: Redakcja Wydawnictw KUL, 1997), 99–108.

210 MGVM, 24–7.

211 E. Schillebeeckx, *Maria, Moeder van de verlossing. Religieuze grondlijnen van het Maria-mysterie* (Antwerpen: Apostolaat van de Rozenkrans, 1955).

212 E. Schillebeeckx, *Mariologie: gisteren, vandaag, morgen*, in Edward Schillebeeckx and Catharina Halkes, *Maria: gisteren, vandaag, morgen* (Baarn: Nelissen, 1992), 23–58; see later translations: Edward Schillebeeckx and Catharina Halkes, *Mary: Yesterday, Today, Tomorrow* (New York: Crossroad, 1993), 12–46; *Mariologia: ieri, oggi, domani* (Brescia: Queriniana, 1995), 25–70.

pre-conciliar and the post-conciliar period. The greatest achievements of Mario-logical work of that period include: the turn to a historical image of Mary based on the Bible and taking into account the results of the latest exegesis; appreciation of Mary's specific corporeal and spiritual motherhood; an attempt to highlight the sacramental and universal nature of motherhood; avoiding simplified and too one-sidedly interpreted parallels between Christ and Mary in order to develop the subject of the relationship between Mary and the Church; the conviction that Mary should be theologically situated more on the side of the community of faith that welcomes Christ; and the emphasis on the representative function of Mary. Biblical exegesis plays a significant role in the development of Mariological thought. Schillebeeckx supplements synoptic Mariology with the more universalist Mariology of John. The image of Mary, the Mother of Jesus, derived from His childhood, is expanded and completed with the image of Mary, the Mother of all believers, by the cross. During the Conciliar discussions, Schillebeeckx (together with the Dutch theologian, Jan Groot) opposed a separate document concerning Mary and postulated (1) the inclusion of the Marian doctrine as Chapter VIII of the *Dogmatic Constitution on the Church* and (2) the abandonment of the title "Mary, Mother of the Church" due to its ambiguity.[213]

According to Schillebeeckx, Chapter VIII of *Lumen Gentium* is an optimal, inter-mediate way between the extremes of Mariological maximalism and minimalism. The factors that shaped the new image of Mary in the dogmatic consciousness of Schillebeeckx included: an increasing ecumenical sensitivity, theology of liberation from Latin America represented mainly by Leonard Boff, and the dynamically developing feminist theology represented in the Netherlands, among others, by Catharina Halkes.[214]

The most important ecclesiotypical elements in Schillebeeckx's Mariology in-clude: the absolute primacy of Christ as the sole Redeemer of mankind; opposition to the isolation of Mariology; the need for complementary Mariological approaches which combine Christology and ecclesiology; recognition of Mary's cooperation in the work of redemption through her active receptivity; demonstrating unique and profound motherly connection with the primordial sacrament; accentuating the spiritual motherhood of Mary and the development of her faith, while omit-ting the issue of co-causing redemption, as well as avoiding the use of the term

---

213 "Met de Nederlandse oecumenische theoloog, mgr. Jan Groot, werd ook ik uitgenodigd door kardinaal König. Wij adviseerden het volgende: ten eerste moet de *Maria-leer* een hoofdstuk worden van en binnen de ecclesiologie van *Lumen Gentium* en ten tweede moet de titel *Maria, moeder van de kerk* worden vermeden." MGVM, 26.

214 MGVM, 23–4; cf. Feder, "Mary, Model of Eschatological Faith," 336; Leonardo Boff, *Der dreieinige Gott* (Düsseldorf: Patmos Verlag, 1987); Catharina Halkes, *Zoekend naar wat verloren ging. Enkele aanzetten voor een feministische theologie* (Baarn: Ten Have, 1984).

"co-redemptrix" (*medeverlosseres*) and preferring the expression "participant in redemption" (*deelgenoote in de verlossing*). Ecclesiotypical elements appeared in Schillebeeckx's Mariology even before the Second Vatican Council. Hence, Conciliar Mariology can be regarded neither as a significant turning point in the Mariological work of the Flemish theologian, nor as a demarcation line between the Christotypical and the ecclesiotypical way of practicing Mariology. The Mariology contained in Chapter VIII of the constitution *Lumen Gentium* rather confirms the correctness of Schillebeeckx's theological reflection to date and, to a large extent, is its effect. It should also be remembered that the Conciliar doctrine of Mary was shaped by the heat of polemics, among which the Flemish theologian always advocated for the ecclesiotypical option. Undoubtedly, the ideas of the Council determined, to a large extent, the further directions of his scientific research. Schillebeeckx's theology cannot be understood without taking into account the achievements of Conciliar thought, just as the Church's reception of the Council cannot ignore the importance of Schillebeeckx's theology.[215]

The Second Vatican Council became (for Schillebeeckx's theological reflection) an important impulse to reinterpret the fundamental theological problems in dialogue with other sciences.[216] The central issues raised in his works concern the relationship between God and man, tradition and contemporary reality, as well as the Church and the world. Positive reference to contemporary experience in intellectual confrontation with the long Judeo-Christian tradition became the starting point for the formulation of new questions. During the Council's deliberations, Schillebeeckx, as the theological adviser to the Dutch episcopate, conducted many meetings during which he assessed, from the theological point of view, the correctness or erroneousness of the statements contained in the documents proposed by the Council.[217]

In terms of chronology, almost all of Schillebeeckx's Mariological work comes from the period preceding the Council. In terms of the content, it is not difficult to notice significant ecclesiotypical threads that have been signaled or comprehensively developed. Schillebeeckx himself describes his Mariological project as pre-Vatican views in the post-Vatican color (*voor-vaticaanse inzichten met een na-vaticaanse kleur*).[218] There is a visible paradigm shift in Edward Schillebeeckx's Mariological

---

215 Hermann Häring, "Met mensen op weg, voor mensen op weg. Over het theologisch denken van Edward Schillebeeckx," in *Mensen maken de kerk. Verslag van het symposion rond 75e verjaardag van Edward Schillebeeckx*, ed. Huub ter Haar (Baarn: Nelissen, 1989), 27.

216 Häring, "Met mensen op weg, voor mensen op weg. Over het theologisch denken van Edward Schillebeeckx," 36.

217 Huub Oosterhuis and Piet Hoogeveen, *God is ieder ogenblik nieuw. Gesprekken met Edward Schillebeeckx* (Baarn: Ambo, 1982), 150.

218 MGVM, 32.

thinking. However, the turning point between the *old* and the *new* is not marked by the event of the Council, but by the period between the first and the second edition of his seminal Mariological work. The original title of the work, "Maria Christus mooiste wonderschepping" ("Mary, Christ's Most Beautiful Creation"),[219] which suggested a rather traditional Christotypical approach, was consistently replaced in the second and the subsequent editions with the title: "Maria moeder van de verlossing" ("Mary, Mother of the Redemption"). The work was rewritten from a more perspective of salvation history and supplemented with a new chapter entitled "The Scriptural Image of the Mother of Jesus" (*Het evangelisch beeld van Jesus' moeder*), which was written using the achievements of the latest exegesis.[220]

At the end of the 1950s, Schillebeeckx turned towards *Mary in history*. The Flemish theologian raised the issue of the historical image of Mary, which led to the question of whether there is a positive connection between the Madonna of Catholic Mariology and the biblical Jewish Miriam, Mother of Jesus.[221] Unfortunately, as Schillebeeckx himself pointed out, the chapter he added was not consistently and coherently integrated into the rest of the work and did not bring the expected results. In the second and the subsequent editions, more emphasis was placed on the fact that mankind has been redeemed by God in Jesus Christ as the only Mediator. Schillebeeckx opposed the prevailing tendency to place Mary in the objective redemption on Christ's side and clearly presented the Mother of God on the side of the community of faith.[222] This idea later became the central postulate of the Conciliar Mariology.

The Flemish theologian consciously avoided using the term *co-redemptrix* (*mede-verlosseres*) with reference to Mary, instead of which he proposed a phrase *partici-pant in redemption* (*deelgenote in de verlossing*). Mary was shown as a person who took her rightful place among all the redeemed, although, thanks to the grace of Christ, her redemption was attained in a unique and privileged way. As the Mother of God, she is our greatest Sister in the Church and, at the same time, the Mother of the whole Christ, i. e. the Head and all members of the Mystical Body (*Maria als de moeder van de gehele Christus, Mater totius Christi*).[223] Schillebeeckx's pre-conciliar Mariology was against both theological and sentimental exaggeration as well as

---

219 Cf. E. Schillebeeckx, *Maria Christus' mooiste wonderschepping. Religieuze grondlijnen van het Maria-mysterie,* Antwerpen: Apostolaat van de Rozenkrans, 1954.

220 MGVM, 29–30; cf. MMV, 13–42.

221 MGVM, 30.

222 "Tegen de toenmalig overheersende mariologische tendens in, met name om Maria een plaats te geven in de zgn. objectieve verlossing, legde ik er de nadruk op dat Maria *niet aan de zijde van Jezus Christus,* maar *aan de zijde van de ontvangende geloofsgemeenschap* moet worden geplaats. Later werd dit ook een centrale affirmatie van de mariologie van Vaticanum II." MGVM, 30.

223 MGVM, 31.

the rationalist belittling of the mystery of Mary. The Flemish theologian proposed appreciation of the ecclesiotypical aspect which was fully approved by the Second Vatican Council (Cf. LG 60–65).

2. The Church as a Sacrament of Dialogue

It is impossible to find a comprehensive ecclesiology in the collection of Edward Schillebeeckx's theological publications. However, ecclesiological issues occupy an important place in many works of the Flemish theologian and were at the center of his theological interests since the Second Vatican Council.[224] The inherently mysterious reality of the Church is in itself so rich in content that it can never be cognitively understood in an adequate and exhaustive way. Hence, in Schillebeeckx's theology, there is no single "spare" definition of the Church that could always be used in scientific explications. Depending on the issues raised, new and diverse images and theories of the Church emerge, which are expressed in religious and secular language. Therefore, the Flemish theologian seeks to express his understanding of the Church rather than provide a comprehensive definition. A significant difficulty in the integral approach to ecclesial issues lies in the coexistence in the reality of the Church of the internal (redemptive, absolute) sphere related to the mystery of the redemption and the external (historical, relative) sphere reaching deep into the mystery of the temporal world.

a) The Church and the Risen Lord
Adoption of the ecclesiotypical model of Mariology postulates the development of a specific concept of the Church. The theologically correct presentation of Mary's relationship with the Church is conditional on understanding the latter's essence. Schillebeeckx understands the Church as a sacrament of the resurrected Christ (*sacramentum Christi*). She is the fruit of His suffering in the messianic sacrifice. Primarily, the Church is Christ Himself in His glorious body. He is both the Head and the members. The Church Militant (*Ecclesia Militans*)[225] is, in turn, a visible

---

224 Ambroos Remi van de Walle, "Theologie over de werkelijkheid. Een betekenis van het werk van Edward Schillebeeckx," *Tijdschrift voor Theologie* 14 (1974): 480; E. Borgman, "... als het ware een sacrament – Naar een theologische visie op de reëel bestaande kerk," *Tijdschrift voor Theologie* 1 (2010): 123–143; Stephan van Erp, "*Sign and Precursor God's Grace for All*: Schillebeeckx's Ecclesiology During the Second Vatican Council," in *T&T Clark Handbook of Edward Schillebeeckx*, eds. Stephan van Erp, Daniel Minch (London: Bloomsbury, 2020), 122–134.

225 The *Ecclesia Militans*, is a traditional name given by Catholics to the part of the Church's body that is still on pilgrimage here on earth, as distinguished from the *Ecclesia Purgans* (the Church in Purgatory) and the *Ecclesia Gloriosa* (the Church in Heaven). The term *Ecclesia Militans* appeared in Christian theology in the second half of the 12th century among French universities. In the

manifestation of the reality of salvation in history. The Church Militant can therefore be defined as a visible community of grace, made up of hierarchy and laity. The inner community of grace with God in Christ becomes visible through the Church and is realized as a social sign. At the same time, the inner community of grace and the legal community of the Church should not be juxtaposed. It would also be a mistake to consider the Church as a means of attaining salvation. The Church is Christ's salvation visibly realized in the world. Since Christ Himself is both the head and the members, the Church as a community remains Christ's reflection in this respect. Hence, despite the community bond, the functions of the laity and the hierarchy in the Church are different. Christ as the head of the People of God is revealed sacramentally in the apostolic office and in the hierarchy, while Christ as the representative of the whole People of God is realized sacramentally in the entire community of the faithful.[226]

b) The Church and Humanity

According to Schillebeeckx, the Church is not an artificial social creation based on biological unity and built on the grounds of loosely related individuals who are bound by some ideology. Instead, the Church arises from the universal calling to create a community of persons that constitutes itself around the community-forming values (*appel des valeurs*). God reveals Himself as the highest value in human life. At the same time, people become the People of God through the self-communication of God. The unity of humanity in the communion of saints (*communio sanctorum*) stems from the will of God Himself. The unity of mankind is not realized by God by means of abstract values, but through values embodied in persons. Hence, in the history of salvation presented in the Old and the New Testament, God chooses representative intermediaries. The final personification of the Father's will is realized by Jesus Christ, in Whom there has been a "great gathering" of all people around God: the church of God – *he Ekklesia tou Theou* (1 Cor 11:22). There has also been a mutual and universal communion around Christ known as the rise of Christ's Church. Through the event of Incarnation, human history found favor with God and reached its fullness. In Jesus, "the eschatological man," the history of

---

post-Tridentine era, it denoted a Church that successfully fights against its enemies, which include the devil, sin and evil lusts, as well as heretics, schismatics and representatives of other religions. In his pre-Vatican II publications, Schillebeeckx occasionally used the term *Ecclesia Militans*. However, in his post-Conciliar works, he definitively abandoned the term, preferring to refer to the Church by such names as people of God, sacrament of salvation, sacrament of dialogue, institutionalized community, story of God (verhaal van God) and story of future (verhaal van toekomst). See Richard McBrien, *The Church. The Evolution of Catholicism* (New York: HarperCollins Publishers, 2008), 136–7.

226 Schillebeeckx, *Christus sacrament van de Godsontmoeting*, 52–4.

each individual has already entered the glory of the Father. Schillebeeckx, however, notices the existence of a dialectical tension between humanity and the Church known as *the sacrament of the future* (*sacramentum futuri*).[227] The new religious meaning given by Christ to all humanity acquires its visible public character only in the Church through the trusting acceptance of the Word of God. The affirmation of God's grace and ecclesial baptism in the name of the Trinity. Following Rahner, Schillebeeckx emphasizes that Christ's triumphant grace becomes an evident, historically recognizable fact thanks to the membership in the community of the Church.[228]

There is a real difference and a dialectical tension between the Church and humanity. This tension extends from the Ascension to the Parousia. The gradual development of Christ's ecclesiogenic activities (exhortation to penance and acceptance of God's message, offer of salvation made first to the Israel and then to the whole world, the calling of twelve apostles) leads to the climax, i. e. the sacrifice of the Redemption made for all people. In the context of death and resurrection, Christ speaks explicitly about the reality of the Church built on the rock of Peter. On the one hand, Christ never mentions the organized form of the Church in His public speeches, thereby making the acceptance of the Good News a condition for entering the Kingdom; but on the other hand, he mentions the founding of the Church in the context of the Sacrifice. It can be concluded that there is a clear connection between the sufferings of Jesus, the Messiah, and the post-Paschal reality of the Church that has become the body of Christ (*soma tou Christou*) through the Paschal mystery. The Church Militant is a community of grace built on the office of Peter. The events of Christ's death and resurrection demonstrated that the condition for entering the Kingdom of God lies in the accession to the sacramental, historically visible community of the Church, which is a sign of the calling for all humanity. As a result, the Church, being the universal sacrament of salvation, is not only a community of grace and the fruit of Christ's redemption, but also a redemptive institution that has been entrusted with the keys to the Kingdom of God.[229]

The distance between humanity and the Church indicated by Schillebeeckx leads to the problem of defining the boundaries between the two. The Flemish theologian distinguishes the universal People of God, significantly extended to all humanity, and the Church, in which the People of God become the Body of Christ. Christ's immanent presence in His Mystical Body is extended to His transcendence in relation to the Church. Christ, being really in the Church, at the same time goes beyond her borders and becomes a gift for all people, including people outside the

---

227 Edward Schillebeeckx, "De sacramentaire structuur van de openbaring," *Kultuurleven* 19 (1952): 797–802.

228 Cf. Karl Rahner, "Kirche und Parusie Christi," *Catholica* 17 (1963): 113–128.

229 Edward Schillebeeckx, "Kościół a ludzkość," *Concilium* 1–10 (1965/66): 30–3.

Church. Thus, Christ's action is not limited only to people who have "historically" encountered Christ's Church, but also applies to all those who have not noticed or experienced the phenomenon of the Church in a historical way. Every action of Christ as the head and the body of the Church is an ecclesial act. Hence, any anonymous relationship with Christ is at the same time a real, strong, though unconscious, relationship with the Church. As a consequence of the assumptions adopted, the distance between the Church and the world becomes radically limited, and, in fact, loses its meaning. Schillebeeckx emphasizes that the Church actually works where her adequate and specific forms do not yet exist historically. Hence, there is no reason to juxtapose the world and the Church. Part of humanity that still remains outside the Church is not an ordinary *non-Church* (*non-Kerk*), but rather a *pre-Church* (*voor-Kerk*). Schillebeeckx probably adopts from Karl Rahner a very strong theological category of "anonymous Christianity" (*anonymes Christentum*) which, though impossible to be directly called the Church, can nevertheless be attributed with an internal aspiration to a historically ecclesial disclosure in the world. In Schillebeeckx's view, all humanity seems to undergo a lengthy process of becoming a Church.[230] The grace of Christ Who operates outside the Church adopts various means of expression, including the pluralism of forms of religion and worship, as well as secular institutions whose deeper meaning is difficult to express explicitly. However, anonymous Christianity is a fragile reality and therefore requires substantiation in its own environment, in the area of ecclesial life where the Word of God, Baptism and the Eucharist are present. In accordance with the principle: *Ecclesia sancta, semper reformanda,* the Church, as a sign that reveals itself to the world, requires constant evangelical renewal in order to prove her credibility.[231] The event of Christ made humanity contain within itself an internal compass, as it were, which points to the Church. Specific desire for the Church (*desiderium Ecclesiae*) is embedded in the human heart. Schillebeeckx notes that the "Incognito Church," which is the fruit of the Holy Spirit, seeks to reveal herself both as a sign of Jesus, the eschatological man, and as a sign of a specific human life: as "Dasein zum Tode" (M. Heidegger) with the inexhaustible immortal hope that death is not the last word.[232]

The secular nature of the world on its deeper level echoes humiliation (*kenosis*) and elevation (*hypsosis*) of Christ Who is a prototype of human fate. Schillebeeckx

---

230 Cf. Giuseppe Silvestre, *Quale salvezza fuori dalla chiesa? Il Cristianesimo anonimo nella teoria di Edward Schillebeeckx* (Cosenza: Progetto, 1995); Stephen Bullivant, "The Myth of Rahnerian Exeptionalism: Edward Schillebeeckx's "Anonymous Christians," *Philosophy and Theology* 22, no. 1–2 (2010): 339–351; Karl Rahner, "Die anonymen Christen," in Karl Rahner, *Schriften zur Theologie*, Vol. VI (Einsiedeln: Benziger, 1965), 545–54.
231 Schillebeeckx, *Mensen als verhaal van God*, 213–15.
232 Schillebeeckx, "Kościół a ludzkość," 35.

advances a bold thesis about the fluidity of the boundaries between humanity and the Church. These boundaries shift in two directions: from the Church to the world and the other way around. The relationship between the Church and the world can be compared to the process of the Church's osmosis towards a world that has not yet been completed. The process of fusing the community of people and the community of saints and the disappearance of the borders is the work of God, not man. The fluidity of the borders does not eliminate the dialectical tension between the Church and the world. However, this tension does not hinder the development of secular tendencies both in the Church and in the world. Analyzing contemporary reality, Schillebeeckx notices the processes of desacralization and secularization which show that what used to be the domain of the Church only has today become the property of universal humanism (charity, education, promoting agronomy) and has taken a desacralised form.[233]

According to Schillebeeckx, secularization is a historical and cultural phenomenon which is closely associated with the development of cognitive horizons and the appreciation of rational human activities. In this sense, secularization recognizes the autonomy of the created reality and is a positive phenomenon. According to Schillebeeckx, one should clearly distinguish between secularization (*la sécularisation*) and secularism (*le sécularisme*).[234] The secularization of the Church in this respect is a positive, purifying and sanctifying process, as it grows out of the transcendent communion with God in Christ (*Het niet-godsdienstige humanisme als "katharsis" van het geloofsdenken en de geloofshouding*).[235] Otherwise, the Church would only be reduced to an institution similar to the United Nations or UNESCO.[236]

According to Schillebeeckx, St. Paul in Ephesians 1:10; 22–23 and Colossians 1:16–20 already showed that there is no ecclesial vacuum in the entire universe, because the whole reality after Resurrection and Ascension is filled with Christ Who is the Church *in sensu stricto*. Schillebeeckx refers to the position of the exegete H. Schlier, who in his commentary to the Letter of St. Paul to the Ephesians wrote: "There is no realm of existence which is not the realm of the Church. Basically, the Church is focused on the whole being. The Church also finds her limits only within this whole. There is no realization of Christ's reign outside the Church or without the Church, just as there is no perfection outside or without the Church. The way the universe rises towards Christ is through the Church that

---

233 Schillebeeckx, *Je suis un théologien heureux*, 83; cf. Schillebeeckx, *God the Future of Man,* 56–90.

234 Paul VI also pointed out the need to distinguish *secularism* understood as the negation of God from *secularization* understood as recognition of the autonomy of the temporal world; cf. EN 55, 56.

235 Cf. Edward Schillebeeckx, *God en mens* (Bilthoven: Nelissen, 1965), 43–6.

236 Schillebeeckx, "Kościół a ludzkość," 34–5.

rises towards Him. Of course, there are spheres that resist and oppose being filled with the Church because they are completely filled with themselves."[237]

For Schillebeeckx, the Church and humanity constitute one and the same perfectly integrated reality in eschatological terms. Recognizing the existence of a real "incognito Church" requires us, at least on a very general level, to indicate the features that enable her identification. Schillebeeckx argues that the basic criterion is not so much interpersonal solidarity as such, but rather the special quality of brotherhood expressed through the love for the little and the weak ones (Mt 25: 31–46). Following Christ's love to the end is always a way of realizing community in Christ, that is, of forming the Church, even if it is done without proper awareness. The parable about the Good Samaritan is the basis for the statement that the "incognito Church" transcends the boundaries of an institutional, historical and visible community of faith, and can arise wherever the abundant love, shown not necessarily by practicing Christians, is authentically experienced. The Church is formed wherever love transforms people into brothers. The essence of the Church is therefore not the hierarchy itself, but the entire People of God relying on brotherly love. Hence, the official Magisterium of the Church always serves an ancillary function for the People of God. Consequently, solidarity with others in Christ has a sacramental quality and is the basis for the general sacramentality of every form of human solidarity.[238]

c) The Dialogic Dimension of the Church

The Church does not exist in a social, cultural and political vacuum, but constantly inculturates into our contemporary reality. According to Schillebeeckx, dogmatic consciousness is currently experiencing a transition from a monological Church shaped by the principles of feudalism to a dialogical Church that takes into account the mentality of contemporary people. The novelty of the present moment is that the Church as a whole has accepted dialogue with the world as her primary task. This state of affairs is confirmed by the documents of the Second Vatican Council and the encyclicals: *Pacem in terries* (John XIII), *Ecclesiam suam* (Paul VI), and *Populorum progressio* (Paul VI). The discovery of the dialogic dimension is the result of a new self-understanding of both the Church and the world.[239]

---

237 Heinrich Schlier, *Die Zeit der Kirche. Exegetische Aufsätze und Vorträge* (Freiburg im Breisgau: Herder, 1956), 69.

238 Schillebeeckx, "Kościół a ludzkość," 38–40.

239 Schillebeeckx, *God the Future of Man*, 124.

The idea of the Church as the *sacrament of the world* (*Ecclesia sacramentum mundi*, LG 1; 9; 48, GS 43; 45)[240] seems to be the key factor here, although it does not often appear in the Conciliar documents. The ambiguous word "the world" should in this case be understood not so much in the physical or cosmic aspect, but more anthropologically as a brotherhood or a human way of existence in dialogue with others.[241] The Vaticanum II (cf. GS 92) emphasizes the specificity of the Church, indicating that she is to be a sign of universal brotherhood. Overcoming the barriers of isolation and making contact with the world becomes an important task for the Church. Schillebeeckx, like Gibson Winter, associates the ministry of conciliation entrusted by Christ to the Church with the task of renewing communication with society.[242]

In the language of the Conciliar documents, the dialogic character of the Church was expressed in the following way: "In Christ, the Church is a kind of sacrament, that is, a sign and an instrument of intimate union with God and the unity of the whole human race" (LG 1, GS 42). The truth itself has a tendency towards dialogicality. The truth of one man, Schillebeeckx emphasizes after Reuel Howe, must be included in the relation to the truth of others so that the full dimension of truth can be known.[243] The relationship of the Church to the world has been reduced here to a dialogic exchange of truths between the Church and the world. In the context of thus formulated problem, the following reservation might be voiced: is a sincere dialogue possible between two partners, one of whom is convinced that (s)he knows the whole truth?

Edward Schillebeeckx opposes the perfectionist vision of the Church (*societas perfecta*) and emphasizes that although the fullness of God's promises does indeed remain in the Church, whose task is to guard, preserve and fulfill them historically, it cannot be argued that the Church always has a ready answer to all problems posed by the modern world. The task of humanizing the world is also part of the religious mission of the Church. This task needs the light of the Divine Revelation that comes through humanity and its experiences. That is why the Church is constantly eschatologically oriented. Being constantly on the way to the Kingdom of God, the Church must take into account the fact that at the current historical stage she is not yet identical with the Kingdom of God (LG 5, 8, 9, GS 1, 40, 45). Only the final reaching of the Kingdom of God will allow the mystery of God, present here

---

240 Cf. Joris Geldhof and Leo Kenis, "The World and History as Sacrament: Schillebeeckx on the Eve of the Second Vatican Council," in *T&T Handbook of Edward Schillebeeckx*, eds. Stephan van Erp and Daniel Minch (London: Bloomsbury 2019), 111–120.

241 Schillebeeckx, *God the Future of Man*, 123; cf. Schillebeeckx, *Gott, Kirche, Welt*, 282.

242 Cf. Gibson Winter, *The New Creation as Metropolis* (New York: Macmillan, 1963), 103.

243 Schillebeeckx, *God the Future of Man*, 124; cf. Reuel Howe, *The Miracle of Dialogue* (New York: Seabury Press, 1963), 121.

and now, to be revealed no longer as an anonymous dialogue, but as a consciously expressed *Amen* to the visible and fully obvious reality. *The Church on the way* proclaims the Kingdom of God, whose powers are already to some extent effective in herself and in the world, but only in a way that is incomplete, limited and integrated into the history marked by sin.[244]

According to the Flemish theologian, the Church can and does thematize the reality to come, but she can never do it adequately. Therefore, in each new social and cultural situation, she must constantly reinterpret her faith in the spirit of fidelity to the sole message of salvation. As a result, the Church cannot fulfill her task of proclaiming the Good News in any other way than through the dialogue with the world and human societies. Honest dialogue is necessary for the unique testimony of the Church, for it belongs to the intrinsic essence of the revelation of the Word of God in the human word.[245]

In Schillebeeckx's view, the task of the Church does not consist in communicating to the world any specific part of the revealed knowledge. In order to communicate, the Church must also receive and hear what comes from the world as the so-called "prophecy from the outside" (*Vreemdprophetie*) that speaks the language of the earthly, temporal circumstances in which, however, the community of believers recognizes the familiar voice of God.[246] The relationship between the Church and the world cannot be defined, as was the case in the past, as a relationship of the teaching Church (*Ecclesia docens*) with the world that is listening and learning (*mundus discens*).[247] The relationship is dialogic: the Church and the world listen to each other and enrich each other. The Council admits that "the Church knows how much she herself has received from the history and the evolution of human kind" (GS 44). Therefore, according to the Flemish theologian, dialogue should be understood as a proper and distinctive way the unique testimony given by the pilgrim Church exists. Through the dialogue with the world, the Church attains her essential character as the Church. Dialogue is the way the Church realizes herself in the temporal reality (*Kerk als sacrament van de dialoog*). The dialogic dimension of the Church as the sacrament of the world does not only consist in accepting dialogue as a more effective method of spreading the redemptive message. Instead, dialogue is realized through openness to others and the ability to listen

---

244 Schillebeeckx, *God the Future of Man*, 125.

245 Schillebeeckx, *God the Future of Man*, 126; cf. D'hert, *Een spoor voor ons getrokken. De Jezustrilogie van Edward Schillebeeckx*, 36–9; Jan Van Wiele, "Edward Schillebeeckx' theologie van de religies," *Tijdschrift voor Theologie* 1 (2010): 103–7.

246 Edward Schillebeeckx, "Zasięg znaczenia teologicznego wypowiedzi Urzędu Nauczycielskiego Kościoła w sprawach społecznych i politycznych," *Concilium* 1–10 (1968): 303.

247 Schillebeeckx, *God the Future of Man,* 126; Schillebeeckx. "Zasięg znaczenia teologicznego wypowiedzi Urzędu Nauczycielskiego Kościoła w sprawach społecznych i politycznych," 299.

to the voice of the world, as well as the ability to materialize in the public life of a democratic society without seeking one's own domination. Ecclesial dialogue must be understood as service to the Kingdom of God and to the good of every human being (*omnium bono inserviens*).[248]

The depiction of the Church in the context of a dialogue leads to the recognition of the formula *Ecclesia semper purificanda* (the Church always purifies herself, cf. LG 8). On the part of the Church, this requires a constant renewal of thinking, consistent conversion, rejection of outdated ideas, and the abandonment of understanding the Church in the spirit of triumphalism for the benefit of a more realistic concept in the spirit of *diakonia*. This does not lead in any way to adopting an attitude of conformism to the real evil in the world, or surrendering to the new triumphalism of destructive dialogue, which can quickly turn into a monologue "from below," replacing the rejected monologue "from above."[249]

Taking into account the dialogic structure of the Church, a question arises about the subject and the content of the dialogue with the world. At first, several levels of dialogue should be distinguished. Referring to Karl Rahner, Schillebeeckx primarily identifies the intra-ecclesial dialogue. It is realized among Christians and concerns the nature of the testimony of faith and, in the broadest sense, the promotion of good in the world and society. This dialogue is carried out in accordance with the principle of the autonomy of the created world. In a pluralist society, there is a transition from the "Church of the Masses" (*Volkskirche*) to the Church of people belonging to her on the basis of personal choice and free decision (*Freiwilligkeitskirche*). As a result, a large part of society remains outside the sphere of the Church (and religion whatsoever) understood as a specific actual sacramental community. Thus, the community of the Church meets the community of people with a different worldview who also take an active part in the world. This is where the possibility of a dialogue between Christians and non-believers, i. e. the Church and the "pre-Church" (*Voor-Kerk*), opens. It should also be remembered that from the sociological point of view, the Church appears to the world as one of the social groups which participate in the work for the good of humanity. Due to the common ground for various activities, the dialogue between the Church and other social groups is possible and necessary. Thanks to the dialogic openness of the Church, the world's distrust is overcome. The subject of the Church's dialogue with the world is always a specific human being and his or her final destiny.[250]

The reality of the dialogue enables the Church and the world to become more and more themselves and help in creating a better reality. The eschatologically

---

248 Schillebeeckx, *God the Future of Man*, 127–8.
249 Schillebeeckx, *God the Future of Man*, 129.
250 Schillebeeckx, *God the Future of Man*, 130–2.

oriented faith of the Church does not generate passive attitude and does not lead to alienation from the world, but becomes a driving force for the commitment to the development of the world and a factor which stimulates the promotion of good in the universal aspect.[251] The Church's contribution can take the form of endorsement, assistance, collaboration, or initiative. It can also be expressed in critical assessment and protest against ideologies based on the reductionist concept of man. The dialogue of the Church with the world must go along the line of seeking answers to the fundamental questions: who is man, and what is the meaning of life, death, suffering, and evil? In the process of technological development and rationalization of culture, Schillebeeckx notices, following Paul Ricoeur, the danger of losing the meaning and obscuring the highest values which results from purely instrumental projects in relation to the world.[252]

In her dialogue with the world, the Church, according to Schillebeeckx, must recognize the autonomous rights of temporal structures and tasks. As *diakonia*, the Church plays a critical role and, in fulfilling her prophetic mission, she must listen to the voice that comes from the depths of secular reality. In the clash between the Revelation and the voice of the world, imperatives and decisions which affect the future of the world are made. The radical experience of contrast (*radicale contrastervaring*) must contain some elements of positive hope for the real possibility of a better future.[253] The authoritative voice of the Church community must be heard in the humanity's endeavour towards a better future which in terms of faith can be considered as the rise in Christ towards the final Kingdom of God. Ethical imperatives arise spontaneously from particular experience of secular life. Only at a later stage are they subjected to theoretical statements and ecclesial declarations.[254] Concluding his lecture, Schillebeeckx emphasizes the need for a pre-reflective dialogue of Christians involved in the world. The dialogue takes the form of existential involvement with the world (*la présence au monde*). The redemptive presence of the Church in the world raises hope for a new heaven and a new earth, a hope that actuates human efforts. The world understood by John as the reality of evil is present not only outside the Church, but also in the Church herself. Hence, the basis of any sincere and effective dialogue at any level must consist in constant

---

251 Schillebeeckx, *God the Future of Man*, 134.
252 Schillebeeckx, *God the Future of Man*, 135.
253 Schillebeeckx, *Mensen als verhaal van God*, 24–6; Edward Schillebeeckx, "Over vergeving en verzoening: De kerk als verhaal van toekomst," *Tijdschrift voor Theologie* 37 (1997): 368–383.
254 Schillebeeckx, "Zasięg znaczenia teologicznego wypowiedzi Urzędu Nauczycielskiego Kościoła w sprawach społecznych i politycznych," 302–4.

metanoia and the implementation of the principle: *Ecclesia semper reformanda et purificanda.*[255]

In conclusion, it should be emphasized that Edward Schillebeeckx abandons the substantialist approach to the Church, typical of Thomism and based on Aristotle's category of substances. Instead, he proposes a concept with its origin in the thought of St. Augustine: the relationalist concept of the Church that becomes herself and fulfills herself through the relation to the world. The sacramental and dialogic vision of the Church presented by the Flemish theologian is an extremely important attempt to overcome both the static, synchronic attitude (excluding history) and the dualistic approach to the relationship between the Church and the world. For the Flemish theologian, not only does the Church have a sacramental character, but also the world is seen in a broader sense as a sacrament of Christ and a sign that reveals God and, to some extent, sanctifies man. Contrary to the former theological opinions which demonstrate contempt for temporality, Schillebeeckx's new ecclesiological concept appreciates all created reality (matter, cosmos, world, community, history) by granting it a sacramental value. The world is no longer an insurmountable obstacle to knowing God and is not considered the enemy of the Church in the Manichean spirit. Thanks to the mystery of Incarnation, the world becomes a real partner in the dialogue with the Church. Throughout history the latter has been constantly transformed into a social sacrament. All mankind is already the Body of Christ in some sense. The thesis about the Church as the sacrament of the world is an expression of a new way of thinking in which the world cannot be treated only as an object of sacramental influence on the part of the Church. Instead, the world in itself is a sign of the living God, subject to the process of ecclesialization on a massive scale. All this is possible thanks to the unity of incarnation, redemption and the perspective of eschatological fulfillment. Although the view about the fluidity of the boundaries between the Church and the world may, as H. de Lubac rightly noted, be disturbing due to its ambiguity resulting from the general nature of the very concepts of the sacrament and the world, and may even seem too optimistic or naive, it is in its essential content correct as a conclusion resulting from basic Christian truths, such as creation, incarnation, redemption, and the eschatic orientation of history and all human activity.[256]

It seems that Schillebeeckx, like H. Küng and K. Rahner, presents the Church more on the factual (material) level, perceiving her rather as a sociological unit, a tool for redeeming the world, a sign of eschatological unity, a specific manner of

---

255 Schillebeeckx, *God the Future of Man*, 137–8; Schillebeeckx, *Mensen als verhaal van God*, 213–5; cf. Ambaum, *Glaubenszeichen. Schillebeeckx' Aufassung von den Sakramenten*, 160–2.

256 Cf. Henri de Lubac, *Petite catéchèse sur nature et grâce* (Paris: Fayard, 1980). See also John Milbank, *The Suspended Middle. Henri de Lubac and the Debate Concerning the Supernatural* (London: SCM Press, 2012).

dialogue and a language in the dialogic communication between man and God. The subjective, personal side of the Church should still be refined, with emphasis on the community of Divine persons and human persons as the source and reason for her existence. Only a synthetic approach to the Church as an objective and, at the same time, subjective reality will make it possible to appreciate the Church's relationship to the human person and to the entire created reality.

Finally, it must be said that the concept of the Church as a sacrament of dialogue with the world, formulated by Schillebeeckx with a clear reference to the views of the French theologians: Victor Poucel, Pierre Charles and Teilhard de Chardin, is an important universalizing factor in shaping a theologically correct image of Mary as the Mother of the Church and the Mother of all people. On the basis of the dynamic ecclesiological foundation, the spiritual motherhood of Mary appears as a reality realized in connection with the mission of the Church, thanks to which Mary's motherhood attains a social and dialogic character of universal scope *par excellence*. It is a valuable idea that may contribute to the development of a more in-depth dogmatic justification for the Christian cult of Mary.

3. Mother of All Believers

For Schillebeeckx, the answer to the question concerning the motive for God's choice of Mary as the Mother of Jesus seems to be the culminating point in the explication of the entire Mariological doctrine.[257] According to the Flemish theologian, any determinism with regard to God should be ruled out in advance, since He always acts in an absolutely free manner. God's will is realized in perfect creative freedom. Hence, Mary, the Mother of the Savior, can never be interpreted in a deterministic, purely sociological or biological way. As a free person, Mary was invited by God to contribute to the history of salvation and carried out the task entrusted to her in the spirit of freedom. God's absolute freedom does not, however, exclude the rationality of His acts. The theological question about the motive for God's action is justified by the fact that God is good and all-knowing. Hence, every act of God has its own meaning, which, to some extent, can be discovered and explained. Schillebeeckx is opposed to theological irrationalism, admitting that a final, complete and absolute understanding of Mary on the level of theological inquiry is impossible and will always remain an unsolved mystery.[258]

---

257 MMV, 95; MThS, col. 3144.
258 MMV, 96.

a) In Search of Mariological Principle

The aim of Schillebeeckx's research is to formulate a basic Mariological principle (*het mariologisch grondbeginsel*) which, as a unifying factor, could provide a
permanent foundation for realistic teaching about the Mother of God.[259] To this
end, Schillebeeckx presents, in a critical manner, a number of significant theological projects which constitute the lasting achievement of Mariological thought
developed throughout its history.

According to Schillebeeckx, even before the emergence of the Nestorian contro-
versy, the Fathers of the Church presented Mary as *New Eve* and *the prototype of
the Church*. After the Council of Ephesus, Mary's motherhood became the central
Mariological theme. Since the time of Scheeben, theologians have attempted to
specify more precisely Mary's motherhood, adding attributes such as: spiritual,
corporeal, adequate, etc. In addition to the patristic definitions of Mary – *New
Eve* and *the prototype of the Church* – other propositions appeared: *the prototype
of redeemed humanity*, or *the first fruit of the Redemption*. As a result, renewed
theological images of Mary, which referred to patristic expressions, emphasized,
above all, the importance of the very act of faith of the Mother of God, omitting or
diminishing the importance of her specific human motherhood. On the basis of St.
Irenaeus' views, Mary was depicted as the antithesis of biblical Eve in the aspect of
faith.[260]

According to Schillebeeckx, another reason for the gradual decline of interest in
the topic of Mary's corporeal motherhood was the difficulty in integrating virginity
with motherhood and individual motherhood with universal spiritual motherhood of all mankind. The idea of formulating two separate Mariological principles
emerged in connection with these aporias. *Principium primum* was the motherhood of Mary realized in the conception and birth of Jesus (the maternal role in
the incarnation), while *principium secundum* was Mary's participation in the work
of redemption (co-redemption of the world with Christ).[261]

Edward Schillebeeckx rejects the complete separation and the alleged opposition
between the reality of the Divine motherhood and Mary's affiliative participation
in the redemption of the world. Because Mary is the Mother of Christ Who is
representative of all humanity, she enters, to some extent, the real relationship
with all redeemed humanity. Moreover, the Incarnation of the Son of God has
in itself an essential redemptive dimension (*incarnatio redemptrix*) and therefore
Mary's *fiat* concerns not only the acceptance of motherhood itself, understood as
the conception and birth of the expected Messiah, but also the implicit consent

---

259 Cf. Edward Schillebeeckx, "Maria," in *Catholica. Geïllustreerd encyclopedisch vademecum voor het
katholiek leven*, ed. A.M. Heidt (Den Haag: Pax, 1961), col. 1040–4.

260 Schillebeeckx, "Maria," col. 1040–1044; MThS, col. 3147–8.

261 MMV, 97.

to the realization of the redemptive sacrifice of the Cross.[262] Hence, Mary's co-suffering in the mystery of the crucifixion is a clear confirmation of her consent to a freely accepted specific motherhood. It should always be remembered that virginity (*maagdelijkheid*) and motherhood (*moederschap*) do not exist in the person of Mary as isolated, contradictory quantities appearing side by side, but constitute a single, complex and mysterious reality that makes it possible to call Mary a virgin mother (*maagdelijke moeder*). Mary's motherhood is not idealistic. Therefore, it cannot be treated *in abstracto*, but as a real and specific reality personally accepted by Mary in faith (*fide concepit*) and related to the absolutely perfect way of her redemption. The fundamental privilege of the Divine motherhood (*goddelijk moederschap)* has become the reason for God's action and, at the same time, the way of redeeming Mary by anticipation in the grace coming from the Cross.[263] There is therefore a permanent link between Mary's redemption and her call to motherhood. This motherhood assumes not only the fulfillment of a biological function, but above all a personal and free act of her will (faith). In Mary's case, the personal consent to motherhood entailed a completely free and conscious decision to participate in the redemptive function of Christ, God-man: "Mary's motherhood and her perfect obedience to the faith are intrinsically linked: Mary's devotion, which is exclusive and full of faith, is internally and essentially directed towards the singular, objective proposal of redemption in the person of Christ, the child of her womb."[264]

The relationship between particular motherhood and personal consent to God's plan of salvation is contained and expressed in the word *fiat*. The basic Mariological principle, according to Schillebeeckx, should be sought in a specific motherhood personally adopted in faith (*in geloof persoonlijk aanvaard concreet moederschap*).[265] Only on the basis of this principle can we properly understand and interpret the patristic attributes describing Mary as New Eve and the prototype of the Church.[266] Developing Mariology solely on the basis of the ideas concerning Marian *fiat* and

---

262 MMV, 97–8.

263 "Haar verlossing is haar moederschap, en haar moederschap maakt haar juist als moeder tot de eerstelinge van de verlossing." MThS, col. 3149; MMV, 98.

264 "Maria's eminent geloofsfiat, en het Moederschap zijn wezenlijk op elkaar betrokken; innerlijk en wezenlijk staat de uitzonderlijke geloofsovergave van Maria gericht op het uitzonderlijk obiectief aanbod van de verlossing in de persoon zelf van Christus als eigen Kind van haar schoot." MCMW, 64–5; MMV, 98–9.

265 MCMW, 61; cf. Edward Schillebeeckx, "Mutua correlatio inter redemptionem obiectivam eamque subiectivam B. M. Virginis in ordine ad eius maternitatem erga Christum et nos, ut principium fundamentale mariologiae," in *Virgo Immaculata. Acta Congressus Mariologici-Mariani Romae anno MCMLIV celebrati*, vol. IX: *De immaculata conceptione aliisque privilegis B. V. Mariae pro statu Christum natum antecedente et concomitante* (Roma: Academia Mariana Internationalis, 1957), 305–21.

266 Cf. SM (part II) 3–4.

her Immaculate Conception, without relating them to the main theme of a specific motherhood towards the Redeemer, risks being a one-sided approach. The primacy of the Divine motherhood in the construction of Marian doctrine does not mean the reduction of this reality to a purely biological, instrumental and passive level. For Schillebeeckx, the privilege of the Divine motherhood (*gooddelijk moederschap*) takes the central place in the hierarchy of the truths of faith and becomes the basis for demonstrating other aspects of Marian mystery and the main reason for God's choice.[267]

b) Sacramental Trait of Marian Motherhood

Schillebeeckx notices an important supernatural dimension in Mary's motherhood. As a person chosen by God to be the Mother of His Son, Mary was redeemed in a unique way through motherhood lived in a qualitatively unique relation to Christ, the universal primordial sacrament.[268]

If a sacrament is understood as the Divine gift of salvation offered in an external historical and discernible form, then the Person of Jesus Christ can be interpreted as the primordial sacrament (*oersacrament*). The Son of God became a real man, as defined by the Council of Chalcedon. Jesus is a true God in a human way. As a man and the Son of God, He is the interpretation and the transposition of the Divine activity into human activity. Jesus is the revealer and the personification of God's redemptive love. Thanks to this, human actions of Jesus are at the same time God's acts in a visible human form and have the redeeming power as the cause of grace. Jesus' humanity is the fulfillment of God's promise of salvation. This truth is realized especially in the great mysteries of Jesus' life: His passion, death, resurrection and exaltation alongside the Father. Jesus as a human being is a visible personal realization of the Divine grace of redemption, because, while being the Son of God, He is, in His humanity, the only way to the reality of redemption (1 Tim 2: 5). For this reason, He is rightly recognized as the primordial sacrament. The presence of Jesus, a man, was for His contemporaries a call to a personal encounter with God. That is why every human encounter with earthly Jesus was an offer of God's grace made in a human way, that is, the sacrament of the encounter with God or the sacrament of religious life understood as the existential realization of faith, hope and love. Jesus' redemptive work is a Divine gift of grace given visibly. It is the cause

---

267 MMV, 99; MThS, col. 3149; MCMW, 67–8. On the importance of the hierarchy of truths in Mario-logy, see: Stanisław C. Napiórkowski, "O właściwe miejsce Bogarodzicy w pobożności katolickiej. Pytania o hierarchię prawd," in *Maryja w tajemnicy Chrystusa*, eds. Stanisław C. Napiórkowski and Stanisław Longosz (Niepokalanów: Wydawnictwo Ojców Franciszkanów, 1997), 187–197.

268 MMV, 99.

of what it means.[269] According to Schillebeeckx, human corporeality is the basic *medium* and the condition for making interpersonal contacts.

The inherently unique incarnational bond between the Mother of God and Jesus the Son throughout their earthly lives is the basis for recognizing motherhood as a kind of sacrament, that is, a visible sign of the gift of salvation that comes through the humanity of the Son of God. For Mary, each encounter with earthly Christ was at the same time the sacrament of an encounter with God, and thus a real, historical experience of redemptive grace.[270] The sacramental character of Mary's motherhood is not to be understood in a reistic way as an additional external quality, accident or privilege. Divine motherhood is not an ordinary functional reality, but it is primarily an incarnate event of a personalistic kind (*het personalistisch, geïncarneerd gebeuren*). This means that Mary's holiness, understood as grace, is not a gift in kind, but a personal communion with the entire Holy Trinity, realized through a maternal bond with Christ, the Son of God. Consequently, Mary's motherhood can be defined as the intimacy of grace with God (*genade intimiteit met God*).[271]

Mary, as the chosen one, was redeemed through the immeasurably profound obedience of faith expressed in the word *fiat* and externalized in a totally free reception of the Universal Primordial Sacrament, i. e. the Person of Jesus Christ, God-man. Hence, the gift of her spiritual and bodily motherhood has an essential sacramental dimension. The Immaculate Conception, the state of perfect holiness and the completely intact orientation towards God are the result of the anticipation in sacramental grace coming from Jesus, the primordial sacrament. On the other hand, Mary's spiritual motherhood towards all people, her participation in the work of the Redemption and in the mediation of graces, her universal intercession and, finally, the Assumption, constitute a consistent confirmation and external expression of the inner efficacy of sacramental grace in the life of the Mother of God.[272]

---

269 Schillebeeckx, *Christus sacrament van de Godsontmoeting*, 22–5.

270 Ambaum, *Glaubenszeichen. Schillebeeckx' Auffassung von den Sakramenten*, 184; Mary C. Hilkert, "Nieuwe paden in een oude tuin. Sacramentele theologie en antropologie," *Tijdschrift voor Theologie* 1 (2010): 109.

271 MThS, col. 3149–50.

272 "Maria is de Uitverkorene, die verlost werd door haar immens-diep *geloofsfiat* veruitwendigd in het lichamelijk *ontvangen* van het universeel oersacrament, de heilige Mens Christus Jesus: de God-mens, door het Moederschap als opgenomen in een persoonlijk vrij engagement van de Moeder. Van dit gelovig ontvangen van het oersacrament-<*fide concepit*>-is Maria's Onbevlekte Ontvange-nis, haar heiligheid van vóór de Boodschap, haar vrijdom van zonden en begeerlijkheid, en haar levenshouding als <*ancilla Domini*> in maagdelijke toewijding aan God, de sacramentele vooraf-werking, terwijl haar geestelijk moederschap over ons, haar specifiek-mariaal deelgenootschap in de verlossing en mede-verdienend middelaarschap van alle genaden en ten slotte haar vervroegde ook

According to Schillebeeckx, the mystery of Jesus' Mother can be considered from two points of view. When interpreting Mary through the prism of faith, it is easy to come to the conclusion that she is a type of the Church and New Eve, a model of every redeemed human life. On the other hand, by taking the objective sacramental gift of Christ's bodily conception as the starting point, one can better understand Mary's participation in her subjective redemption and in the redemption of all people. The two approaches to interpreting the mystery of Mary are not mutually exclusive but complement each other.[273]

For Schillebeeckx, a realistic and rational Mariological doctrine should function as an organic whole, the keystone of which must be a single Mariological principle that possibly takes into account all aspects of objective and subjective Redemption.[274] The key to understanding Mary's greatness lies in the mystery of her motherhood, which she undertook in the atmosphere of faith and in a completely free manner. The objective fact of the Divine motherhood does not necessitate theological isolation of Mary from the community of the Church. Mary's motherhood is a gift for the Church community and unites the Mother of God with the members of the Mystical Body even more. The clearly ecclesiotypical character of Schillebeeckx's Mariology does not mean acceptance of ecclesiological egalitarianism. Because of the privilege of the Divine motherhood, Mary remains in a double relationship to the humanity redeemed by Christ. In the community of the Church, she is not only our sister, but also our mother, the mother of the whole Christ, both the Head and the members.[275]

Schillebeeckx emphasizes that the person of Mary has been entrusted by God with a universal task in the work of objective redemption of the world, which she has fulfilled through the spiritual acceptance and bodily conception of the sole Redeemer, Jesus Christ. On the basis of an act of God's free will, Mary's motherhood plays an important role in the economy (distribution) of graces. The role of Mary, however, does not lie in the autonomous and arbitrary administration of the treasury of Christ's merits, but in her maternal commitment to the mystery of the Incarnation, which underlies the economy of graces.

---

lichamelijke verheerlijking, er de *consequente sacramentele intrinsieke efficaciteit* van uitmaken." MCMW, 66–7; MMV, 99–100.

273 MCMW, 67.

274 MMV, 100.

275 "Maria is niet alleen onze zuster, maar ook onze moeder: de moeder van <de gehele Christus, hoofd en ledematen>, *de mater Creatoris:* <de geëngageerde> en derhalve *moederlijke* moeder van al-scheppende almacht." MMV, 100–1; MGVM, 30–1; cf. HK, 239: "Die Kirche, deren Bild sie [Maria] also ist, sind wir zusammen. So gesehen, ist Maria unsere Schwester. Doch die Kirche ist für jeden von uns wie eine Mutter um uns. So gesehen, ist Maria, die lebende Personifikation der Kirche, unsere Mutter."

c) Epiphanic Character of Mary's Motherhood

Theological analysis of Mary's motherhood reveals an essential element in Christ's very act of redemption. It is the feminine and maternal dimension of the good.[276] The Bible reveals the goodness of God's redemptive love both in paternal and maternal dimensions. Several Old Testament passages describe God's love by comparing it to motherly love (Jer 30:3; Hos 11:4; Is 49:15–16). Tenderness, delicacy and sensitivity are unique attributes of a mother and therefore could not have been developed and shown in the Person of Jesus, a male. Only a woman is able to reveal the depth of her subtle maternal love. Hence, one of God's reasons for choosing Mary as the Mother of God was to manifest through her the maternal dimension of the Divine love.[277]

Schillebeeckx puts great emphasis on the truth that Mary, as a gentle woman and a tender mother, played a unique and irreducible role in the work of the Redemption.[278] Of course, the maternal function of Mary in the work of the Redemption does not have totally autonomous characteristics and is not realized without the necessary connection with Christ, the sole Redeemer. Every activity of Mary is always perfectly harmonized with Christ's mission. Mary is a Mother *sui generis* because, while remaining a virgin, she concentrated her motherly care on the only Son, Christ. Mary's virgin and motherly love directs all people towards Christ. In this sense, Mary fulfills the function of a caring guide in faith and love towards the Church community, which was expressed in the traditional expression "Mater amabilis."[279]

Edward Schillebeeckx recalls that Mary's kindness, tenderness, sacrifice and maternal concern found their permanent expression in Catholic piety, which is characterized by greater warmth than Protestant piety. Mary enables us to participate in Christ's sacrifice in the spirit of gentle and kind obedience. The actual birth of Christ *ex Maria virgine* is not an accident, but an expression of a profound knowledge of the psyche and respect for the human heart on the part of the Holy Trinity.[280] Christ and Mary form an inseparable dyad that allows man to better understand the *tremendum* of the Cross. The drama of the redemptive death on the cross is humanized by the presence of Mary – a tender woman and a loving Virgin

---

276 "Zo wordt Maria door God uitverkoren om het vrouwelijke en moederlijke aspect van Gods zowel man als vrouw transcenderende goedheid en liefde te vertegenwoordigen." MGVM, 34; cf. MMV, 101.

277 MMV, 101–2.

278 "Nochtans kan in de man Jesus die moederlijke mildheid, die zacht tederheid, *ja dat <quid* nesciam> van <Moeder> niet als zodanig geëxpliciteerd worden. Dat kan alleen in een vrouwelijke Moeder." MCMW, 58–9.

279 MCMW, 59–60.

280 MMV, 102–3.

Mother. From this perspective, Schillebeeckx perceives the work of the Redemption as the highest elevation of humanity (*de hoogste verheffing van de mensheid*). In the Christian tradition, Mary has therefore been rightly called *dulcedo* (sweetness) because of the perfect realization of the role of New Eve in the plan of salvation.[281]

d) Motherhood as Diakonia

Edward Schillebeeckx also attempts to yield significant implications for Mariology from the analysis of the phenomenon of motherhood. It is a complex, dynamic and developmental reality.

Mary's motherhood is associated not only with the gift of life to her Son, but also with the task of upbringing and educating Jesus, Who, as a human being, was subject to all the laws of developmental psychology and pedagogy. Mary introduces Jesus to history, religion, language, culture, national tradition and the world of human values. Her motherhood is also expressed through the social gift consisting of engaging Jesus in social life. Schillebeeckx demonstrates, in a realistic way, Mary's influence as a mother on shaping the human character of her Son. Since the Bible shows Christ as a pilgrim doing good, it should be borne in mind that Mary had to play the motherly role in Christ's interpretation of the Divine love.[282]

Christ, as Mary's Son, is therefore a particular personal reflection and extension of His mother in the real sense of the word. Schillebeeckx appreciates the importance of the family environment in the process of Jesus' growth and upbringing. Although in the proper sense only Christ as the Messiah, as God in humanity, took responsibility for the realization of the redemption in the world, Mary, nevertheless, became Christ's maternal partner on the historical level – in the environment of the holy family of Nazareth – and, being a mother, she in fact had a particular influence on all life events. We should accept the thesis that Mary, as part of Jesus' upbringing, also took responsibility for the fate of the Redemption. The whole person of Mary, i. e. all her inner and outer activity as a mother, was a principle that continually transformed, in a maternal way, all the thoughts, desires and feelings of Christ that concerned the realization of the redemption.[283] In the Flemish theologian's view, Mary is the effective expression and motherly translation of the Divine language of grace, mercy and redemptive love, revealed in visible and expressive form in the Person of Christ the Redeemer.[284] The specific bodily and spiritual motherhood

---

281 MCMW, 60; MMV, 103.

282 MMV, 103–4; Schillebeeckx, *Jezus, het verhaal van een levende,* 150; cf. Snijdewind, *Leeswijzer bij "Jezus, het verhaal van een Levende" van Edward Schillebeeckx,* 34–5; Logister, "De passie van en voor Jezus Christus," 47–8.

283 MMV, 104.

284 "Heel het wezen van Maria is niets anders dan *voortdurende omzetting* in *moederlijkheid* van al wat Christus denkt, voelt en doet voor ons heil: Zij is de genaderijke *vertaling in moederlijke termen,*

of Mary is the theological basis and at the same time a necessary condition for understanding the dogmatic development of all Marian doctrine.[285]

Simple scripturistic formula: *Mary, the mother of Jesus*, contains the entire theological depth of *mysterium Mariae*, which constantly finds new interpretations in the history of theological thought. Mary's motherhood cannot be limited to the mere act of Christ's birth, but should be seen in a broader perspective as a long and heterogeneous process of development and growth throughout her life. Schillebeeckx notes that full and mature motherhood is always the result of constant action and reaction in the relationship between a mother and a child. Hence, Mary's motherhood, according to Schillbeeckx, is a dynamic and progressive reality (*progressieve werkelijkheid*), which can be schematically expressed by means of the following stages:

1) The preparatory stage – Immaculate Conception and virgin life as an essential and indispensable element of the preparation for accepting motherhood in the service of the Kingdom of God.
2) The Nazareth stage – Annunciation as the event of Mary's actual acceptance of the incarnational motherhood to the Redeemer and of the spiritual motherhood to all humanity awaiting Christ's redemption.
3) The Calvary Stage – Maternal communion with the suffering Christ as an expression of spiritual motherhood to all the redeemed.
4) The pentecostal stage – the experience of Pentecost as the achievement of full awareness of the maternal mission in the community of the redeemed (within the redeemed world).
5) The eschatic stage – the appointment of Mary as mother and queen in the mystery of the Assumption as the consequence of her motherly love for the sake of the final realization of the Kingdom of her Son.[286]

In the context of the dynamic concept of Mary's progressive motherhood adopted by Schillebeeckx, the traditional Marian titles: "co-redemptrix," "mediator of grace," or "intercessor of all people" must be interpreted not as autonomous, individual functions or abilities, but in a more personalistic spirit as the expression of Mary's personal communion with Christ which reaches its fullness in heaven. The Assumed Mary, as the glorified *Mother of the Redemption* (*Moeder van de verlossing*) in the community of saints, clearly identifies herself in maternal love with the redemptive

---

van Gods barmhartige verlossingsliefde die ons in Christus verscheen." Edward Schillebeeckx, "De Schrift zwijgt over Maria!," *De Bazuin* 38, no. 16 (1955): 2.

285 MMV, 104; cf. OTh, 196–200.

286 MMV, 105; Schillebeeckx, "De Schrift zwijgt over Maria!," 2.

acts of her Son, the Redeemer. Other numerous Marian titles express the same reality in different ways and must be applied in the correct proportions.[287]

e) Mary as a Type of the Church

To define Mary's relationship to the Church, it is, first of all, necessary to explain the reality formulated in the word *Ecclesia* as precisely as possible. Schillebeeckx emphasizes that Christ, as the representative of the human race, is Himself the Church. The sacrifice made by God on the cross was made in the name of all mankind. The Flemish theologian recalls Augustine's famous adage: "Christ died so that the Church might arise" (*moritur Christus ut fiat Ecclesia*).[288] Therefore, the Church born of Christ must be understood more in a personal than a material way. The Church is a community of faith inspired by the Holy Spirit. The members of the Church constitute the New People of God, a community of grace and faith, a communion of persons belonging to Christ and hopefully waiting for the glorious parousia. Due to the social nature of man, the invisible community of grace and faith takes the visible form of a community of persons, although in terms of her origins, the Church is not a social creation of humanity's community aspirations, but comes "from above" – from Christ.[289]

For Schillebeeckx, the Church is a visible community established on earth by Christ in order to continue the work of redemption. Christ immortalizes and makes visible His redemptive work in the word and in the sacramental life of the Church. As a result, the Church has a double function:

1) She is the visible sacramentalization of the heavenly Christ. During the Savior's earthly life, each meeting with Jesus was at the same time a sacramental meeting with the living God substantiated in the holy and effective sign of Jesus' humanity. Likewise, after Jesus' Ascension, the encounter with God takes place in the external, visible Church, where Christ's holy humanity can be encountered in a sacramental way. Hence, the Church is rightly called a sanctifying community.

2) She reveals the hidden inner communion of faith and love of all those baptized in Christ. In this sense, the Church is a community of worship. The Church as one

---

287 "Within the Communion of Saints, the Mother of Jesus enjoys the most intimate human communion with the sole Redeemer. The various titles given to Mary are but other expressions of this one fundamental reality. On the basis of this same reality, moreover, all these titles are reduced to their proportions." MMR, 148; cf. MMV, 105.

288 Schillebeeckx, *Christus sacrament van de Godsontmoeting*, 52.

289 MMV, 107.

Mystical Body of Christ consists of two interconnected elements: the internal community of grace and the external, sacramental, institutional structure.[290]

Historically and chronologically speaking, the Church was called our mother (*Ecclesia Mater*) earlier than Mary, although there were certainly intuitions to recognize Mary as the mother of all redeemed (*Mater Ecclesiae*). According to Schillebeeckx, already in the first centuries of Christianity the Church was figuratively defined through the prism of the Mother of God, whom God chose and loved.[291] The biblical category of election (*electio*) is one of the most frequent methods of God's intervention in the history of the world, particular nations and individuals. In the Old Testament, Israel – the Chosen People – was a harbinger of the New People of God, i. e. the Church. The process of selecting and calling the appropriate figures initiated by God was aimed at preparing humanity for the coming of the Redeemer. This process continued until the idea of the God Who was to come gradually crystallized in human consciousness.[292]

According to Schillebeeckx, the development of the history of the world and the mankind guided by God's grace progressed towards the fullness of time and, as a process of purification, it reached the highest and the most sublime expression in the person of Immaculate Mary who is the personification of the Chosen People. As the most receptive representative of the Chosen People, Mary became a border and a bridge between the Old and the New Covenant. To confirm this idea, Schillebeeckx cites the words of St. Thomas: "It is said that the Blessed Virgin was the boundary between the Old and the New Law, just as the dawn was the boundary between day and night" (*Dicendum quod beata Virgo fuit confinium Veteris et Novae Legis, sicut aurora diei et noctis*).[293] The mediating function of the Chosen People is transferred onto the Jewish girl, Mary, who is the personification of the Daughter of Zion. Hosea's prophecy contained in Hosea 2:20–24 can be interpreted from Mariological perspective.[294] Granting Mary the function of a mediatrix in the work of salvation of mankind is solely the work of the Divine love, in accordance with the words: *elegit eam Deus et praeelegit eam*. However, the fact of being elected required of Mary a faith that would be unconditionally ready for sacrifice. This faith is the primary condition for fulfilling God's promise. Unconditionality, total flexibility

---

290 MMV, 107–8; Schillebeeckx, *Christus sacrament van de Godsontmoeting*, 55–6. On the historical development of magisterium/authority in the Church, see: Edward Schillebeeckx, *Kerkelijk ambt. Voorgangers in de gemeente van Jezus Christus* (Bloemendaal: Nelissen, 1980).

291 MMV, 108; Schillebeeckx, "Verschillend standpunt van exegese en dogmatiek," 66–8.

292 Schillebeeckx, *Christus sacrament van de Godsontmoeting*, 17–22.

293 MMV, 108.

294 Cf. Michaele G. Masciarelli, "Maria «figlia di Sion» e «Chiesa nascente» nella riflessione di Joseph Ratzinger," *Marianum* 68 (2006): 321–415.

and constant readiness to make sacrifices are the hallmarks of a truly Christian faith. Schillebeeckx analyzes the faith of three typological biblical figures: Adam, Abraham and Mary, in terms of the above-mentioned attributes.[295]

Adam's faith was put to the test of obedience by God. Unfortunately, due to his sinful fall, Adam became a type of fallen humanity. The faith of the patriarch Abraham was put to a double test by God: first in connection with the order to leave his native country, and then in connection with the order to sacrifice his only son, Isaac. Abraham believed God against all hope (*contra spem*) and thus became the Father of all believers. Finally, Mary underwent a paradoxical test of faith among contradictions. The death of her Son on the cross was the climax of Mary's test of faith. According to Schillebeeckx, Mary's faith in the hour of the cross turned out to be greater than that of Abraham, who, as a result of God's intervention, ultimately did not sacrifice His Son. Following Saint Augustine, Schillebeeckx emphasizes that Mary became the mother of the New People of God because of her *cooperatio caritatis*,[296] that is, an unconditionally selfless love.[297]

Mary was chosen by God to become the first fruit of the Redemption. She was redeemed in a special way so that, as a mother, she could typologically represent the Church that is to be maidenly faithful to Christ and fruitful as mother. The vision of the Church perfectly united with Christ in an eschatic reality was fully realized in the person of Christ's Mother (cf. Eph 5:25–27). The whole life of the Church that unfolded in history can be described as growth towards the fullness revealed in the Mother of God. With regard to Mary, one can rightly speak of an individual parousia understood as a spiritual and bodily union in glory with the risen Christ. The reality of the ideal, true, eschatic Church has already been realized in the person of Mary, although in the temporal dimension the Church is still *in via*. In this sense, it can be argued that Mary is the prototype of both the earthly Church and the spiritual life of every believer, and so far only she has been the eschatic Church in the full sense.[298]

Schillebeeckx does not limit the meaning of the words *type* and *prototype* to the objective dimension understood as a static example, ideal, model, convention, or canon, but associates them more closely with the personal dimension of Mary.

---

295 MMV, 109.

296 "Sed plane mater membrorum eius, quod nos sumus; quia cooperata est caritate, ut fideles in Ecclesia nascereur quae illius capitis membra sunt, corpore vero ipsius capitis mater." St. Augustine, *De sancta virginitate* 6, 6, PL 40, 399.

297 MMV, 111.

298 "De hemelse moeder Gods is aldus het oertype van de aardse kerk en van het geestelijk leven van elke gelovige." MThS, col. 3142; Ambaum, *Glaubenszeichen. Schillebeeckx' Auffassung von den Sakramenten*, 185.

Christ's mother is not an objective, "cold" and perfect model, but a personal manifestation and a vivid summary of God's purposes in relation to the Church. The word *type*, already used by the Fathers of the Church, should not be understood as a static, ideal image to be admired and imitated. In Mary as a type of the Church, one should see a more dynamic element, which is the real presence of the redeeming power (*een dynamische heilskracht*). As a result, Mary, as a type of the Church, personally and effectively helps the community of believers to achieve all that has already been typically realized by Christ in her person.[299] Schillebeeckx seems not to deny Mary a specific form of agency with regard to the subjective realization of the redemption in the community of the Church. However, Mary's influence on the realization of the subjective redemption in relation to all people is very delicate and discreet. The pro-ecclesial dimension can be discerned in Mary's maternal activity. Mary, as the mother and the type of the Church, collaborates maternally with the Church formed by Christ in the work of the latter's development.[300]

The expression "maternal cooperation" (*moederlijke medewerking*) used by Schillebeeckx may constitute a theological justification for describing Mary as the Mother of the Church (*Moeder van de Kerk*). This does not mean granting Mary the function of the creator of the Church, which is unquestionably the work of Christ and the Holy Spirit. Instead, the title should be understood in the sense that the Church discerns in the perfect icon of the Immaculate Mother her ideal eschatological image revealed by God and the model of the sacramental meeting (*sacramentele ontmoeting*) with the mystery of Christ.[301] In this way, the Church becomes aware of the truth that she really owes her maternal character to Mary. Together with Mary and in imitation of Mary, the Church becomes more and more virginal and maternal, breeds new Christians, develops a personal relationship between man and God, sanctifies and educates. Any theological attempts to position Mary above or beyond the Church are, according to the Flemish theologian, completely wrong, because, despite undisputed merits and privileges, she will always remain a member of the Church, which was beautifully expressed by St. Augustine: "Mary is part of the Church, a holy member, a unique member, superior to others, but a member of the whole body."[302] It must not be forgotten that Mary plays the wonderful, irreplaceable role of the spiritual and

---

299 MThS, col. 3142.

300 "Daar Maria als *moeder* het typus van de kerk is, werkt zij nu op hemels-moederlijke wijze mede aan de kerk die door Christus wordt uitgebouwd en opgetrokken." MThS, col. 3142; MMV, 111–2.

301 Ambaum, *Glaubenszeichen. Schillebeeckx' Auffassung von den Sakramenten*, 185–6.

302 "Maria portio est Ecclesiae, sanctum membrum, excellens membrum, supereminens membrum, sed tamen totius corporis membrum." St. Augustine, *Sermo XXV*, PL 46, col. 938. For more on St. Augustine's contextual Mariology, see: Marek Gilski, *Mariologia kontekstualna św. Augustyna* (Lublin: Wydawnictwo KUL, 2006).

physical womb of the Church.[303] The idea seems to be particularly theologically useful for Schillebeeckx in explicating the relationship between Mary and the Church.

f) Mary in Relation to the Sacramental and Hierarchical Church

When making theological comparisons between Mary and the Church, it is necessary to take into account the fundamental distinction which implies two irreducible aspects of the Church: the community of grace and the hierarchical institution. The Church, understood as the visible community of the hierarchy and the lay faithful, is an earthly sign of the grace of redemption. Schillebeeckx definitely rejects the earlier division into the soul (the internal communion of grace with Christ) and the body of the Church (a visible communion with her members and authorities). According to the teaching of Pope Pius XII, the visible Church is the Mystical Body of Christ in which there is no duality of internal and legal community. The unity of the community of faith does not, however, abolish the ecclesiastical differences between the sacramental functions of the laity and the hierarchy. The difference between the hierarchy and the faithful in general is based on the dual function of the glorious Christ, Who is in Himself both the head of the Church and her members. The Church, i. e. the sacramental Christ, is a reflection of this reality. As the Head of the People of God, Christ is revealed formally and functionally in the historically shaped apostolic office, while Christ as members of the People of God is revealed in the entire community of the faithful, both in the laity and in the hierarchy. The visible presence of grace and its granting are realized in two ways:

1) Through the apostolic function exercised in the Church by virtue of the sacrament of the Holy Orders;
2) Thanks to the universal mission of the faithful by virtue of the sacraments of Baptism and Confirmation.[304]

According to Schillebeeckx, Mary can be regarded as a type of the Church understood only in the aspect of a visible community of grace and not as a hierarchical institution. She is rightly called a figure, an image, or a perfect realization of the Church understood as a community of graces (*communio gratiae*). As a human person redeemed by Christ, Mary enjoys the privilege of being filled with grace as if in excess. It is not about the quantitative dimension, but about the social character of grace, which is a gift received by a particular, individual person in the service of others. On this basis it can be concluded that the fullness of grace enjoyed by Mary

---

303 "Doch in die Kerk is Zij [Maria] de geestelijk-lichamelijke moederschoot van de Kerk. Als *moeder* wekt Zij de Kerk ten leven." MMV, 112.

304 Schillebeeckx, *Christus sacrament van de Godsontmoeting*, 53–5.

is a gift of an ecclesial, *diakonia* and community-forming character. The abundance of grace generates in Mary a universal causative power for all people. The grace of the Immaculate Mother of God has the ability to effectively influence people in a way that is adequate to the subject of grace, i. e. the person of Mary. It is always a maternal influence, the source of which is in Mary's caring love as a mother.[305]

On the other hand, grace received from God through the sacramental activity of the Church has a priestly character and is by no means mediated by Mary, because it does not belong strictly to the hierarchy of the Church. Schillebeeckx unequivocally states that Mary is not a priest and does not perform sacramental functions in the Church, which does not mean, however, that the grace received from the sacraments is completely beyond her influence. Sacramental grace is always the grace of Christ, Who, historically, shared many of His Mother's characteristic features. Schillebeeckx tries to point out that the mother-son relationship between Mary and Jesus is realized not only in the functional dimension (mother-son, parent-child, caregiver-ward), but also in the deepest dimension of the ontic relationship between a mother and a son (mother's personality – son's personality). Hence, it can be said that the grace which is solely a gift of Christ contains specific Marian features.[306]

The task of the Church, which is a visible community of grace, is to make the work of redemption present and to distribute redemptive grace among people in an institutional way that is specific for her. As a redemptive institution, the Church fulfills the function of the mediator of grace elaborated by Christ and co-elaborated by Mary.[307] It should be remembered that the Mother of Christ is not a structural principle of the hierarchical Church. This does not diminish in any way Mary's importance, since she fulfilled the maternal function entrusted to her by God from the very beginning of Christ's redemptive act. Communicating redemption to people is the task of the sacramental Church, not Mary's.[308]

Schillebeeckx notes that all sacramental activity of the Church in the mediation of graces, understood as a personal reception in faith and love of the gift of Christ's redemption, can be seen as a reality previously and typically announced and realized in the earthly life of the Mother of God. Mary did not receive grace from any specific sacrament, but as the Mother of Jesus, she received the primordial sacrament in her life, that is, the historical Person of Jesus Christ Who is the embodiment of God.[309] As a result, the reception of Jesus Christ as the primordial sacrament allowed Mary to become the prototype of the Church's sacramental life from the point of view of

---

305 MMV, 112.
306 MMV, 112–13.
307 MMV, 113.
308 MMV, 113.
309 MMV, 72.

the person receiving grace (*ex parte recipientis*).[310] The reality of the sacramental reception of Christ by Mary on the basis of anticipation towards other members of the Church was presented in an interesting way by Leo the Great in the words: "He gave to water that which He bestowed upon His mother" (*Dedit aquae quod dedit matri*).[311] This means that the Power of the Most High, which was first the principle of Christ's conception in the Virgin's womb, today sanctifies the baptismal water, making it capable of realizing new birth in the Holy Spirit.[312] The dispenser (*minister*) of the sacraments is primarily Christ Himself and the sacramental Church in His power. Mary is not a minister of the sacraments instituted by Christ. Rather, she takes her place on the side of those who receive the sacraments, although her sacramental life is realized in a unique way based on maternal self-identification with Christ's work of redemption. She was the first Christian to accept Christ, the primordial sacrament, in perfect faith and love. We receive the sacraments surrounded by her active receptivity.[313]

Theological model of Mary's relationship with the Church constructed by Schillebeeckx allows us to avoid the erroneous imputation of priestly attributes to Mary, while maintaining the essential relationship of the hierarchical aspect of the Church with the universal and maternal function of Mary's mediation in the mystery of redemption. Schillebeeckx emphasizes Christ's unique and inviolable position as the sole Redeemer. Mary identifies herself materially with the redemptive work of Christ, which leads to the discovery of the truth that Christ's grace is at the same time a specific gift of Mary who is rightly called the intercessor of grace.[314]

With regard to the sacraments, it must be strongly emphasized that Mary is outside the structural aspect of the sacraments, but not outside the sacramental life. It would be a mistake to assign Mary the function of concelebrating and carrying out with the priest the act of co-consecration of the offerings during the Holy Mass. On the other hand, it is not entirely correct to place Mary only on the side of those taking part in the Eucharist. Mary is the mother of the whole Church, both clergy and laity. The hierarchical aspect of the Church is completely inscribed in Mary's universal mediating function. If we recognize the Eucharist as an ecclesiastical sacramental *anamnesis* (remembrance) of the sacrifice of the cross carried out in the historical dimension by Christ Himself and co-carried out in a maternal way by Mary, then we should see a typical personification of the ecclesial community of grace in the Mother of Sorrows standing by the cross. Holy Orders are one of the

---

310 "Zij [Maria] is het prototype, het oerbeeld van een waarachtig christelijk, *sacramenteel geloofsleven*." Schillebeeckx, "Het geloofsleven van de *dienstmaagd des Heren*," 263.

311 St. Leo the Great, *Sermo XXV*, 4, PL 54, col. 211.

312 MMV, 113.

313 MMV, 113.

314 MMV, 113.

fruits of Christ's redemption in which Mary really participated through the most intimate maternal communion with her Son. Hence Mary, although she does not carry out the act of consecration herself, embraces with her universal and maternal influence both the act of priestly consecration and co-offering, as well as the active participation of the faithful People of God.[315]

Finally, it can be rightly said that Mary is present both on the side of Christ the High Priest as His Mother and on the side of the redeemed humanity as the Mother of all redeemed. According to Schillebeeckx, describing Mary as the Mother of the priesthood is basically correct. It should be remembered that Mary's mediation does not have a priestly and sacramental character, and therefore in Christian art she cannot be artistically represented with priestly symbols, which was emphasized by St. Bonaventure and pseudo-Anselm, among others.[316]

Maternal love binds Mary's lasting communion with the redemptive actions of her Son. Although Mary does not belong directly to the hierarchical sphere of the Church, she is the Mother of the Church in all her aspects, because of the former's privileged place in the work of redeeming the world. Mary translates into maternal language all the redeeming actions of Christ that reach people through sacramental and priestly acts.[317] Thus, Mary has a maternal, comprehensive and universal share in the historical work of redemption of all mankind carried out by Christ, the primordial sacrament, and in the subjective redemption and sanctification of all people through the reception of individual sacraments. As the Mother of objective redemption, i. e. Christ, Mary is at the same time the Mother of all people and nations (*moeder van alle volkeren*), including those who do not yet believe in Christ. In a special way, she is the Mother of all Christians who participate in the sacramental life of the Church.[318]

***

Presenting Mary's relationship with the Church, Schillebeeckx emphasizes the completely free act of electing the Virgin of Nazareth as the Mother of the Redeemer. Mary's role in the history of salvation is part of her maternal mission. Mary is presented as the Mother of the whole Christ, i. e. the Head and the Members of the Mystical Body. Mary's motherhood is a progressive reality which did not end with the earthly life of Jesus and His mother. Historical and individual motherhood is extended in a supra-historical, mystical and social form. The category of universal spiritual motherhood for all members of the ecclesial community of faith and for all people becomes essential for the theological understanding of Mary's function within the ecclesial community of faith. It is a continuous motherhood (*maternitas*

---

315 MMV, 114.
316 MMV, 114.
317 MMV, 115; cf. Schillebeeckx, "De Schrift zwijgt over Maria!," 2.
318 MCMW, 41–2; MMV, 114–15.

continua). Mary, as the type and the personification of the eschatic Church, can rightly be called both our Sister in faith and the mother of the ecclesial community. The complementary approach to Mary as a mother and a sister allows us to better demonstrate her place in the history of salvation.

An important novelty in Schillebeeckx's Mariological project is constituted by an attempt at a sacramentological interpretation of Mary's motherhood which harmoniously develops a unique and extremely creative relationship with Christ as the primordial sacrament. As a result, all Mary's activities bear true sacramental features in the sense of being the result of a profound mysterious communion with Christ Who is the historical, visible embodiment of God. In the context of natural and genuinely human mother-son relations, a strange exchange of the gift of grace takes place at the deepest interpersonal level, which determines the transcendent dimension of Mary's relationship with Jesus. Edward Schillebeeckx's appreciation for the category of Mary's spiritual motherhood brings an essential and invaluable element of universalism to contemporary Mariology.

IV. Liturgical Icon of Mary

After discussing internal relations between Mary and the Church, Schillebeeckx undertakes reflection on Mariological *praxis* expressed in specific forms of Marian devotions. The Flemish theologian makes a fundamental distinction between liturgical and non-liturgical Marian devotions. He perceives liturgy as a very important theological place, which, in accordance with the principle *lex orandi – lex credendi* (the law of prayer is the law of faith), allows us to determine the dogmatic correctness of the veneration of the Mother of God.

The specificity of Marian devotions results, among other things, from the privileged position Mary occupies in the history of salvation. Schillebeeckx gives priority to the Christocentric liturgical Marian devotions. Private Marian apparitions are only an actualization and a cultural adaptation of the permanently closed public revelation made in the Person of Christ. Yet, they have an important motivational function in deepening the faith.

Schillebeeckx notices in Marian folk piety marked with a strong emotional tinge a natural expressive function resulting directly from the psycho-physical structure of a personal being who externalizes the act of faith. One of the tasks of Mariology is to evaluate Marian devotions in terms of dogmatic correctness and to formulate their theological foundations.

1. Liturgy as the Source of Mariology

In the early 20th century, a new discipline called theological epistemology or gnoseology emerged from fundamental and dogmatic theology. It deals with the problems of pre-religious, religious and theological knowledge, and examines all reality in order to give final reasons for the credibility (truthfulness) of the truths of Christian religion.[319] The primary object of theological knowledge is the redemptive revelation realized in the Person of Jesus Christ. The secondary object is all reality considered in the light of Christ's revelation, as long as the deepest meaning of the temporal world is revealed and there is a positive mutual correlation between knowledge from the revelation and knowledge from below (grassroots knowledge). There are essentially two subjects of theological knowledge: a particular human

---

319 Czesław Bartnik, *Poznanie teologiczne* (Lublin: Pracownia Poligraficzna PKLO, 1998), 71.

being (in the proper sense) and the whole community of the Church (in the broader sense).[320]

Since the time of Melchior Cano (1509–1560), theological methodology has focused its attention on the problem of the so-called theological places (*loci theologici*), i. e. sources of theological knowledge and argumentation. The most frequently mentioned theological places are:

a) constitutive – the Bible and the Tradition;

b) declarative – motivating and justifying awareness of the Church expressed especially in doctrinal acts;

c) medial – ontic reality of the Church where the encounter between the revelation and the awareness and knowledge of the faithful takes place; includes the history of the Church, Christian experience, liturgy, spiritual life, and Christian *praxis*;

d) auxiliary and external – all worldly knowledge, i. e. philosophical, historical, natural, sociological, as well as the whole world of the human person.[321]

Edward Schillebeeckx assigns liturgy the status of an important theological place (*theologische vindplaats*).[322] In his justification, Schillebeeckx emphasizes the truth that the whole Church is the subject of the tradition of faith. The faith of the Church (*fides Ecclesiae*) is infallible in itself, while the sense of faith of the whole Church community (*sensus fidelium*) is regulated by the unanimity of the Magisterium of the Church. It is expressed, inter alia, in the liturgical prayers officially recognized by the Church. One of the most important tasks of the liturgical prayer is the authentic expression of the integral faith of the entire Church. If this task is fulfilled, prayer becomes *ipso facto* a vehicle of dogmatic value, which, in turn, makes the liturgy a reliable source for theological knowledge of faith. The essential relationship between the liturgy and the faith has been expressed in the formula *lex orandi – lex credendi* (the law of prayer is the law of faith), known since the fifth century.[323]

The dogmatic value of liturgical prayers has been noticed by the popes of recent times. For Schillebeeckx, liturgical prayer is dogma experienced in a practical way. Although it is initially unconscious, the dogma is actually present in the life of the Church from the very beginning, even before it is fully and clearly realized. As part of her historical self-realization, the Church has been gradually making her dogmatic consciousness more explicit. In its own way, liturgical prayer can contribute, in the course of centuries of tradition, to the Church's discovery of

---

320 Bartnik, *Poznanie teologiczne*, 73.

321 Bartnik, *Poznanie teologiczne*, 258–260.

322 Edward Schillebeeckx, "Loci theologici," in *Theologisch Woordenboek*, vol. II, ed. H. Brink (Roermond en Maasaik: J.J. Romen & Zonen, 1957), col. 3004–6.

323 Cf. Edward Schillebeeckx, "Lex orandi, lex credendi," in *Theologisch Woordenboek*, vol. II, col. 2926–8.

the existence of a particular truth of faith as of yet unrealized and theologically undefined. The Church's liturgical prayer is one of the essential ways of expressing the Church's living Tradition and faith.[324]

Schillebeeckx emphasizes that the solemn proclamation of the dogma is always an act of the Magisterium of the Church which is clearly religious and liturgical by nature. The dogma does not function in the liturgical life of the Church in an academic way. The liturgy is a prayerful expression of universal unanimity in faith, in which the hierarchical Church professes her faith with all believers. The liturgy experienced by the entire ecclesial community of persons is a special manifestation of the ecclesial faith in its dogmatic aspect. In this way, the liturgy can be rightly interpreted as a devotional confession and expression of the dogma, and thus become an important theological place (*locus theologicus, theologische vindplaats*).[325]

In adopting the valid principle of *lex orandi – lex credendi*, emphasis, according to Schillebeeckx, should be placed on the primacy of the objective reality of the dogma which is practically experienced in the liturgy. In modernist circles, there is a claim that the liturgy not so much expresses as creates the dogma.[326] Strong reaction to this misconception was expressed by Pope Pius XII in his encyclical *Mediator Dei*, which emphasized the truth that liturgical piety was only a manifestation and not an arbitrary creation of the dogma.[327] According to Schillebeeckx, liturgy remains an important, though not the only, source of the manifestation of faith. Above all, it is an important theological place for sacramentology and theology of spirituality. For Schillebeeckx, the liturgical argument from Tradition is identical with what St. Thomas Aquinas calls the custom of the Church (*consuetudo Ecclesiae*), which is of greater importance for the resolution of theological problems than the teaching of theologians or the Fathers of the Church. The Flemish theologian reminds us that although liturgical practice is a real ecclesial manifestation of faith, one should always bear in mind that liturgical prayers have not been constructed with the same precision as theological dogmatic definitions and treatises. Therefore, dogmatic conclusions drawn from the analysis of liturgical texts must be subject to critical scrutiny. Liturgy and dogmatics are closely related and influence each other. Liturgy tries to be an adequate, correct expression of the truth of the dogma, while dogmatic theology draws inspiration for theological research from liturgy and watches over its correctness. Following the encyclical *Mediator Dei*, Schillebeeckx notices that an in-depth knowledge of liturgical texts *per se* does not lead to the development of dogmatic consciousness. The liturgy, like all theology, is subject to the law of

---

324 OTh, 156.

325 OTh, 157.

326 Cf. George Tyrell, *Lex orandi, or Prayer and Creed* (London: Longmans, Green & Co., 1903).

327 Cf. Pius XII, *Mediator Dei*, AAS 39 (1947), 528–80.

aging and, from time to time, needs renewal and content adaptation. Hence, many liturgical formulas today constitute venerable anachronisms which cannot be the absolute criterion of dogmatic correctness for contemporary theology. Therefore, one should not indiscriminately juxtapose or contrast inaccurate or theologically obsolete liturgical formulas that articulate the insufficiently expressed dogmatic consciousness of the Church with the later, perhaps more accurately conveyed dogmatic theses. The encyclical *Mediator Dei* points to the nonsense of the so-called "unhealthy archeologism" (*ongezond archeologisme*).[328]

In addition to the traditional consideration of liturgy *in se* with the emphasis on the principle *lex orandi – lex credendi*, Schillebeeckx develops a parallel relational concept, according to which, liturgy and the sphere of temporal human activity in the world create a dynamic unbreakable dyad. The tendency to devalue Church liturgy and to diminish the supernatural dimension in theology (a secularist trend within "the death of God theology"), which exists in the circles of radical Protestant theologians (D. Bonhoeffer, P. van Buren, W. Hamilton, H. Cox, G. Vahanian, T. Altizer),[329] is a challenge for the Flemish theologian which leads to the critical analysis of the relationship between the liturgy and the life of a specific contemporary man. The cause of significant misunderstandings regarding the meaning of the external forms of Christian worship lies in a deep split and the lack of continuity between liturgical and secular activities among people.[330]

Taking up the thought of E. Käsemann, Schillebeeckx constructs the notion of the so called "secular liturgy" based on Romans 12:1–2 and Hebrews 7:13. Secular liturgy should be understood as the whole of human existence experienced and lived as a permanent act of worshiping God. The New Testament (Phil 2:17; 4:18; Heb 13:16; Rev 21:22) lays the foundation for the new understanding of worship, in which religious categories characteristic of the Old Testament law and burdened with formalism are complemented by the notion of spiritual sacrifice in everyday life made by Christians who identify themselves as the priestly People of God (1 Pet 2:5). The Bible clearly indicates the need for "secular worship" understood in a broader sense as the realization of truth, goodness, love, help, and solidarity among people. Jesus' self-offering on the cross took place not in the context of a solemn celebration, but in a specific dramatic existential situation, which, in turn, allows for the postulate that all human life should be treated as an existential form of offering a

---

328 OTh, 158.

329 Cf. Dietrich Bonhoeffer, *Letters and Papers from Prison* (New York: Macmillan, 1963); Thomas Altizer and William Hamilton, *Radical Theology and the Death of God* (New York: Bobbs-Merrill, 1966); Thomas Altizer, *The Gospel of Christian Atheism* (Philadelphia: Westminster Press, 1966); Harvey Cox, *The Secular City. Secularization and Urbanization in Theological Perspective* (Princeton: University Press, 2013).

330 Schillebeeckx, *God the Future of Man*, 95–6.

spiritual sacrifice to God. The reserve for building altars and temples which existed in the first three centuries after Christ's birth, and the eminently eschatic orientation of the early Christianity, favored the understanding of all positive temporal human activity as an expression of spiritual worship of God. St. Paul's words: "whether you eat or drink or whatever you do, do it all for the glory of God" (1 Cor 10:31) are an expression of the unity between the sacred and the profane. As a result of redemption, all reality was freed from the domination of evil forces and subjected to Christ (1 Cor 3:22–23). Redemption was then understood as a kind of exorcism: de-deification and de-demonization of secular reality, as well as breaking the cycle of absolute fate proclaimed by the ancient world. Striving to implement the principles of justice, love and brotherhood was considered by Christian communities as a social imperative stemming from the liturgy they experienced.[331]

As an insightful analyst who follows the changes in modern mentality, Schillebeeckx notices transition from the cosmocentric to the anthropocentric type of thinking. While within the cosmocentric approach the elements of nature, such as water, oil, and icons, were signs that expressed transcendent reality, within the anthropocentric approach, ethical values, such as love, social justice, and solidarity, are experienced as a sacramental manifestation of God. In the consciousness of modern man, elements of the material world are progressively losing their function of revealing God (theophany), giving way to ethical values which become an epiphanic *millieu*. According to the Flemish theologian, both the cosmocentric orientation towards the nature of the world and the anthropocentric orientation towards human history are expressions of the sacramentality of the world and should be considered in relation to each other. The sphere of humanistic values must be considered as a sacramental and historical revelation of God's presence, even more than the material world.[332] The stance of the Flemish theologian emphasizes, above all, the human person as an important center of theophany that perfectly corresponds to the humanistic sensitivity in the contemporary world. Hence, the reflection undertaken within the theology of creation must develop a personalistic thread, in which a person (*persona*) attains the status of chief methodological category in the overall cognitive process.

Christian faith should not be treated as an escape from the temporal world into the "ghetto" of Church liturgy understood as a *sui generis* asylum against the alleged evil of the material reality.[333] The Second Vatican Council emphasizes that the eschatic waiting of Christians does not eliminate undertaking worldly tasks, but motivates and impels them even more to work for a better world (cf. GS 21,

---

331 Schillebeeckx, *God the Future of Man*, 98–102.
332 Schillebeeckx, *God the Future of Man*, 110–12; cf. Schillebeeckx, *Gott, Kirche, Welt*, 41–56.
333 Schillebeeckx, *God the Future of Man*, 102; see Schillebeeckx, *God the Future of Man*, 146–164.

39, 43). Ancient Christian feasts of love (*agape*) are an example of a harmonious combination of strictly liturgical celebrations with the "secular worship."[334] Personal bond between human being and God is never realized in an existential vacuum, but is grounded in human relationships and experiences. This does not mean, however, a reduction of the vertical dimension to a purely horizontal one, which is so typical of the representatives of the death of God theology. Approval of "secular" worship entails the need to express explicitly the praise and thanksgiving to God through the participation in Church liturgy. "Secular liturgy" lived in the sphere of everyday human experiences is in its deepest dimension a gift of grace received and lived in the Church liturgy.[335]

As a result, Christian Church liturgy and "secular liturgy" cannot be considered in isolation or in opposition to each other, but as one, organic, correlative and bipolar reality. Evangelical relationship between the washing of the apostles' feet by Christ (*mandatum novum*) and the institution of the Eucharist indicates the need to perceive the sacramental dimension in a secular activity and to link the liturgical life of the Church with the realization of the ministerial brotherhood in Christ. Agapetological perspective adopted by Schillebeeckx, i. e. theological reflection on reality through the prism of the category of love shows that thanksgiving to God during the liturgy requires intensification of efforts to implement human love, solidarity, justice, and freedom, and to promote all good in the world. The reality celebrated during the Eucharist extends and, in a way, completes itself socially in human history which can thus become the history of salvation. The unity of the Church liturgy and the "secular liturgy" makes a lay person (*homo mundanus*) a real religious person (*homo religiosus*).[336]

Concluding his thought, Schillebeeckx emphasizes that liturgical worship cannot ignore the entire sphere of "secular worship" realized within the history of the world, in which the eschatic trend has already begun and is developing. Not only the physical, natural and cosmic reality, but even more everything that belongs to *humanitas* is experienced as a sacramental manifestation of God's presence, by which the Church, together with her liturgy, becomes a sacrament of world history (*sacramentum historiae mundi*) and advances towards eschatological fullness.[337] For Schillebeeckx, the profane does not identify itself with the sacred and is not a part of the transcendent reality in the pantheistic sense, but it is an autonomous

---

334 Schillebeeckx, *God the Future of Man*, 103.
335 Schillebeeckx, *God the Future of Man*, 106.
336 Schillebeeckx, *God the Future of Man*, 108–9; cf. Schillebeeckx, *Mensen als verhaal van God*, 195–7.
337 Schillebeeckx, *God the Future of Man*, 111–12; cf. Schillebeeckx, *Mensen als verhaal van God*, 201–3.

and at the same time provisional category in relation to the eschatic kingdom of God that is to come.[338]

Finally, it must be stated that the concept of a dynamic relationship between Church liturgy and "secular worship" developed by Edward Schillebeeckx has a considerable substantive and formal significance. "Secular liturgy" is not only an external test for the authenticity and sincerity of liturgical prayer or the consequence of professed faith, but it is a methodologically important condition for constructing proper theology. "Secular liturgy" plays an irreplaceable role of a preventive factor that protects theology against the danger of ideologization in the form of creating an isolated, completely abstract theoretical superstructure which is inconsistent with the world.

Schillebeeckx appreciates creative dynamism in a human person. Moreover, every positive human act, effort, effect of work, result of thought or outcome of an action has a meaning-generating function in relation to the Church liturgy. The traditional principle *lex orandi – lex credendi*, which is rightly applied to the interpretation of liturgical texts, must be supplemented by the category of "secular liturgy" understood as the existential *praxis* of the liturgically professed faith. As a result, the well-known Latin formula should be extended with yet another element, finally taking the form: *lex orandi – lex credendi – lex vivendi* (the law of prayer is the law of faith and the law of life). Therefore, theological reflection should not be limited to treating as a theological place only the collection of liturgical prayers from which theological and dogmatic content can be read, but should refer to the richness of contemporary experiences and thoroughly evaluate temporal human activity in terms of its orthopraxy. The proposal formulated by Schillebeeckx – an extremely interesting and, at the same time, deeply personalistic one – allows for a complementary approach to the liturgy by connecting it with the dynamics of human experiences, which is a valuable methodological novelty for the development of contemporary Mariology. Ultimately, the theological image of the Mother of God is influenced by both liturgical orthodoxy and living orthopraxy, which, interrelated, create a relational theological place (*locus theologicus*).

2. The Specificity of Marian Devotions

According to Edward Schillebeeckx, the cult of Mary is not autonomous and therefore should be considered in connection with the veneration of saints. It is always an act of faith, hope and love, and on the part of the human subject, it is a personal

---

338 Schillebeeckx, *God the Future of Man*, 113.

experience of the synthesis of theological virtues.[339] In this sense, the veneration of saints is identified with the Christian love for God. The veneration of saints is based on the community of the redeemed united perfectly with Christ and Mary. Christ occupies the highest place in the *communio sanctorum*. He is the fullness of grace and the head of humankind. As *caput gratiae*, He is the absolute source of grace. The unity of the community of saints is the result of life in Christ. Consequently, every human holiness, including that of Mary's, constitutes a pure participation in the holiness of Christ. Hence, every explicitly religious experience of Christ is, at the same time, an act of glorifying the saints, and vice versa, the veneration of saints logically and ontically entails the worship of Christ.[340]

a) The Veneration of Mary and the Life of the Church

The life of grace has in itself a community-forming factor. The unity of people endowed with grace is an objective fact, independent of thoughts, feelings, or will. However, the dynamics of grace tend to increase the mutual relationships which can be then experienced. The human condition sanctified by grace is expressed in Christian *caritas*. Hence, on the one hand, the veneration of saints is the most important fruit of fraternal love, and, on the other hand, the help provided by saints is essentially connected with and conditioned by their glorious state of grace.[341]

Just as our love for Christ cannot be separated from our love for our brothers and sisters, so does the worship of Christ include the veneration of saints. Christ is the crown of all saints (*de kroon van alle heiligen*). Thus, in the act of glorifying Christ, we cannot omit all His saints. Holiness, understood as participation in Christ's holiness and as Christ's gift received freely and personally by human beings, is connected with the recognition of the irreplaceable role that the saints play in God's economy of grace. All the saints are essential in the plan of salvation for the entire community of grace. Every conscious experience of Christ in faith must develop into conscious veneration of the saints. In the direct religious experience of Christ, there is also an unconscious act of devotion to Mary because of her exceptional holiness and maternal bond with Christ. Schillebeeckx emphasizes that the veneration of Mary is an essential expression of Christian life which is objectively and fundamentally co-defined by her.

---

339 MCMW, 69; cf. Edward Schillebeeckx, "Gebed als daad van geloof, hoop en liefde," *De Heraut van het Heilig Hart* 92 (1961): 186–8; KH, 526–7.

340 "Heiligenverering is immers voor katholieken een explicitering van de uitdrukkelijke Christus-beleving. Alle heiligheid, ook die van Maria, is louter deelname aan de heiligheid van God in Christus Jezus." MGVM, 36.

341 MMV, 120; cf. Edward Schillebeeckx, "Het gebed als liefdesgesprek," *De Heraut van het Heilig Hart* 92 (1961): 153–6.

From the historical point of view, Marian piety did not take a clear shape in the lives of many saints, but was harmoniously and completely naturally integrated into the background of their spiritual life. Every attempt to live in the spirit of faith, hope and love is at the same time an act of following Mary. Hence, the model of piety "towards Mary" is completed by the model of piety "in the image of Mary." Dogmatic analysis of Marian devotions allows us to discover a special dimension that distinguishes the cult of Mary from the cult of other saints. Marian veneration cannot be reduced to the veneration of the saints, because Mary occupies a unique place in the history of salvation, in God's economy of grace and in the life of each person. When compared to the cult of saints, the specificity of Marian devotions differs not only in degree but also in quality. Catholic dogmas confirm the fact that Mary, as a person, really belongs to the reality of God's revelation. The epiphanic function understood in this way cannot be attributed to any other saint.[342]

Christian experience of Mary as the Mother of the Redeemer and the Mother of all believers is, at the same time, a religious experience of the universalism of faith and Christian life. Schillebeeckx sees in Church dogmas a specific call from God to man, one that demands man's response. Therefore, the theological image of Mary is a Divine appeal from the heart of the Redemption calling for the practice of Marian devotions. Given the thesis that Mary is an essential, real, structural principle and an integral part of the redemptive mystery of Christ, we can conclude that she has an objective and universal relationship with each individual Christian life.[343]

Referring to Pius XII's encyclical *Fulgens corona*, Schillebeeckx warns against the erroneous creation in Catholic piety of such an image of Mary which would suggest that she is an external addition to the reality of the Redemption served by Christ Himself. Mary cannot improve the work of Christ in any way. However, she has the essential and irreplaceable function in God's plan of salvation as the maternal expression of the Divine love revealed in the redemption of the world. Mary does not so much bring "something new" to the Redemption; rather, she emphasizes, historically specifies and reveals the Redemption in a maternal way.[344] Just as a fully Christian life can be realized only in the community of the Church, so must a fully mature Christian spirituality be truly Marian because of the irreplaceable function which the Mother of God performs in the redemptive order. As a person, Mary has undeniable value, but on the level of the mystery of the Redemption, she appears as Christ's most beautiful creation (*Christus' mooiste wonderschepping*).[345]

---

342 MMV, 119–120.

343 MMV, 121; MGVM, 36.

344 MMV, 122.

345 "Zo is Maria op het plan van de verlossing Christus' mooiste wonderschepping, die haar eigen onvervangbare taak bezit in het heilsbestel en toch niet kan opgeteld worden met Christus' verlossingswerk." MMV, 123.

For Schillebeeckx, Marian cult is not accidental, arbitrary or marginal, but constitutes a necessary element in the process of the integral growth of faith. Conscious and profound Marian devotion is a necessary condition for the full development of the spiritual life and full Christian maturity. Specificity of Marian devotions results, above all, from the objective fact of the unique place given to Mary by God in the context of salvation history.[346] This fact also contains a task for humanity to discover the real relations that exist between Mary and all people, and to consciously develop human relationships. According to the Flemish theologian, renewed awareness of the existing relationship between Mary and all mankind will lead to the transformation of an objective, vital relationship into an effective, motivating force for the growth of personal holiness and commitment to the external apostolate. It is no coincidence that as the Church became more and more aware of Mary's unique role in the history of salvation, the lives of the great saints were marked by special Marian devotions.[347]

In conclusion, it should be emphasized that the history of the Church, treated by Schillebeeckx as *locus theologicus*, confirms the existence of a significant relationship between the practice of Marian devotion and the maturity of Christian life. Mary's motherhood of Jesus and all believers is perceived by Schillebeeckx as an important element in the work of divine grace and is a sign of God's concern for the spiritual development of man. To diminish Mary's importance in the process of developing the life of faith would be an expression of a complete misunderstanding of the Christian way of life and an injustice to God's call for every human being to achieve full and mature holiness The Catholic cult of Mary has no origin in the ancient pagan cults of mother goddesses practiced in the Mediterranean region or in the worship of Celtic and Germanic goddesses, as suggested by some Protestant theologians (W. Künneth, W. Delius, G. Miegge, F. Heiler). It is a mistake to indiscriminately associate Marian piety with pagan cults, both formally and genetically. Opposing the above views, Schillebeeckx emphasizes that Catholic Marian devotions are an important implication for the history of salvation, which is understood not only as their source and justification, but also as their fundamental norm.

b) "Magnificat" as the Biblical Basis for Marian Devotion
According to Schillebeeckx, justification for Christian Marian devotions cannot be provided only by means of theological speculation, but must refer to the source, i. e. the Holy Bible. The Canticle of Mary contained in the Gospel of Saint Luke (Lk 1: 46–55) is the biblical basis for Marian devotions and their structure based on salvation history. The *Redaktionsgeschichte* method allows us to perceive the

---

346 MMV, 123; MCMW, 73; MGVM, 36.
347 MMV, 123; MCMW, 75.

Magnificat as a compilation of many characteristic Old Testament motifs typical of Israelite piety. There are numerous biblical examples of prayers offered to God by mothers. The structure of those prayers corresponds to that of the *Magnificat*.[348]

Each biblical *Magnificat* has its own *Sitz im Leben* and contains the mystery of the life of a specific Jewish woman, whose personal experience (contained in the words of the uttered prayer) remains largely non-transferable to others. Mary's expectation of the birth of the Messiah must be interpreted not only on a natural level as a motherly joy at the unfolding new life that is the beginning of a new possibility within human history, but more from a religious perspective as a joy at the coming birth of the herald of the definitive coming of the Kingdom of God. The meeting of two pregnant women, Mary and Elizabeth, and the joy of their motherly expectation constitute a particular reason for the Mother of God to utter the words of praise and thanksgiving to God for the wonderful works of His goodness. The text of the *Magnificat*, provided by St. Luke *ex post* the paschal events, ultimately takes the form of a meditative hymn which, as an early Christian liturgical transcript confirming Marian devotion reveals the basic structure of authentic Christian prayer. Therefore, for the Flemish Theologian, the *Magnificat* contained in the gospel should be seen both as Mary's individual prayer in a specific existential context, and as the expression of the theocentric Marian devotions of the first Christian communities.[349]

The *Magnificat* is above all a prayer of thanksgiving and praise to God for Himself. At the center of the Canticle of Mary is the living God Who works for salvation in the history of the world. The *Magnificat* shows God Who comes to man through history, providing salvation and freedom. The words of the *Magnificat* are the most personal expression of thanksgiving on Mary's part. This thanksgiving springs from the depths of realities defined by the concepts of *psyche* and *pneuma*.[350] As a conscious subject, Mary gives thanks to God both individually (for the gift of Jesus the Redeemer) and in a community (for all God's redemptive interventions in the history of Israel). The *Magnificat* clearly defines the shape of Christian prayer, which is not realized as an individualistic radical novelty, but in a close connection with the entire tradition of prayer (*in een gebedstraditie*) from which it naturally grows. The *Magnificat* prayer is a solemn anamnesis of God's great works in history.[351] It

---

348 Schillebeeckx, "Het geloofsleven van de *dienstmaagd des Heren*," 246–8.

349 "Het Magnificat uit het Lucas-evangelie is dan ook de eerste onbetwijfelde uiting van Mariadevotie in de oerkerk. Vers bij vers is dit Magnificat opgesteld met impliciete citaten uit het Oude Testament." MGVM, 56–7.

350 Edward Schillebeeckx, *Evangelie verhalen* (Baarn: Nelissen, 1982), 26.

351 "Daaruit leren we tegelijkertijd, dat een persoonlijk gebed nooit volkomen nieuw, on-uitgegeven is, maar een heropnemen van en een persoonlijke nieuwe vormgeving aan gebeden die anderen vóór ons reeds hebben gebeden." Schillebeeckx, *Evangelie verhalen*, 27.

reveals the universalism of God's promises fulfilled in the history of salvation. It commemorates *magnalia Dei* understood as:

a) permanent and constantly renewed mercy of God shown to the poor of Yahweh (*anawim*), to the God-fearing and those pushed to the social margin (individual dimension),

b) God's mercy towards all Israel understood collectively as the suffering Son of God and the Servant of Yahweh (community dimension).[352]

By expressing her gratitude for the fulfillment of God's salvific promises, Mary demonstrates that Christian prayer cannot be limited only to the personal dimension, but must take into account the broader supra-personal perspective of God's plan. The *anamnesis* of the fulfillment of God's promises in the past justifies the effectiveness of requests contained in prayers. Prayer of supplication is always an expression and recognition of God's creative fidelity in human history. The human response is to give thanks to God (*dankende felicitatie aan God*) in the form of a communal liturgical celebration. Therefore, the meaning of prayer is not exhausted only in mutual fraternal reinforcement or admonition, or in the creation of communion, but in the transcendent reality, and in God Himself Who enters into a relationship of love with a human being. Prayer then becomes not so much a carrier and a transmitter of new information between man and God, but rather it has an emphatic function within the already existing love relationship.[353]

Schillebeeckx notices that the *Magnificat* has a clear eschatological trait, which underlines the tension between what "has already been" and what "has not been yet" (*reeds en nog niet*). History stretches between a human beginning and a human end. Mary is presented here as an eschatological personification of Israel in contrast to Abraham, the father of all believers, who is its protological (original) icon.[354] Abraham's faith was always, as Pope Francis stresses, an act of remembering God's promise and entrusting himself to God's word. However, this remembrance is not limited to the past, but can open the new future. It is capable of becoming a memory of the future (*memoria futuri*).[355] Consequently, Marian devotions reveal the hidden eschatic dimension, directing Christian piety towards the final completion of the Divine redemption. Mary's meditative prayer contained in the *Magnificat* becomes an echo of God's promises, a resonance of the history of salvation, without which

---

352 Schillebeeckx, *Evangelie verhalen*, 27; cf. Schillebeeckx, "Het geloofsleven van de *dienstmaagd des Heren*," 264–5.

353 Schillebeeckx, *Evangelie verhalen*, 28–9.

354 "In het Magnificat is Maria de eschatologische, dat is laatste personificatie van Israël, terwijl Abraham, de *vader van alle gelovigen* de protologische, dat is eerste personificatie van datzelfde Israël is." Schillebeeckx, *Evangelie verhalen*, 29.

355 Cf. LF 9–10.

it would be just an ordinary, unfounded, human projection of the future. Mary's prayer and, consequently, the entire Christian devotion to Mary, contains elements of the so-called living dogmatics, i. e. personally experienced truths of faith. The *Magnificat* clearly shows that in the experience of human prayer the initiative belongs absolutely to God, Who makes it a free gift of grace (1 John 4:10). Since God's grace manifests itself specifically in a visible way in history, which becomes a specific accumulation of God's redemptive work and His provocative presence, the prayer is never an entirely introverted act. It also contains a strong *ad extra* tendency.[356]

In Schillebeeckx's view, prayer (*gebed*) is a state of personal openness to God's visit (*open staan voor visitatio, het Gods bezoek*), an attitude of submission to God's action (*pati divina, God ondergaan*), and a subjective readiness and availability to receive God Who comes in and through history (*open staan voor het komen Gods in onze geschiedenis*).[357] The *Magnificat* presents prayer as the ability to receive God's gift without cold calculation and without imposing any specific conditions on God, but in an attitude of evangelical, childlike fascination (Mk 10:15). In the *Magnificat*, Mary interprets all created objective and subjective reality as a pure gift of God (*puur geschenk*) that prompts the human person to express a heartfelt thanks (*extra-dankje*). She points to the necessity to link the attitude of faith with the tradition of prayer. Mary appears to be a teacher of authentic Christian piety at the center of which there is the living God Who manifests Himself in the history of salvation. Verbal dimension of the prayer must find its extension and confirmation in the love of one's neighbor thus becoming an existential *prayer-in-action* (*gebed-in-actie*).[358] Schillebeeckx attempts to present Marian piety as piety in the image of Mary (to pray like Mary), thereby trying to counterbalance the one-sided proposition of devotion to Mary (to pray to Mary). Piety in the image of Mary is a deep fascination with the greatness and goodness of God, Who, within history, gives meaning to all the nonsense resulting from some of human activities.[359]

Summing up the analysis of the *Magnificat* carried out by Edward Schillebeeckx, we should first of all emphasize the need for a theocentric orientation of Christian Marian piety. Thankful affirmation of God expressed in the stanzas of the Canticle of Mary takes place not so much because of cosmic theophany, but rather as a human response to the mystery of historical theophany. Therefore, proper biblically inspired Marian devotions must necessarily take into account the dimension of salvation history, and not focus on the formulation and multiplication of Marian privileges and titles.

---

356 Schillebeeckx, *Evangelie verhalen*, 29–30.
357 Schillebeeckx, *Evangelie verhalen*, 30.
358 Schillebeeckx, *Evangelie verhalen*, 31.
359 Schillebeeckx, *Evangelie verhalen*, 30–1.

History consists of the words and works of God (*verba et gesta Dei*). *Magnificat* is the theologically authored basis for the Christian veneration of Mary because of the great things that the Almighty has done to her. It is a model example of Christian, historico-salvific, personalistic Marian prayer. Marian devotions, which are part of the entire Christian cult, are presented by Schillebeeckx as prayers based on the scheme: to God the Father through Jesus Christ in the Holy Spirit and in an ecclesial and ontological union with Mary and the saints. Consequently, on the basis of the theological analysis of the *Magnificat*, Marian devotions should be understood more as prayer with Mary (communion aspect) and like Mary (exemplary aspect) than as a prayer to Mary which wrongly implies that the Mother of God is the ultimate object of Christian worship, and not God Himself.

Treating Marian devotions as a separate, absolutely autonomous, competitive or even opposing form to Christian Trinitarian worship is contrary to the sacramental structure of salvation history which theologically defines the role of Mary in God's plan. At the same time, this [sacramental structure] confirms the legitimacy of venerating the Mother of God for the sake of *magnalia Dei* accomplished in and for her sake. Apart from giving thanks to God with Mary and like Mary, Schillebeeckx also seems to see the need to thank God for Mary. Moreover, Marian devotions are not limited only to the dimension of the liturgical celebration (*veneratio*), but are completed and verified on the existential and interpersonal level (*imitatio, communio personarum*).

3. The Phenomenon of Popular Piety and the Experience of Marian Apparitions

Schillebeeckx begins the analysis of popular Marian piety (*mariale volksdevotie*) with the description of some of the most characteristic human behaviors displayed on pilgrimages and while visiting places of worship. The most typical and common are: lighting candles in front of a statue of Mary, touching the rock in the places of Marian apparitions, enthusiastic processions around the sanctuaries, walking the Way of the Cross on one's knees, or buying devotional items at famous pilgrimage sites. From the psychological point of view, the driving force behind such behavior is the fundamental and primary need to manifest internal religious experience. Religiosity is not narrowed down to the intellectual sphere only but covers the entire human person. The act of faith cannot be reduced to an intellectual act.[360]

---

360 MMV, 124–9.

a) Expressive Function of Popular Piety

Schillebeeckx notes that the remarkable power of universal symbolic human activity (*symboolactiviteit*) comes into play in popular piety. It consists in treating material reality as a medium expressing the inner longing for God, a longing which resides in the depths of human personality. For the human person, the material world is the closest experimental area and life context in which a person realizes himself or herself as a spiritual being. Material reality is marked with human personality subjected to continuous development. The corporeality of human existence is the basis for the tendency to create a world of symbols.[361] Referring to the anthropological and philosophical analyzes of Dominique De Petter, Schillebeeckx notices that man borrows the objective element from the world to express a subjective, spiritual reality.[362]

Internal religious experiences in the relationship between God and man concern the transcendent plane and cannot be expressed verbally. That is why the human subject reaches for ordinary material objects in order not only to express religious experiences, but also to enable their intensification. The objects of the material world then become symbols that allow us to know the transcendent reality better and to express that reality more eloquently. In religious life, internal signs become an expression of faith, creating an external cult which is of a social nature. Symbolic forms that express human religiosity have a universal character and are almost identical in their structure in all religions of the world. Repeating the terminology of Gustav Jung, Schillebeeckx calls them original human archetypes of religious sign-generating activity. They form a reality that St. Thomas described as "the sacraments of nature" (*sacramenta naturae*).[363]

On the other hand, apart from the symbolic expression of a deep religious experience, candle-lighting, processions and other typical forms of human behavior confirm the reality of the pilgrimage participants' experience. Gestures typical of popular piety can be seen as symbols of helplessness, powerlessness and moral weakness of a Christian. The lighted candle then becomes an expression of one's inability to fully entrust oneself to God. In this case, the candle serves as a substitute and represents a man who is unable to properly answer God's call. Lighting a candle becomes a visible cry of a human being who is longing for God. Given the unquestionable strength of their authenticity, the forms of popular piety should not be subjected to careless criticism and hasty elimination, but rather should be treated as an attempt to forge a lasting link between the external element and the

---

361 Schillebeeckx, *Christus sacrament van de Godsontmoeting*, 67.
362 Ambaum, *Glaubenszeichen. Schillebeeckx' Auffassung von den Sakramenten*, 88; cf. Dominicus M. De Petter, "De oorsprong van de zijnskennis volgens de H. Thomas van Aquino," *Tijdschrift voor Philosophie* 17 (1955): 199–254.
363 Schillebeeckx, *Christus sacrament van de Godsontmoeting*, 67–8.

religious authenticity of internal experience. All gestures related to popular piety are an expression of a restless human heart that tends to rest in the vicinity of God and Mary. The very structure of a personal being requires the creation of a visible environment in which man will be able to establish contact with God by means of the world of symbols.[364]

Schillebeeckx notices the ambivalent character of popular piety. On the one hand, religiosity cannot develop in a cultural vacuum, but is internally connected with a specific society and its folklore. In this sense, it would be wrong to deprive a religious act of its cultural aspect. The task of theologians is to develop an in-depth critical reflection on the phenomenon of popular piety, and not to replace it with a cool, completely rationalized and over-intellectualized cult. On the other hand, one should beware of the triumph of external forms of expression over content (inner religious life). Failure to maintain balance in this regard may lead to the disappearance of genuine piety for the benefit of ritualism reduced to extensive elements of folklore. Religious enthusiasm has a great potential but must be properly channeled. Each renewal of religious life entails the emergence of new forms of its manifestation, and therefore recognition of multiple forms of piety is essential for the development of the inner religious life. Ultimately, according to Schillebeeckx, popular piety needs constant support from dogmatic theology in order to preserve its genuine value.[365]

b) The Function of Marian Apparitions in Religious Life

The extraordinary and, at the same time, very complex phenomenon of Marian apparitions requires a critical dogmatic assessment. Schillebeeckx does not provide a detailed review of the content of individual Marian apparitions, but tries to determine their proper function within Marian piety by means of theological and dogmatic analysis. Every miraculous phenomenon must be considered with reference to public revelation and interpreted in its light. The starting point in Schillebeeckx's reasoning is the statement that the peak and the center of God's revelation are constituted by historical, visible, singular and complete revelation realized in the Person of Christ. In accordance with contemporary hermeneutics, Schillebeeckx, following R. Pesch, raises the problem of the timeless meaning of Jesus' miracles aimed primarily at helping the poor and the suffering. Expressing Christological content of Jesus' miracles by means of the formulas: "Jesus went around doing good" (Acts 10:38) and "He has done everything well" (Mk 7:37), Schillebeeckx and Pesch emphasize the humane conduct of the historical Jesus as a

---

364 MMV, 128–9.
365 MMV, 130.

manifestation of God's power and a sign of messianic activity.[366] Moreover, as L. Monden rightly points out, Jesus' miracles are a model for modern miracles and their hermeneutic key.[367] Hence, all other miraculous events in the history of salvation, including the present-day Marian apparitions, must be related and subordinated to Christ, the greatest miracle, in the light of Whom all other extraordinary phenomena take on meaning and become understandable.

In principle, Schillebeeckx accepts the traditional teaching that the Public Revelation ended with the death of Christ's last apostolic witness. This does not mean, however, that there is no Divine intervention in the subsequent history of the world. Yet, the purpose of God's work in history is not to introduce new order of revelation or salvation, but to focus human attention on the historical fact of revelation in Christ, in which Mary also played a unique and irreplaceable role. One cannot speak of a new revelation that would bring any radical "difference" to the truth about human salvation. The living faith of the Church and the sacramental life make it possible to experience objective redemption and thus make personal, subjective redemption possible. The sacramentality of the Church realized in the environment of faith is a sufficient condition for the real sanctification of man. Revelation-in-reality (*openbaring-in-werkelijkhied*) and revelation-in-word (*openbaring-in-woord*) interpreted by the Magisterium of the Church are the factors which objectify the faith of the Church.[368] Private revelation therefore does not constitute the objective norm of the Church's faith. Despite their authenticity officially confirmed by the Church, private revelations of both the Heart of Jesus and Mary do not constitute structural principles of the Church established for the salvation of humanity.

According to Schillebeeckx, authentic private Marian apparitions should be interpreted in the context of the prophetic and charismatic dimension which exists side by side with the service in the sacramental community of the Church. The grace of redemption becomes visible in the Church through the service and the charism. The service comprises of the priestly activity of the hierarchy, including administering the sacraments, preaching the word, preaching to the Church and pastoral, i. e. spiritual, care for the lay faithful who fulfill ecclesial functions they are entitled to because of their baptism and confirmation. Charism is the activity of both the hierarchy and the laity insofar as it expresses their internal communion with God in grace. The reality of the service and the reality of the charism are truly ecclesial elements and cannot be separated from each other in the Church as a whole.[369]

---

366 Schillebeeckx, *Jezus, het verhaal van een levende*, 147–159; Rudolf Pesch, *Jesu ureigene Taten? Ein Beitrag zur Wunderfrage* (Freiburg im Breisgau: Herder, 1970), 19.

367 Luis Monden, *Le miracle signe de salut* (Bruges-Paris: Desclée de Brouwer, 1960), 99.

368 MMV, 131; O'lh, 126.

369 Schillebeeckx, *Christus sacrament van de Godsontmoeting*, 56–7.

The work of the Holy Spirit in the Church manifests itself both "from above" through the hierarchy, and "from below" as the effect of influencing specific individuals who, while not belonging to the hierarchy, have a special role to play for the good of the entire Church. The Church has both the official and the charismatic dimension. Schillebeeckx states clearly that "various authentic Marian apparitions really belong to the prophetic or charismatic side of the ecclesial life."[370] Private Marian apparitions cannot be treated equally to public revelation made in Christ. On the doctrinal level, the former do not contain any elements that could supplement or extend the scope of the latter. They never introduce new dogmas or moral laws. With regard to the constitutive elements of the Church, private revelations play a secondary role and cannot be used as arguments to justify doctrinal doubts arising from public revelation.[371]

Private status of Marian apparitions, however, does not mean that they are of no value to the life of the Church.[372] Schillebeeckx, like Rahner and Laurentin,[373] sees in private revelations the loving care for man shown by God and the Mother of Jesus. In order to avoid theological misunderstandings, one should perceive private revelations as a confrontation of the objective, dogmatic, moral content of faith with the current historical situation in which God, motivated by love, wishes to reveal His will to man in a specific, unique, charismatic way.[374] In particular circumstances of life, a person may receive spiritual support from the Church community, both from the hierarchical and the charismatic side. In both cases, it is the same Holy Spirit Who acts and reveals himself within the community of the Church. Private revelations are essentially individual by nature, as they refer to specific individuals and frequently contain very personal content related to the life story of a given person. Nevertheless, due to their charismatic structure, private revelations have broader social meaning, sometimes even of a worldwide reach. It should be remembered that the charismatic element present in the life of the Church must be objectified through the action of the Magisterium.[375]

In further analysis of Marian apparitions, Schillebeeckx no longer takes into account the psychological and "technical" aspects, but tries to present the Church's

---

370 "Wij zijn van mening dat de authentieke Maria-verschijningen werkelijk behoren tot dit prophetisch of charismatisch element van het kerkelijke leven. Men noemt ze private openbaringen, in tegenstelling tot de publieke openbaring." MCMW, 90; MMV, 132.

371 MMV, 132.

372 Cf. Edward Schillebeeckx, "De Mariaverschijningen in het leven van de kerk," De Rozenkrans 84 (1957/58): 131–3; Edward Schillebeeckx, "Het charisma der verschijningen," De Bazuin 41, no. 19 (February 8th, 1958): 1–2.

373 See Karl Rahner, Visions and prophecies (London: Burns & Oates, 1963); René Laurentin, The Apparitions of the Blessed Virgin Mary Today (Dublin: Veritas, 1990).

374 MMV, 133.

375 MMV, 134.

position on the acceptance of private revelations in a synthetic way. From the dogmatic point of view, two facts are important for Schillebeeckx: the visionary's personal contact with Mary, and the sign as the form by means of which this interpersonal contact takes place directly.[376] According to the Flemish theologian, when formulating a stance on the phenomenon of private Marian apparitions, the following indications should be taken into account:

1) The charismatic element in the Church must always be subordinated to the moral and religious life of grace expressed through the dogma. Private revelations can internally move people who have a weak faith and may lead them to discovering the true sign of God, that is, Christ. However, they cannot and will not help people whose hearts are completely closed. For people of a strong faith, private revelations are an expression of God's love and concern shown by Mary in difficult times. Acceptance and gratitude constitute the response from deeply religious individuals.

2) Private revelations do not require the assent of divine faith, but are received on the basis of human ecclesial authority.

3) Ecclesial approval of private revelations is not an infallible proof of their historical truth and authenticity. Instead, it confirms the fact that their authenticity can be reliably assumed on the basis of the research carried out. Ultimately, the problem concerns the authoritative opinion of the Church, not historical truth. The Church officially allows Mary to be venerated in places of her apparitions, refraining positively from assessing the specific content of these apparitions. The position of the Church on private revelations can be briefly described as a *nihil obstat* opinion.

4) Ecclesial approval of private revelations does not imply an absolute obligation to accept them. According to Schillebeeckx, the Church emphasizes the lack of dogmatic and moral contradictions between private and public revelations, leaving the faithful with individual freedom of critical choice.

5) The Church has the right to authorize the erection of a place of worship at the site of the apparitions, to establish new liturgical feast or to consent to the promotion of a new form of piety by wearing a scapular or a holy medal. However, this does not mean recognition of the historical truth of the apparitions. As a result, a situation may arise in which the veneration of the miraculous medal does not equate with faith in private apparitions, because Marian devotion is positive in itself and comes from the depths of the Church's sacramental life. The will to establish a liturgical feast results not so much from the imperative

---

376 Edward Schillebeeckx, "Betekenis en waarde van de Maria-verschijningen," in *Hoe preken wij over O. L. Vrouw*, ed. Ambrosius M. Bogaerts (Antwerpen: Apostolaat van de Rozenkrans, 1954), 35–6.

stemming from the content of specific apparitions, but rather from the dogmatic consciousness of the entire Church, which has been growing throughout the Tradition. For example, the petitions for the institution of the Feast of the Immaculate Heart of Mary, formulated at the Eucharistic Congress in Lourdes in 1914, were filed earlier than the apparitions in Fatima, which took place only in 1917. The prophetic element present in private revelation constitutes, as it were, the concentration of the impulse of the Holy Spirit, Who is constantly present in the life of the Church.[377]

According to Schillebeeckx, Public Revelation always remains the basis and the norm of faith. Thus, the cult that arises from a specific private Marian apparition has a relative value, while the very legitimacy of venerating Mary does not raise any theological doubts. The specific veneration given to the Mother of God by virtue of her apparitions in Fatima or Lourdes[378] is voluntary, while the veneration of the Mother of God as such is expressly recommended by the Church. The multiplicity of Marian apparitions cannot be misunderstood as the multiplicity of "incarnations" of the various forms of Mary (Mariological modalism, Mariological polymorphism). Instead, it must be considered as a manifestation of the richness of aspects of a single person, i. e. the Mother of God. Moreover, devotional practices resulting from private revelation cannot be made obligatory.[379]

c) Mary in Preaching

According to Schillebeeckx, it is a serious mistake in Marian preaching to overly focus on the extraordinary events of private revelation, while ignoring the biblical and theological image of Mary. In the ministry of the word, dogmas should not be treated as "reference" arguments to confirm and justify the truthfulness of private revelation. It would be an abuse on the part of the preachers to put any verbal pressure on the laity to recognize and absolutely accept private revelations. It is also unacceptable to try to arouse a feeling of unjustified guilt in case of emerging doubts. From the psychological point of view, man is constantly open to miracles. The expectation of a miracle is especially heightened in difficult moments of life. Human search for the extraordinary can lead to the loss of genuine faith. Therefore, the task of preachers is to avoid any exaggeration related to the miraculous circumstances of private revelations for the benefit of a clear and profound presentation of the evangelical icon of Mary.[380]

---

377 MMV, 134–7; MCMW, 94–5.
378 Cf. Edward Schillebeeckx, "Het Lourdes-dossier," *Tijdschrift voor Geestelijk Leven* 14 (1958): 256–260.
379 MMV, 137–8.
380 MMV, 139; MGVM, 45.

The content of private revelations never appears in a pure, isolated form, but is integrated into the entire mental life of the visionaries, which includes their cognitive capacity and imagination.[381] The transmission of the content of private revelations is not accompanied by a charism of inspiration as is the case with Public Revelation. Therefore, any attempt to construct theological views on hell on the basis of the Fatima revelations is bound to fail, because it was the children who were the addressees of the messages. Hence, the descriptions of their Marian visions contain elements typical of a child's psyche. Particular prudence should be exercised in Marian sermons with regard to presenting sensational details that fuel human curiosity in matters related to the future of the world. Otherwise, a misinterpretation of private revelations can lead to the loss of the essence of religion, the abandonment of spiritual effort, and seeking a convenient *alibi* for religious laziness.[382]

The first and foremost task of the preachers is to proclaim the message of the Gospel. Private revelations can only be used to illustrate and exemplify selected issues discussed in Marian sermons. One cannot understand the full meaning of a miracle while remaining at the level of considering the phenomenon of extra-ordinariness.[383] According to Schillebeeckx, a miracle does not keep people's attention on its spectacular side, but refers to ordinary Christian life, and has a therapeutic and motivational function. Preachers should avoid arbitrary interpretations of Marian apparitions and refrain from introducing sensational elements of dubious dogmatic value. The splendor of private revelations cannot obscure the richness of biblical and theological images of the Mother of God. It is not the individualism of one's own beliefs but rather experiencing Marian piety within the community of the Church that is a significant help in the process of shaping the correct image of Mary.[384]

Finally, it must be admitted that Schillebeeckx's position on the issue of Marian apparitions is characterized by a clear recognition of the primacy of public revelation and its normative role in the evaluation of private revelations. The multitude of Marian apparitions in the last two centuries has provoked solid critical research. Therefore, the content of Marian apparitions should not be absolutized, as they do not constitute a substantive extension of the revelation permanently realized in the Person of Christ. Instead, Marian apparitions serve as a motivating factor in the development of faith. They become a specific, historical and cultural adaptation of the evangelical message. However, all elements that distort the theologically correct

---

381 Schillebeeckx, "Betekenis en waarde van de Maria-verschijningen," 44.
382 MMV, 140.
383 Schillebeeckx, "Betekenis en waarde van de Maria-verschijningen," 45.
384 MMV, 141; MCMW, 105.

image of the Mother of God should be avoided in spontaneous and highly emotional popular piety. Based on the solid foundation of exegesis, the preaching activity of the Church should also play an important role in promoting the evangelical image of Mary.

4. Marian Prayer

A theologically precise definition of Marian prayer, i. e. of prayers to Mary and prayers with Mary, requires, first of all, a proper understanding of the meaning of Christian prayer as such. In Schillebeeckx's view, prayer is not a passive, unoriginal, imitative reality, but contains an essential creative dimension that actually triggers a dynamism capable of renewing the face of the earth. Prayer cannot be understood in a reistic way as a formulaic monologue. In its essence, it is an interpersonal experience based on the relationship between "you" and "me." Two free persons, God and man, are involved in the prayer and they establish personal communication in an environment of mutual love.[385]

a) General Characteristics of Prayer

There is no place in Christian prayer for passive surrender to inevitable destiny, meaningless fate, or the crushing determinism of the cosmos. The *fiat* expressed by man in a prayer refers primarily to the will of God, Whom the human "I" addresses in a personal way. God stimulates human initiative from the very beginning of the prayer. Thanks to this, the prayer is not an exclusively human work, but the fruit of God's cooperation with man. The relationship between the temporal human being and the eternal being of God causes many difficulties in terms of science. The *aeternitas* of the divine order is a dynamic quantity in motion and cannot be understood as passivity, petrification, or stillness typical of a monumental granite massif. One should not imagine God as a despotic person Who has finally and totally shaped reality, regardless of the content of human prayers. Schillebeeckx takes up G. Marcel's idea that the deepest understanding of our worldly decisions and requests takes place in eternity. Prayer then becomes a genuine initiative of free human beings directed to the divine "You."[386]

---

385 "Het gebed is immers een innige ik-Gij-beleving, een persoonlijke levenscommunie van twee *vrije wezens* die in liefde tot elkaar nijgen: God en de mens." MMV, 141–2; cf. Schillebeeckx, *Evangelie verhalen*, 29–30; Edward Schillebeeckx, "Het gebed, centrale daad van het menselijk leven," *Tijdschrift voor Geestelijk Leven* 10 (1954): 469–490.

386 MMV, 142–3; cf. Edward Schillebeeckx, "Het mysterie van het gebed," *De Heraut van het Heilig Hart* 92 (1961): 91–3.

As a result, prayer is not a simple request, or knocking on a "closed door" behind which there is a specific collection of gifts previously prepared by God. Prayerful entrusting oneself to God leads to the creation of a spiritual harmony between the will of man and the loving will of God. Human initiative in prayer has an important creative quality. In it, the will of man meets the will of God. The more one is united with God, the more effective one's prayer becomes. Prayer is consequently a dynamic, creative dialogue and a really effective co-creation of reality by God and man.[387]

The above principle of the effectiveness of Christian prayer may, according to Schillebeeckx, concern both the pleading prayers offered by Mary and the human prayers associated with them. Human prayer, which is an expression of deep faith and trust in God as the Lord of the created world, does not negate the effects of temporal cause and effect relationships. Hence, the grace for which we ask God in our prayer can actually be fulfilled for us thanks to the positive coincidence of life circumstances, including (and above all) the conscious and purposeful actions of other people. This does not mean that there is no interference from God. Likewise, praying to God through the mediation or intercession of Mary does not imply that Mary is given absolute agency in fulfilling human supplications. According to Schillebeeckx, prayer *to* and *with* Mary should be interpreted in a personalistic way, as creating a community of people who turn to God together in the spirit of faith, hope and love. Mary's prayerful influence on God's actions cannot be ruled out. Although God has absolute dominion over the world He has created and carries out His will in a completely sovereign manner, the prayer brought to Christ through Mary makes the events of everyday human life ultimately related to God.[388] Hence, the theology of creation (*scheppingsgeloof*) can be rightly considered the basis of Christian prayer and mysticism (*grondslag van gebed en mystiek*).[389]

b) The Prayer of the Rosary

The Rosary is currently one of the most popular forms of Marian devotion recommended by the Church. Its creation was not the result of a one-time inspiration, but took place in a long process of development during which many adaptations and changes were made. According to Schillebeeckx, the form of counting and repeating the same prayers that are framed in a specific structure is a widespread practice among almost all religions of the ancient world.[390]

---

387 MMV, 142; cf. Edward Schillebeeckx, "Gebedsdialoog," *De Heraut van het Heilig Hart* 92 (1961): 121–5.

388 MMV, 142–3.

389 Schillebeeckx, *Evangelie verhalen*, 103.

390 MMV, 143. For the detailed history of the Rosary, see: Edward Schillebeeckx, "De Gezins-rozenkrans," *Tijdschrift voor Geestelijk Leven* 6 (1950): 523–5.

In analyzing the phenomenon of the Rosary, the Flemish theologian distinguishes two aspects: psychological and strictly dogmatic. From the psychological point of view, the Rosary resembles the Breviary as the structure of the latter also consists in the properly ordered repetition of the same prayer texts in a given cycle. The Rosary and the breviary are both an oral and an internal form of prayer. The essential difference lies in the form of the Rosary itself. The Rosary has two dimensions: the external one, which consists in repeating the same prayers orally, and the internal one, which is an expression of the soul's prayer. Prayer is an event that is carried out, above all, *in forum internum*. The external reality is also a prayer, as long as it is an authentic expression of the prayer of the soul. According to Schillebeeckx, it would be a mistake to treat the repetitive formulas of "Hail Mary" only as an external, purely technical aspect of the Rosary that helps the soul to contemplate. Repeating the prayers externally is not a technique, but an actual prayer.[391]

Schillebeeckx's valuable intuitions on the importance of the Rosary were further developed in the subsequent teaching of the *Magisterium Ecclesiae*. The contemplative dimension of the Rosary was theologically deepened and clearly expressed by John Paul II in his apostolic letter on the Rosary *Rosarium Virginis Mariae* published in 2002. The Pope stresses that the rosary is a typically meditative prayer and corresponds to the Eastern Christian practice of "prayer of the heart." The purpose of the Rosary is to contemplate the face of Christ together with Mary. She is for the Church a great model of contemplation of Christ, an example of an adoring gaze, a gaze inflamed by the presence of the Holy Spirit. Contemplating Christ during the Rosary means remembering Christ with Mary, learning Christ from Mary, being conformed to Christ with Mary, praying Christ with Mary, and proclaiming Christ with Mary. In the papal interpretation, the Rosary is understood as a true school of prayer, in which Mary cares for the pilgrim Church and constantly reminds her of the "mysteries of her Son," so that people can experience their full salvific power through contemplation.[392] In this perspective, Mary, united with the Holy Spirit, appears as the living Memory of the Church (*Memoria Ecclesiae*).

Many spiritual writers, not mentioned by Schillebeeckx by name, say that the monotonous recitation of the Rosary leads to quieting the mind and enables meditative prayer. The Rosary is a relatively free form of prayer in which a person can focus one's attention on the words of the "Hail Mary" or let one's mind ponder the redemptive events attributed to each mystery of the Rosary. In the event of distraction, the regularity and the rhythm of the prayers continually uttered with

---

391 Schillebeeckx, "De gezinsrozenkrans," 525–6; cf. Edward Schillebeeckx, "De eigen techniek van de Rozenkrans," *De Rozenkrans* 85 (1958/59): 208–211.

392 Cf. RVM 9–17.

the mouth allow the mind to return to the content of the prayer. As a living experience of faith, hope and love, prayer should be said despite fatigue, lethargy and absent-mindedness, because it creates a wonderful atmosphere for the development of spiritual life. Schillebeeckx considers this concept of the Rosary presented above to be a purely theoretical interpretation; it is too idealistic and does not take into account the significant difficulties that arise during this type of prayer.[393]

The Flemish theologian likewise presents the so-called realistic concept of the Rosary, which arose on account of pastoral experiences. In his opinion, the monotonous repetition of the Hail Mary formulas prevents young people from a deeper concentration of the mind on the mysteries of salvation. The mind of modern man encounters many difficulties in fully accepting the value of praying the Rosary, leading to a kind of spiritual lethargy. The very limited dynamic of feelings that accompany the Rosary makes the Rosary seem a lengthy, wearisome and unconvincing form of prayer. The above-mentioned observations are by no means a sufficient reason to give up praying the Rosary. The regularly recited Rosary can become a tool for mystical experience in which the beads fall out of one's hands and the prayer takes on a purely internal form. However, in the period of spiritual coldness (impassiveness), the Rosary remains the support of prayer.[394]

Ultimately, human presence before God (*het daar-zijn voor God*) is the essential value of the Rosary. The Rosary stimulates and constantly renews Christian awareness of living in the presence of God, regardless of the feelings that a person currently experiences. That is why the practice of praying the Rosary regularly, even in a situation of impassiveness and spiritual heaviness, is a factor developing the prayerful life.

Schillebeeckx, probably following Freud's ideas, distinguishes three levels in the human psyche: the light zone, the semi-light zone and the dark zone. In the dark zone there are visions, impressions, beliefs, and dormant truths. All of these subconscious elements can be moved and activated through affects and ideas. Mechanically repeated words have the power to awaken truths dormant in the human subconscious and to bring them to the surface of consciousness. Likewise, the Rosary, through mechanically repeated prayers, can awaken Christian truths that lie dormant in the human mind without much inner effort. Thus, the Rosary does indeed have an evocative function.[395]

The Rosary does not require such exertion of strength as to be able to say the prayers externally and at the same time contemplate the individual mysteries of

---

393 Edward Schillebeeckx, "Rozenkrans bidden in nuchtere werkelijkheid," *De Bazuin* 33, no. 1 (1949): 5.

394 MMV, 212–3; Schillebeeckx, "De gezinsrozenkrans," 527; Schillebeeckx, "Rozenkrans bidden in nuchtere werkelijkheid," 5.

395 Schillebeeckx, "De gezinsrozenkrans," 527–8.

salvation internally. In praying the Rosary, one should allow God to embrace and touch one's entire human existence, because the essence of every act of prayer is to harmonize the will of man with the will of God. When the tensions of the human psyche are subdued in the framework of the Rosary, peaceful harmony between the human will and God's will is established in a real and extremely delicate way.[396] Schillebeeckx considers the Rosary not so much as the opposite of the factors activating our spiritual life, but rather as an echo of the inner prayer of a person whose mind is still or even tired. The human soul is activated mainly by such factors as the sacraments (especially the Eucharist), conversion (*metanoia*), private meditation, or public recitation of the breviary.[397]

c) The Dogmatic Aspect of the Rosary

Contrary to popular belief, Mary is not at the center of the Rosary. The Rosary focuses primarily on the mystery of the Redemption. It points to Christ as the sole Redeemer of the world, although it does not ignore the person of Mary who is actively present in the entire historical order of the Redemption. The Rosary is a specific synthesis of faith, a Christological *creed* and a doctrinal *compendium* expressed in the form of a meditative prayer.[398]

Prayer as such always strengthens the faith of the Church in its dogmatic aspect. In a prayer, it is possible to go back in space and time and become truly united with the person of Mary. The Rosary allows believers to follow the path of Mary's development and growth in faith. Thanks to prayer, man can experience all the stages of the mystery of Christ – from His birth to His reaching the state of glorification with Mary – in an atmosphere of faith and love. In the Rosary, the praying subject focuses internally on the living mysteries of Christ while simultaneously repeating the well-known words of *Ave Maria* (*Hail Mary*) externally. The content of the inner prayer of the Rosary is a great thanksgiving for the work of the Incarnation and the Redemption in which Mary also played her role. Therefore, the Rosary also has a didactic function. It points to Mary as a typical model of the earthly and heavenly Church,[399] a model of a positive human response to God's calling and of personal consent to the fulfillment of God's will in every moment of life. The

---

396 Schillebeeckx, "De gezinsrozenkrans," 528; Schillebeeckx, "Rozenkrans bidden is nuchtere werkelijkheid," 5.

397 MMV, 145–6; cf. HK, 355.

398 "Zachte overweging van het heilsmysterie van Christus, bezien van uit het bevoorrecht standpunt van de Moeder van het Christusgeheim: dit is de diepere inhoud van het rozenkransgebed." Schillebeeckx, "De gezinsrozenkrans," 530; MMV, 146.

399 "Zo reeds is Maria het prototype van de aardse pelgrimerende Kerk, zoals Zij als *Assumpta* het prototype is van de definitieve, hemelse Kerk." Schillebeeckx, "Het geloofsleven van de *dienstmaagd des Heren*," 257.

person of Mary mentioned in the Rosary teaches all Christians the readiness to endure the difficult circumstances of life and to draw strength from the reality of the Redemption. Schillebeeckx clearly emphasizes that Christ, being personified redemption, is at the center of Marian prayer.[400]

Apart from the Christological aspect, the Rosary has an important anthropological dimension. It presents the human condition in all its realism from a Christian perspective. The incarnation of God gave a new interpretation to all human existence. The final stage of Jesus' human life was not death but His resurrection. That is why the Rosary in all its dogmatic depth makes one aware of the fundamental truth that life is born from death, i. e. from Christ's sacrifice (*vita ex morte*). The Rosary is a summary of our Christian life.[401] Living like Christ is a religious and moral task for Christians that is to be carried out on earth. The Rosary is a request to Jesus and His Mother for strength to carry out this task. The Rosary is an invitation to follow Mary in meditating on the Word of God (cf. Lk 2:51). It was in prayerful reflection that Mary came to know the mystery of Christ and realized her special place in the economy of salvation. The contemporary Christian understanding of one's place and specific vocation in the redeemed world is achieved through a deep reflection on the mystery of Christ which contains the mystery of Mary.[402]

Every request presented to God in the Rosary is always brought by Christ to the Father (*per Christum ad Patrem*). The prayer addressed to the Father through Christ is at the same time mediated by Mary, Queen of the World. The inseparable unity of the mystery of Christ and Mary allows us to see in the person of the Mother of God the maternal identification with the sanctifying action of her Son. The maternal love and perfect personal union of Mary and Jesus in glory make Mary know the heart of Jesus so well that, when asking for gifts, she receives *a priori* consent from her Son. It should be remembered that the heart of Jesus is the source of all grace. The gifts received through Mary are always the result of grace emanating from the Sacred Heart.[403]

d) Rosary as a Family Prayer

Schillebeeckx suggests that the Rosary should be considered a communal form of family prayer. The Rosary recited by all family members, along with other modern

---

400 MMV, 146; cf. Edward Schillebeeckx, "De leer van het Rozenkransgebed," *De Rozenkrans* 82 (1955/56): 53–4.

401 "Zo is de rozenkrans het eenvoudige résumé van onze Christelijke levensbeschouwing." Schillebeeckx, "De gezinsrozenkrans," 531; Schillebeeckx, "Rozenkrans bidden is nuchtere werkelijkheid," 6.

402 MMV, 146–7; cf. Edward Schillebeeckx, "Rozenkransgebed: verantwoord gebed," *De Rozenkrans* 84 (1957/58): 4–7.

403 MMV, 146–7.

forms of prayer, may become a real family liturgy and a school of faith based on solid dogmatic foundations. Schillebeeckx makes an explicit reference to the ancient idea of the domestic Church (*Ecclesia domus*). The Rosary is a great community-forming force and leads the whole family to God's throne, where they can remain close to Christ and His Mother. During the Rosary, a kind of presentation of the family before God takes place. The recitation of the Rosary by a family constitutes a privileged time of God's grace which enables the family to experience themselves as a community united by God.[404] The Rosary then strengthens the bond of mutual love, creates a microcosmic redemptive community in the family and organizes the hierarchy of temporal values, emphasizing the primacy of the Kingdom of God. The rhythm of the Rosary covers all family problems, worries, anxieties and difficulties, and introduces them to the sphere of God's salvific mysteries and His work. Schillebeeckx perceives practicing the Rosary as the process of growing in spiritual life which is full of peace and simplicity, and which enables the family to learn to entrust themselves completely to Mary, the Mother of the Miracle of Cana of Galilee and the Mother of the Redemption.[405]

In conclusion, it is worth emphasizing that according to Edward Schillebeeckx, Christian prayer has a personalistic, dialogic and communal character. The effectiveness of prayer is not understood as a simple fulfillment of human request by God, but as a result of personal cooperation between two entities: man and God. Marian prayer practiced by Christians is not an attempt to use Mary's authority in order to gain God's favor in the implementation of personal plans. Marian devotions fall within the community character of the ecclesial cult and are realized in personal communion with the Mother of the Redeemer. The Rosary is a perfect example of Marian devotion. It has a biblical, salvation history and Christocentric dimension. Mary is the model of authentic Christian piety. The latter does not consist in the formal fulfillment of religious practices, but is expressed in existential union with the living God through sacrificial love. Edward Schillebeeckx's thought was an attempt to synthesize two trends in piety: *to Mary* and *in imitation of Mary*.

---

404 "Het bidden van de gezinsrozenkrans is de bevoorrechte tijd waarin het gezin, als gemeenschap, God als haar bindende factor beleeft en waardoor de familiale liefdeband bewuster en hechter wordt gemaakt." Schillebeeckx, "De gezinsrozenkrans," 529; MMV, 147.

405 MMV, 148; cf. Edward Schillebeeckx, "Providentieel Redmiddel," *De Rozenkrans* 82 (1955–1956): 18–21.

5. Distortions of Marian Devotion

In the absence of a proper critical sense and due to the omission of basic methodological principles, the cult of Mary and its dogmatic justification may appear in
a distorted form. As a result, a negative dogmatic phenomenon, called by Schillebeeckx "Marianism," comes to the fore.[406] It consists of an erroneous hierarchy of
Jesus and Mary. Instead of considering the theological mystery of Mary in the light
of Christ, an erroneous view is created, in which Mary is treated as the only prism
in looking at the Person of Christ. This approach is based on a misinterpretation of
the mother-son relationship between Mary and Jesus. Christ is interpreted only
through the person of Mary. Consequently, there is a paradoxical situation in which
Mary becomes the meaning and the key to understanding all reality, thereby taking
over the task entrusted to Christ. Marian piety built on the idea of subordinating
the Person of Christ to the person of Mary leads to the disappearance of the Christocentric dimension in Christian piety and the development of a dwarfish form
of spiritual life. The person of Mary is then at the center of Christian veneration,
and the figure of the sole Redeemer is lost in the glory of the Redeemer's Mother.
In this way, the true greatness of Mary, expressed in the mystery of the unconditional reception of Christ and in anticipation of the coming of the sole Mediator, is
destroyed.[407]

Edward Schillebeeckx indicated the basic reasons for the distortions in the theological image of Mary.

*a) Incorrect Interpretation of the Principle "per Mariam ad Iesum" (through Mary
to Jesus)*
There is a serious danger of distancing Jesus the man from all humanity and treating
Mary as the sole, individual and necessary bridge between the two distant poles.
This idea affects the deepest sense of the Incarnation through which the Word
became flesh: a real man and our brother. Moreover, there is a complete falsification
of the meaning of Christ's holy humanity, that humanity which is God's instrument
of salvation (*de heilige mensheid van Christus als het heilsorgaan van de Godheid*).
The phrase *qui natus est de Virgine Maria* (He was born of the Virgin Mary) indicates
the special closeness of Jesus and His full solidarity with all mankind due to His real
humanity. Consequently, there is a direct relationship between Christ and every
human being and only Christ can be called the sole Mediator between God and
humanity. However, the gift of the Redemption earned solely by Christ comes to us
in a special, universal and personal form, that is, in Mary, who accepted the gift

---

406 MCMW, 79.
407 MCMW, 80.

of Christ for all humanity by means of her *Fiat*. Hence, one can reasonably claim that the Marian *fiat* includes the individual *fiat* of every person. That is why we can meet Jesus, the man, directly with Mary and because of her.[408]

According to Schillebeeckx, theological doubts may arise if we put together the following two statements: Mary gave us Christ as our Redeemer and Christ gave us Mary as our Mother. Although both concepts are dogmatically correct, Schillebeeckx prefers the statement Christ gives us a Mother.[409] One can see here a rather timid attempt to formulate new Mariological principle *per Iesum ad Mariam (through Jesus to Mary)*, which was explicitly expressed by Pope John Paul II in his homily at the end of the 20th Mariological Marian International Congress in Rome on 24 September 2000,[410] and had already been analyzed much earlier by the French theologian, Yves Congar.[411]

Indeed, Mary became the real mother of Jesus and the real mother of all believers by being chosen by God. Thus, she gave the world the Redeemer. On the other hand, Mary found grace with God and was blessed with the fullness of grace (*kecharitomene*, Lk 1:28; 1:30). In this way, she became God's gift to the Church. Therefore, every person can also find favor with God thanks to the union with Mary. However, Mary should not be understood as a bridge between God and humanity, but rather as a universal spiritual womb in which people are born as brothers and sisters of Christ. Mary creates a personal environment in which a direct encounter with Christ takes place. A person's union with Mary not only does not cancel, but also highlights the essential, Christocentric dimension of Christian piety even more. That is why Christian prayer related to the Marian *Fiat* makes it possible to experience in faith and love even deeper levels of the mystery of Christ's Redemption. Mary as "supplicant omnipotence" (*smekende Almacht*), understood on a purely receptive basis (*puur ontvangende almacht*), accompanies our prayers, enabling Christ to grow in our lives. Christian prayer is never carried out in total isolation. It is connected with the prayers of the community of saints who in glory participate in the universal power of the prayers uttered by the Mother of the Mystical Body.[412]

---

408 MMV, 125–6.

409 "Tezamen met Maria, maar onder haar wezenlijke beïnvloeding ontmoeten we rechtstreeks de heilige mens Jesus die ons bij de Vader binnenleidt. In die zin is het veeleer Christus die ons Maria geeft als onze Moeder dan Maria die ons Christus geeft: <*Ecce Mater tua*>." MCMW, 80–1.

410 Jan Paweł II, "Tajemnica Trójcy Świętej a Maryja," *L'Osservatore Romano (Polish edition)* no. 11–12 (2000): 16.

411 Cf. K. Pek, *Per Spiritum ad Mariam. Implikacje mariologiczne pneumatologii Y. Congara* (Lublin: Wydawnictwo KUL, 2000).

412 MMV, 126: MCMW, 81.

b) Misapplication of Human Analogies

The principle of analogy is widely applied in theological knowledge. Supernatural reality must be expressed in a human way. A clear presentation of the function that Mary performs in the order of Redemption requires particular precision and sensitivity in applying human comparisons. A serious dogmatic mistake with repercussions in Marian piety is constituted by the juxtaposition of both the punishing hand of Christ the Judge and the strict justice of God with the maternal mercy of Mary. The phenomenon is known as the incomplementarity of the images of God and Mary.

According to Schillebeeckx, it should be remembered that pity, compassion, mercy and, in general, all good shown and done by Mary, stem entirely from the mercy of Christ, Who showed an excess of kindness to His Mother, the first fruit of the Redemption. Although Mary reveals in herself the maternal aspect of divine mercy, setting Mary's motherhood against God's mercy does not have dogmatic justification and does not stand up to theological criticism. Schillebeeckx does not deny Mary real effectiveness in her intervention for the benefit of the sinners, but he strongly rejects the possibility of interpreting Mary's maternal actions as a counterweight to Christ's justice.[413]

c) Instrumental Treatment of Marian Devotion

Marian devotion as part of mature Christian piety does not in any way relieve us from fulfilling our obligations arising from faith in Christ. In practice, there are attempts to treat Marian devotions as a substitute form of personal commitment to following Christ *(substitutie-praktijk)*.[414] Mary is then recognized as a higher authority, fulfilling for us certain obligations arising from faith and constituting a compensation for our sins and neglect before God. At the root of this view there is a misinterpretation of human weakness and helplessness which in a way predetermines our failures. In the context of this assumption, there is an attempt to completely shift human tasks and the hardships associated with them onto the person of Mary without taking personal responsibility. Although union with the person of Mary during prayer and work is justified and constitutes a great opportunity to deepen the faith, the instrumental treatment of Marian devotions leads to the weakening or even the disappearance of a living relationship with God and faith in the redemptive power of Christ. As a consequence, the development of holiness is inhibited, because in relation to God, a personal and free response to God's call has been questioned on the part of man. For every human being, a fully personal consent to the fulfillment of God's will is possible together with Mary and

---

413 MMV, 127.
414 MCMW, 82.

through the power of her love. This can never be achieved by trying to recruit Mary to compensate God for human sins. The phenomenon of substitution, i. e. putting Mary in place of one's own Christian and human obligations, should therefore be assessed negatively.[415]

d) Linguistic Anachronism

Absolutization of one specific form of piety is a significant danger that leads to the degeneration of Marian devotions. The pluralism of religious practices is considered to be a factor that guarantees proper development of spiritually fruitful Marian devotions. The variety of Marian prayers prevents the tendency to develop a monopoly on one form of veneration and significantly reduces the risk of fanatic devotion. In practicing a certain type of Marian piety, it is necessary to take into account the historical character of the ecclesial language which is subject to the process of aging. The verbal layer of the prayer always reflects the mentality of a given epoch. Hence, terminology and the manner of expressing piety which were commonly understood and accepted in the past do not always correspond to the current state of the human mind. Therefore, it is necessary for Marian piety to constantly search for adequate means of linguistic expression. A prime example of a terminological anachronism in today's piety can be found in St. Louis Grignion de Montfort's phrase, "slave of Mary."[416] It forms rather negative associations in the minds of modern people, and leads to many misunderstandings. Today, love for Mary cannot be presented in terms of slavish submission. The interests of contemporary anthropology increasingly focus on the issues related to the person and his or her freedom. Hence, the idea of Marian slavery is not an appropriate way to promote Marian devotions in the context of a contemporary sensitivity to the problem of human freedom, more and more commonly regarded as the foundation of integrally understood human rights. Schillebeeckx puts forward the idea to promote such forms of Marian devotion that would harmonize with the Trinitarian and Christological orientation of Christian worship.[417]

On the basis of the analysis of the four types of distortions in Marian devotions presented by the Flemish theologian, four parallel postulates regarding the renewal of Marian devotions can be formulated.

---

415 "De Maria-devotie ontslaat ons dus niet van een gedeelte van onze religieuze inzet voor Christus. Daarom mag men het ook nooit zo voorstellen alsof deze devotie het ons door *substitutie* gemakkelijker zou maken christelijk te leven." MMV, 126.

416 Św. Ludwik Maria Grignion de Montfort, *Traktat o prawdziwym nabożeństwie do Najświętszej Maryi Panny* (Warszawa: Wydawnictwo Księży Marianów, 1996), no. 76–7.

417 MMV, 124–5.

a) Appreciation of the Trinitarian and Christological Dimensions

Marian devotions should be seen as an integral part of Christian devotion which is by nature Christocentric and applies to the whole Trinity. The autonomy of Marian devotions is in clear contradiction with God's plan of salvation. It is necessary to emphasize the truth that the veneration of Mary results from her maternal communion with Christ, the sole Redeemer of the world and the only Mediator to the Father.[418]

b) Appreciation of the Anthropological Dimension

Marian devotions require a realistic image of Mary as a human person. The idealized, fairy-tale, static and fictitious interpretations of Mary should be rejected. Contrasting the merciful Mary with the ruthlessly punishing Father must give way to the correct concept of God and man in the perspective of the history of salvation.[419]

c) Appreciation of the Exemplary Dimension

It is necessary to acknowledge the truth that Mary is a model and a teacher of Christian piety for the whole Church and not a substitute in taking up and fulfilling the duties arising from faith.[420]

d) Appreciation of the Linguistic Dimension

The language of Marian devotions cannot diverge from the modern mentality of man. Obsolete theological and liturgical formulas that are not properly understood in the present historical and cultural context should be avoided.[421]

***

Summarizing the analyzes carried out in this section, it is worth emphasizing that, according to Edward Schillebeeckx, distortions of Marian cult are the result of

---

418 Cf. MC 25; Stanisław C. Napiórkowski, "Ku odnowie kultu maryjnego," *Ateneum Kapłańskie* 110, no. 475 (1988): 416–429; Stanisław Budzik, "Odnowa kultu maryjnego według adhortacji *Marialis cultus*," *Resovia Sacra* 3 (1996): 61–5.

419 Cf. MC 34–7; Ewa Durlak, "Antropologiczna droga odnowy kultu maryjnego," in *Nauczycielka i Matka. Adhortacja Pawła VI "Marialis cultus" na temat rozwoju należycie pojętego kultu maryjnego. Tekst i komentarze*, ed. Stanisław C. Napiórkowski (Lublin: Redakcja Wydawnictw KUL, 1991), 405–426.

420 Cf. MC 26–7; SM (part II) 5–7; Napiórkowski, *Maryja jest piękna. Zarys mariologii i maryjności*, 197; Stanisław Gręś, *Maryja wzorem życia w Duchu Świętym* (Włocławek: Włocławskie Wydawnictwo Diecezjalne, 1995).

421 Cf. MC 31; Józef Sroka, "Liturgiczna droga odnowy kultu maryjnego," in *Nauczycielka i Matka. Adhortacja Pawła VI "Marialis cultus" na temat rozwoju należycie pojętego kultu maryjnego. Tekst i komentarze*, ed. Stanisław C. Napiórkowski (Lublin: Redakcja Wydawnictw KUL, 1991), 285–324; Napiórkowski, *Maryja jest piękna. Zarys mariologii i maryjności*, 196.

insufficient consideration of the perspective of salvation history, undervaluing the mystery of the Incarnation, exaggerated anthropomorphization of God, imprecise application of human analogies, instrumental treatment of Marian devotion and disregard for the historical dimension of theological language. In shaping Marian devotions, it is therefore necessary to refine the biblical, historical, Christological, Trinitological, and anthropological aspects, and to take into account the category of experience understood in the broad sense as an important factor in the development of the cult that presents Mary as an adequate model for modern man.

V. The Future of Mariology

A tendency to ask questions about the future is becoming more and more visible in the thinking of contemporary societies. Radical changes taking place in social and cultural life have led to highlighting the future (*futurum*) as the guiding principle that dominates all human activity – especially science. Current reality should be interpreted not only in the light of the past, but also from the perspective of the future. The formulation of forecasts of development is now a common part of many scientific methods. The primacy of the category of the future is clearly marked in the field of the theological sciences in which Christian eschatology plays an enormous role.[422]

For Edward Schillebeeckx, the image of God, Christ, Mary, the Church and all religious reality is closely connected with the development of human self-awareness which is significantly influenced by cultural conditions. Hence, the question about the future of Mariology acquires a truly scientific value. Proper recognition of the specificity of the mind and taking into account the dynamics of modern man's cognitive interests are of great importance here. The fulfillment of these conditions makes it possible to set the right direction for further research in the field of Mariology.[423]

1. Substantive Perspectives

According to Schillebeeckx, the "Protoevangelium of James" and other apocryphal writings are the source of erroneous Mariological views. Ideas taken from apocryphal literature are burdened with elements of Docetism and Gnosticism, and despite their pious character, they do not correspond with evangelical images. Numerous instances of pious folk fantasy contained in the non-canonical writings exclude these writings from being a sufficient basis for proper Mariology. Specifically, docetic concepts, which deny Jesus' full and authentic humanity, consequently lead to a completely unrealistic Mariology in which the Mother of God takes place

---

422 Cf. Schillebeeckx, *God the Future of Man*, 169–207; Jürgen Moltmann, *Theologie der Hoffnung* (München: Kaiser, 1964), Jürgen Moltmann, *The Coming of God. Christian Eschatology* (Minneapolis: Fortress Press, 1996); Ernest Gellner, *Thought and Change* (Chicago: University of Chicago Press, 1964); Joseph Ratzinger, *Bilder der Hoffnung* (Freiburg im Breisgau: Herder, 1997); Góźdź, *Jesus Christus als Sinn der Geschichte bei Wolfhart Pannenberg*, 75–93, Góźdź, *Teologia historii zbawienia według Oscara Cullmanna*, 54–75.

423 Schillebeeckx, *God the Future of Man*, 178–185.

between Jesus, true God and an incomplete man, and the rest of absolutely true humanity. A realistic Mariology based on the Bible should be an argument against Docetism in Christology rather than an apology for it.[424]

The Flemish theologian quite boldly puts forward the postulate of reinterpreting the issue of the virginal birth of Christ based on the biblical, historical and theological knowledge. In his opinion, we should depart from understanding the virgin birth of Jesus in the literal and biological sense, as it does not correspond with the contemporary image of the world and man.[425] Schillebeeckx focuses only on resolving the aporia related to the traditionally recognized virginity of Mary *in partu*, not bothering to interpret the dogma of *Maria semper virgo* in an integral way. The Dominican theologian does not address the issue of Mary's virginity *ante partum* and *post partum* at all. However, he proposes to further consider the issue related to the person of Joseph and to clarify his role in the birth of Jesus from the perspective of the history of salvation.

Schillebeeckx quite shyly raises the problem of extending to Joseph the titles hitherto traditionally assigned to Mary. Consequently, one should ask whether considering Mary as the *first among the believers* should not also be true for Joseph, the righteous husband of Mary the Mother of Jesus. The issues raised by the Flemish theologian are undoubtedly an impulse to supplement current Mariology with an adequate Josephology. In the evangelical narratives there are two different ways of reporting the events of Jesus' childhood. In Matthew's version, the birth of Jesus is shown more in connection with Joseph, while Luke relates the same event by emphasizing the important role of Mary. Therefore, the results of biblical exegesis provide a sufficient basis for the further development of Mariology in conjunction with the theological study of Joseph.[426]

Another important thematic section that needs to be refined in the near future is the relationship between Mary and the Holy Spirit.[427] According to Schillebeeckx,

---

424 MGVM, 38.

425 "Vooral de maagdelijke geboorte van Jezus wordt, mede op historisch-bijbelse en theologische gronden, op het ogenblik door menig theoloog anders geinterpreteerd dan in een, gezien het vroeger vanzelfsprekend mens-en wereldbeeld, begrijpelijk letterlijk-biologische zin." MGVM, 38.

426 MGVM, 38–39; cf. HK, 84.

427 Currently, Mariological literature devotes more and more space to the problem of the relationship between Mary and the Holy Spirit, see: Joseph Ratzinger, *Die Tochter Zion. Betrachtungen über den Marienglauben der Kirche* (Einsiedeln: Johannes Verlag, 1978); Lucjan Balter, "Duch Święty w tajemnicy Maryi i Kościoła," in *Matka Jezusa pośród pielgrzymującego Kościoła*, eds. Jan S. Gajek and Kazimierz Pek (Warszawa: Wydawnictwo Księży Marianów, 1993), 243–257; Alfonso Langella, *Maria e lo Spirito nella teologia cattolica post-conciliare*, (Napoli: D'Auria, 1993); Leo Scheffczyk and Anton Ziegenaus, *Maria in der Heilsgeschichte. Mariologie* (Aachen: M-Verlag, 1998); Wolfgang Beinert, ed., *Cześć Maryi dzisiaj. Propozycje pastoralne* (Warszawa: Wydawnictwo Księży Marianów, 1992); Hugolin Langkammer, *Maryja w Nowym Testamencie* (Gorzów Wielkopolski: Gorzowskie

the Holy Spirit cannot be treated as a person taking over the tasks intended to be fulfilled by man. It is a mistake to say that the conception of Jesus in Mary's womb is the result of the work of the Holy Spirit alone, i. e. without the participation of a male. Rather, it is about an exceptional presence of God (*Gods unieke aanwezigheid*) in the emergence of a new life in Joseph and Mary's marriage.[428] It seems that Schillebeeckx is defending himself against Mariological Docetism, which could take the form of an idealized interpretation of the Mother of God, while questioning her full humanity. However, it does not include Mary's virginity even, as Max Thurian wants it, in the category of a triple sign: exclusivity in the service of God, spiritual poverty that expects everything from the Lord, and the eschatological kingdom of God.[429] Therefore, a justified doubt arises whether the abandonment of the traditionally recognized dogma of the virgin conception and birth of Jesus does not depreciate the fact of the preexistence and transcendence of the Son of God Who, in becoming a man, did not cease to be God. There is a concern that Schillebeeckx's proposal is very difficult to reconcile with the Chalcedonian dogma and the doctrine of the Holy Trinity.

According to the Dominican theologian, the analysis of the relationship between Mary and the Holy Spirit needs, from the very outset, to outline precisely the semantic field of the following biblical concepts: *holy spirit* (*pneuma hagion* written with the lowercase letters and without the definite article) and the *Holy Spirit* (the *Pneuma Hagion* written with the capital letters and the definite article).[430]

In the Annunciation, Schillebeeckx perceives the work of holy spirit (*pneuma hagion*), understood not as a personal being, but in the Old Testament sense of God's creative power, revealed externally in the sign of an obscuring cloud, which indicates God's particular presence. Due to this, Jesus becomes the Son of God at the moment of a truly human conception, which takes place in God's unique presence.

Wydawnictwo Diecezjalne, 1991); Stanisław C. Napiórkowski and B. Kochaniewicz, eds., *Maryja w Katechizmie Kościoła Katolickiego* (Kraków: Bratni Zew, 1996); Julian Wojtkowski and Stanisław C. Napiórkowski, eds., *Nosicielka Ducha. Pneumatofora* (Lublin: Redakcja Wydawnictw KUL, 1998); Stanisław C. Napiórkowski, Teofil Siudy and Krzysztof Kowalik, eds., *Duch Święty a Maryja* (Częstochowa: Wydawnictwo "Regina Poloniae," 1999); Kazimierz Pek and Teofil Siudy, eds., *Trójca Święta a Maryja* Częstochowa: Wydawnictwo "Regina Poloniae," 2000; Jacek Bolewski, *Misterium Mądrości. Traktat sofio-mariologiczny* (Kraków: Wydawnictwo WAM, 2012).

428 "In het kindsheidevangelie van Lucas gaat het om een goddelijke presentie die haar schaduw laat vallen op Maria. *Overschaduwing door heilige geest* en *zoon van God* genoemd worden roepen hier elkaar op. Dit betekent in deze context van Jezus' conceptie in Maria's moederschoot zeker niet dat de Geest de rol overneemt van de man bij het voortbrengen van een kind, het gaat om Gods unieke aanwezigheid bij het ontstaan van nieuw leven; het leven van dit mensenkind Jezus." MGVM, 41.

429 Cf. Max Thurian, *Maryja Matka Pana. Figura Kościoła* (Warszawa: Wydawnictwo Księży Marianów, 1990), 39–56.

430 MGVM, 40.

Later events, such as the baptism in the Jordan, the resurrection or ascension to heaven, are merely the confirmation and solemn proclamation of this distinction.[431]

According to Schillebeeckx, Mary received a double gift from God: in the pre-paschal period connected with the conception of the Son of God, she individually experienced the action of holy spirit (*pneuma hagion*) as God's unique creative power, while during the post-paschal period, she participated in the Church's reception of the Holy Spirit (*the Pneuma Hagion*) on the day of the Pentecost.[432]

The topic discussed above reveals Schillebeeckx's disturbing tendency to treat the Holy Spirit in an impersonal way. In his opinion, at the time of the Annunciation, Mary did not fulfill her mission with an interpersonal relationship with the Holy Spirit in mind, but experienced in her life the dynamics of the undefined creative power of God's presence, called holy spirit. The omission of the personal attributes of the Holy Spirit in the mystery of the Annunciation is undoubtedly a weakness in Schillebeeckx's Mariological project, as it poses an obstacle in the path to creating a Trinitological interpretation of Mary.

Another topic that requires theological attention is the relationship between the Holy Spirit and the Church. According to Schillebeeckx, it is not correct to define Mary as the Mother of the Church, because the Holy Spirit, and not Mary, is the source of all life, including that of the Church. In the proper sense, the Holy Spirit is the mother of all believers and the true Mother of the Church.[433] The real relationship between Mary and the Holy Spirit attested to by the Bible cannot be interpreted, as proposed by Leonardo Boff, as a hypostatic union analogous to the union of the hypostatic Person of Jesus and the Word of God.[434] Schillebeeckx objects to this over-interpretation and aims to clearly show and emphasize Mary's relationship with the community of believers in the Church, rather than taking her out of ecclesial communion in favor of creating a hypostatic union with the Holy Spirit which would ultimately destroy the traditional concept of the Trinity.

According to Schillebeeckx, Mariological titles contained in the Litany of Loreto (The Litany of the Blessed Virgin Mary) should be interpreted not only ecclesiologically, but also – in their most basic and primal layer – pneumatologically

---

431 MGVM, 40–1.

432 MGVM, 39–40.

433 "Zelf zou ik – kritisch ten aanzien van Boffs mariologische overdrijvingen en ook kritisch ten aanzien van sommige details in mijn vroeger werk over Maria – nu willen zeggen, dat *niet Maria, maar de heilige Geest de bron van alle leven is, ook van de kerk*. Dat wist ik toen wel reeds, maar thematiseerde dat niet in mijn mariologische publikaties. Vanuit deze voor mij nu duidelijke, nieuwe (overigens oud christelijke) blik is niet Maria, maar de *heilige Geest de moeder van alle gelovigen*: ware moeder ven de kerk." MGVM, 42–3.

434 Leonardo Boff, *Ave Maria. Das Weibliche und der Geist* (Düsseldorf: Patmos-Verlag, 1982); Leonardo Boff, *Das mütterliche Antlitz Gottes* (Düsseldorf: Patmos-Verlag, 1985).

(christelijk-oerspronkelijke eretitels van de heilige Geest). The litany of Mariological titles constitutes a transposition of the second degree. The titles were transferred from the Holy Spirit first to the Church and then to Mary as the first distinguished member of the ecclesial community of faith. Schillebeeckx makes the postulate of updating the entire existing Mariology with the basic idea that the Holy Spirit is the Mother of the Church.[435] Probably following Congar, he accepts the need for a critical revision of pneumatological titles attributed to Mary.[436]

Contemporary Mariology, according to Schillebeeckx, still faces the task of developing a particularly important idea of Mary's universal spiritual motherhood. Apart from the specific bodily and spiritual motherhood of Mary towards her Son, it is necessary to appreciate and theologically clarify Mary's spiritual motherhood which has its source in her attitude of infinite faith. In addition to the Infancy Gospels (Mt, Lk), which focus mainly on the mystery of biological motherhood, relevant fragments from the synoptic Gospels should be highlighted as they present Mary as a motherly model of faith, obedience, listening to the Word of God and consistent implementation of that Word in life (cf. Mk 3:31–35; Mt 12:46–50; Lk 8:19–21). These texts point to Mary as the universal model of a true believer and Jesus' disciple *(leefmodel van de ware gelovige en de ware leerling)*. Mary's greatness results not only from her biological motherhood of Jesus, but even more from the obedience to faith.[437]

Gospel according to St. John brings to contemporary Mariology more universal ideas than the synoptic Gospels.[438] Mary's presence by the cross is recognized by Schillebeeckx as a historical event of universal importance. It is the biblical basis for recognizing Mary as the Mother of *all believers (Maria moeder van alle gelovigen)*. The great appreciation for His Mother's faith expressed by Jesus in the aforementioned passages of the Gospels and the positive reaction of the early Church towards Mary recorded in the New Testament allow us to discover a universal model of true mature faith in the Mother of God.[439]

---

435 "Heel de kerkelijke mariologie zal daarom opnieuw geactualiseerd moeten worden vanuit de grondidee dat *de heilige Geest de moeder ven de kerk is.*" MGVM, 43; cf. Schillebeeckx, *Je suis un théologien heureux*, 108.

436 Cf. Yves Congar, *Wierzę w Ducha Świętego. Vol. I, Duch Święty w ekonomii. Objawienie i doświadczenie Ducha* (Warszawa: Wydawnictwo Księży Marianów, 1995), 224–6; Christopher Ruddy, "A Very Considerable Place in the Mystery of Christ and the Church? Yves Congar on Mary," in *Mary on the Eve of the Second Vatican Council*, eds. John C. Cavadini and Danielle M. Peters (Notre Dame: University of Notre Dame Press, 2017), 113–132.

437 MGVM, 49.

438 HK, 105–6.

439 "In zowel de reactie van Jezus als die van de vroege kerk op Maria gaat het om een zaligprijzing van de ware gelovige, en wel van het door Jezus zelf geschetste *model* van ware gelovige, waarvan de glans en glorie wordt weerkaatst op de figuur van Maria als gelovige moeder van deze Jezus."

Influenced by the developing feminist theology, Schillebeeckx suggests emphasizing the sisterly aspect of Mary, who, within the ecclesial community of the redeemed, appears as our Sister in faith (*Maria onze zuster in geloof*).[440] The truth about Mary's divine motherhood has been the fundamental principle of Mariology to date, which has consequently made it one-sided. According to the Flemish theologian, greater emphasis should be placed today on Mary's sisterly solidarity with all the redeemed, which was already emphasized by Pope Paul VI in the apostolic exhortation *Marialis cultus*.[441]

According to Schillebeeckx, the issue of Marian devotion still requires theological exploration. Marian piety has as its natural source in the general human experience of deep respect for the mothers of significant historical figures. The words of the evangelical woman, "Happy the womb that bore you and the breasts you sucked" (Lk 11:27), are an example of spontaneous respect for the role of the mother in the lives of outstanding individuals. Jesus' answer, "Still happier those who hear the word of God and keep it!" is the basis for constructing a pisteological interpretation of Marian devotions. Also, the words of welcome uttered by Elizabeth indicate that Mary should be glorified primarily for the depth of her faith.[442]

In addition to the universal tendency to affirm motherhood, in Schillebeeckx's view, the biblical foundation of Marian devotions, which is expressed in the *Magnificat* based on Old Testament quotations, should also be appreciated.[443] The *Magnificat* has a pre-scriptural genesis. As a pre-Luke tradition incorporated into the Gospel during the editorial work, it is an example and proof of the living Marian

---

MGVM, 56. John Paul II draws attention to the universal nature of Mary's motherhood in the Church and through the Church, presenting the Mother of Christ as "the spiritual mother of humanity." Cf. RM 47.

440 "Men zal dus in de toekomst de betekenis van Maria's vrouwelijkheid theologisch meer moeten zoeken in de lijn van haar *vrijmakend* zusterschap dan van haar *kindbindend* moederschap." MGVM, 35; cf. Catharina Halkes, "Maria," in *Wörterbuch der feministischen Theologie* (Gütersloh: Verlagshaus Gerd Mohn, 1991); Wolfgang Beinert, *Maria in der Feministischen Theologie* (Kevelaer: Butzon & Becker, 1988); Rosemary Ruether, *Mary – The Feminine Face of the Church* (Philadelphia: The Westminster Press, 1977); Bruno Forte, *Maria, Mutter und Schwester des Glaubens* (Zürich: Benziger, 1990); Johnson, *Truly Our Sister: A Theology of Mary in the Communion of Saints*, New York – London: Continuum, 2003; Amy J. Levine and Maria Mayo, *A Feminist Companion to Mariology* (New York – London: T&T Clark, 2005).

441 "Marie est la grande sœur de tous les chrétiens. C'est un point de vue féministe: l'accent est mis sur la sororité de Marie plutôt que sur la maternité de l'Église." Schillebeeckx, *Je suis un théologien heureux*, 108. The title "Sister" in relation to Mary was already used by Pope Paul VI in *Marialis Cultus* 56.

442 MGVM, 53–54.

443 Schillebeeckx, *Evangelie verhalen*, 25–31.

devotion of the early Church in the period before the New Testament was even written.[444]

The *Magnificat* contains a theological synthesis in which Schillebeeckx finds two main motives that justify the veneration of Mary. These motives are Mary's messianic motherhood and her unconditional faith, by which – beside Abraham, the father of faith – she became the mother of all believers.[445] The idea of *Mary as the Mother of all believers* (*Maria Moeder van alle gelovigen*) becomes an innovative impulse to develop Marian devotions based on the thorough study of the Bible. Marian devotions should turn more towards the ecclesial expression of gratitude to God for the gift of Mary; this is in line with the etymology of the name *Miriam*, which means the Gift of God. Schillebeeckx seems to prefer praying with Mary rather than to Mary. The limits of healthy Marian devotions should be sought in the person of Mary. At the same time, the Mother of God can never become an object onto which human dreams or frustrations are projected. In accordance with Augustine's adage: *Iesus, solutio omnium difficultatum* (Jesus is the solution to all difficulties), Marian piety must, according to Schillebeeckx, have a Christocentric dimension.[446]

Conciliar ideas expressed in the constitution *Sacrosanctum Concilium*[447] inspired Schillebeeckx to link Marian devotions more closely with the liturgy – the source and the summit of ecclesial life. For the Flemish theologian, the primacy of the liturgy in the life of the Church becomes the ordering principle of Marian devotions which should be coordinated with the liturgical year. Marian piety is not an absolutely autonomous value, but it is closely related to the Catholic cult of saints, which is always an expression of veneration of Christ.[448]

In accordance with Chapter VIII of the constitution *Lumen Gentium*,[449] Schillebeeckx advocates moderate Marian devotions and a balanced folk Marian piety, the extent of which should be proportional to Mary's place in the history of salvation. True religion is not a Neo-Platonic turn to an isolated God, but an encounter with God Who loved the world. Therefore, professing Christ (*Christusbeleving*) means

---

444 MGVM, 56; cf. Luise Schottroff, "Das Magnificat und die älteste Tradition von Jesus von Nazareth," *Evangelische Theologie* 38 (1978): 298–313; Serra, *Myriam, fille de Sion*, 111–145; Marek Jagodziński, "Communional Marian Anthropology," *Roczniki Teologiczne* 62, no. 7 (2015): 84–5.

445 MGVM, 55–56. See Carlo Ghidelli, *Magnificat. Il cantico di Maria, la donna che ha creduto* (Milano: Edizioni Paoline, 1990), 61–5.

446 MGVM, 55.

447 Cf. SC 9–13.

448 Cf. MC 1–23.

449 LG 67.

at the same time venerating Mary, who belongs to the reality of the Revelation.[450] Schillebeeckx recalls that, in the end, the Second Vatican Council did not obligatorily recommend one particular form of Marian devotion but gave a free choice in this matter.

Summing up, it should be emphasized that according to Edward Schillebeeckx, the future of Mariology in the substantive aspect is associated with a clear appreciation for the pneumatological and ecclesiological context, with the simultaneous elimination of Gnostic elements of apocryphal origin and giving priority to the liturgical Marian devotions.

2. Methodological Perspectives

In his publications on Mariology, Schillebeeckx devotes little attention to methodological problems. It is impossible to indicate in his work a systematized presentation of the methods that should be used in constructing new Mariology. Nevertheless, the substantive reorganization of the existing classical Mariology proposed by him is based on several new methodological assumptions.[451] In general, the methods used by Schillebeeckx in Christological research should be used in the field of Mariology. Schillebeeckx's evident reference to *Leben-Jesu-Forschung* has led to the postulate of applying such exegetical methods that would ultimately allow to obtain a historical-critical image of Mary.[452]

Schillebeeckx assumes that any theological synthesis is temporary and changeable. Along with the development of human consciousness in the individual and social dimension, theological synthesis must undergo constant reinterpretation based on the Bible and the Tradition. The task of Mariology in its formal aspect is to develop a method that will allow to present Mary to modern people in a credible way. Therefore, it is necessary to try to present the historical *Miriam* of Nazareth in

---

450 MGVM, 36; cf. HK, 87: "Maria, die das klarste Bild des harrenden Israel war, wird das Urbild der Kirche, die Jesus empfängt. [...] Sie ist mit ihrer ganzen Person in die Ereignisse einbezogen. [...] Ihre Verehrung wegen ihrer besonderen Stellung im Christusmysterium ist echt evangelisch."

451 For epistemological assumptions in Schillebeeckx's theology, see: Philip Kennedy, *Deus humanissimus: the knowability of God in the theology of Edward Schillebeeckx* (Fribourg: University Press 1993); Pieter van Rossum, "L'epistemologia di Schillebeeckx e la dottrina della fede," *La Rivista del Clero Italiano* 57 (1976): 988–999; Romas S. Chamoso, *La teoría hermenéutica de E. Schillebeeckx. La reinterpretación de la fe: contexto, presupuestos, principios y criterios* (Salamanca: Universidad Pontificia de Salamanca, 1978); Daniel S. Thompson, "Epistemological Frameworks in the Theology of Edward Schillebeeckx," *Philosophy and Theology* 15, no. 1 (2003): 19–56.

452 MGVM, 30.

the context of a specific historical, social and religious experiences that were in a scripturistic manner expressed in the New Testament.[453]

A historical-critical approach to Mary requires not only a simple reconstruction of life events, or a chronological order of biographical facts. But it also, above all, requires the identification of the historically defined horizon of experiences and religious expectations of the Jewish community from the times of Mary and Jesus and understanding the motives behind the positive reactions of people at that time towards the Mother and the Son. The *historical Miriam* presented in the Bible is the criterion and, at the same time, the norm of any subsequent theological interpretation.[454]

The historical reconstruction of Mary of Nazareth does not rule out further dogmatic systematization. However, in order to avoid the danger of ideologization, the category of experience should also be valued in Mariology, both in the individual and community dimension. Revelation, in fact, is closely related to experience and, in some respects, identifies itself with the latter. Revelation that comes from God is always realized in the context of a particular human experience.[455]

Contrary to F. Schleiermacher, Schillebeeckx sees a transcendent element in the revelation, which makes it impossible to speak of a genetic relationship between revelation and experience. Mariology begins with a specific, original human experience of the meeting between Jesus and His Mother, which, thematized and interpreted, was then recorded in the New Testament, where the pluralism of Mariological interpretations appears from the outset (synoptic Mariology, John's Mariology, Paul's Mariology, Mariology of the Acts, etc.). The process of interpreting the original experience extends onto the entire history and continues today.[456]

The contemporary historical and social context demands a new, fully human image of Mary, devoid of docetic and Gnostic burdens. For this purpose, according to Schillebeeckx, the biblical image of the Mother of God should be confronted with current human experiences. Hadewych Snijdewind lists Schillebeeckx as a

---

453 MGVM, 30.

454 MGVM, 47; cf. Schillebeeckx, *Jezus, het verhaal van een levende*, 57–61. For more information about the method used by Schillebeeckx in Christology, see: Snijdewind, *Leeswijzer bij "Jezus, het verhal van een Levende" van Edward Schillebeeckx*, 23–7; Franco G. Brambilla, *La cristologia di Schillebeeckx. La singolarità di Gesù come problema di ermeneutica teologica* (Brescia: Morcelliana, 1989); Luigi Iammarrone, *La cristologia di E. Schillebeeckx* (Genova: Quadrivium, 1985); Pieter van Rossum, "La christologie du R. P. Schillebeeckx," *Esprit et Vie* 85 (1975): 129–135; Piet Schoonenberg, "Schillebeeckx en de exegese. Enige gedachten bij *Jezus, het verhaal van een levende*," *Tijdschrift voor Theologie* 15 (1975): 255–268.

455 Cf. E. Schillebeeckx, *Interim Report on the Books Jesus & Christ*, 10–19; Schillebeeckx, *Menschliche Erfahrung und Glaube an Jesus Christus*, 31–6.

456 Schillebeeckx, "Verschillend standpunt van exegese en dogmatiek," 62–3; Schillebeeckx, *Gerechtigheid en liefde. Genade en bevrijding*, 26–56.

pioneer in the use of systematic historical hermeneutics in Catholic theology,[457] the basic elements of which are:

a) analysis of contemporary experience,
b) identification of permanent elements in basic Christian experience *(christliche Grunderfahrung)* which was recorded in the New Testament and passed down in later Tradition,
c) critical reference of both sources to each other.[458]

Thanks to this methodological procedure, realistic Mariology will be created. Such Mariology will be faithful to both the Bible and the Tradition, and at the same time, it will be updated.[459]

Research must take into account the tension between the Mary of history and the Madonna of Christian faith. Contrary to Bultmann's extreme opinions which depreciate historical elements in the evangelical narrative, Schillebeeckx sees a positive relationship between *Miriam of history* and *Mary of the Christian faith* expressed in the evangelical formula: *Mary, the Mother of Jesus.*[460] In this way, Schillebeeckx overcomes the skeptical attitude towards the historical value of the Gospel represented by the 19th-century liberal theology. In Schillebeeckx's work, one can notice the adoption of moderate historicism, by which he distances himself from the dogmatic formulas of Catholic Mariology. Schillebeeckx does not start biblically oriented Mariology with the analysis of the content of dogmas, but goes back to the original Christian experience, considered as prior and normative to the dogmas.[461] Hence, he proposes to construct a new updated Mariology of the pneumatological and Christological type based on the exegesis of historical testimonies contained in the New Testament.[462]

Edward Schillebeeckx does not underestimate the linguistic problem. Updating Mariology entails the need to develop a new meaningful language that will be able to present Mary by taking into account characteristic features of a secularized man's mind. As a result, Marian spirituality cannot be built on fictional, illusory

---

457 Snijdewind, *Leeswijzer bij "Jezus, het verhaal van een Levende" van Edward Schillebeeckx*, 11–2.

458 Schillebeeckx, *Menschliche Erfahrung und Glaube an Jesus Christus*, 40.

459 "Vanuit deze, mijns inziens in feite authentiek-evangelische visie kunnen we – trouw aan de kern van de bijbelse en nabijbelse, christelijke geloofstraditie – een niet alleen postmoderne en evangelich-trouwe, maar tegelijk ook *geactualiseerde mariologie* uitwerken." MGVM, 43–4.

460 "Uit de ontleding van de twee kindsheidverhalen leer ik dat de hoofdtitel van mogelijk andere legitieme titels van Maria, in eerste instantie althans, gelegen is in het feit dat zij historisch *de moeder van Jezus is*." MGVM, 55.

461 Rosino Gibellini, *La teologia del XX secolo* (Brescia: Queriniana, 1992), 368–70.

462 "Binnen mijn zoeken naar een juiste, christelijk verantwoorde, authentieke christologie zou ik nu, om een begin te maken, willen spreken van mijn zoeken naar een *pneuma-christologische mariologie*, en wel op zuiver nieuwtestamentische grondslag." MGVM, 39.

elements, but should arise from reliable exegesis in conjunction with the spiritual needs of contemporary people. At this level, Mariology must refer to the actual human experience.[463]

In the context of the historically changing mentality of man, there is, according to Schillebeeckx, an urgent need for an in-depth reflection on theology as a science. According to the Flemish intellectual, there is a close relationship between theology and faith, although these realities are not the same. "Theology is the faith of the thinking man: it is reflection on faith."[464] Unlike spontaneous reflection of a religious person on the reality of his or her faith, theology is characterized by systematic and methodically organized knowledge. Theology as a science is not a private work of a theologian, but is a reflection of the entire community of faith expressed in the work of theologians. It grows out of the depth of faith and returns to it at the same time.[465]

For the renewal of theological thinking, it is important, according to Schillebeeckx, to see the essential difference between faith as an existential human act and theology as a theory of the reality of faith. Theology never detaches the redemptive value from the redemptive truth, but it is in the redemptive truth that it sees the value of the Divine Revelation to all people. Theology aims to know the truth as a practical life value. The act of theological reflection arises from human life and at the same time serves this life, being a kind of intellectual reflection on its depth. Theology is primarily about the reality of faith which, in its own absoluteness, makes sense to man.[466]

According to Schillebeeckx, theology is neither a science only of God in Himself, nor only of man in an abstract way, but it is a methodical reflection on the mystery of God in relation to the human person and to the whole supra-personal reality. The mystery of God and His Revelation cannot be understood as the manifestation of a new, static supra-metaphysics. It takes place within the framework of the redemptive acts carried out in human history in which God appears not only as the Creator, but also as man's life partner. Hence, the Divine Revelation by nature has a history-shaping character and, being directed to man, does not take the form of supernatural concepts and words, but is deeply embedded in the structure of existential experience. God is cognitively defined by names derived from temporal

---

463 "Een op Jezus gecentreerde mariologie die bovendien hedendaagse, zelfs geseculariseerde mensen zinvol kan aanspreken. En ten slotte een moderne mariale spiritualiteit voedt, één van symbiose van innerlijkheid en uiterlijkheid, een ook naar buiten – naar mensen en wereld – toegewende levenshouding." MGVM, 44; cf. Schillebeeckx, *Menschliche Erfahrung und Glaube an Jesus Christus*, 41–53.

464 "Theologie is het geloof van de denkende mens: zij is een bezinning op het geloof." OTh, 286.

465 OTh, 286.

466 OTh, 287.

experience and Christ's self-awareness, which he expressed in words, images, and concepts appropriate for him. Thus, the full experience of the supernatural aspect of our life will be realized only in the reality defined as *visio beatifica* (Col 3:3–4).[467]

Schillebeeckx, like many contemporary theologians including K. Rahner, Y. Congar, or W. Kasper, distinguishes the history of salvation in a specific Judeo-Christian and general sense, which includes all redemptive experience realized within all religions, especially in the great religions of the world. Religions and Churches understood as the sacrament of salvation in the world (*sacrament van het heil-in-de-wereld*) constitute an *anamnesis* of God's universal and, at the same time, effective redemptive presence in the history of the world, which becomes an important source for theological renewal.[468] Theological concepts arise from the current experience of real, temporal relations in which the human subject is involved. The very historical structure of a personal communion with God defines the method of dogmatic theology. The constitutive elements of the phenomenology of human encounters provide the basis for the construction of theological approaches that demonstrate the inter-subjective and dialogic nature of the relationship between God and man. Therefore, according to Schillebeeckx, theology cannot break cognitive contact with a specific world of human experience.[469] The analysis of Schillebeeckx's views shows that essentialist scholastic and neo-scholastic theology based on a purely conceptual way of thinking must be complemented by the phenomenological concepts of existential nature. The crisis of contemporary theology, including Mariology, undoubtedly has its cause in the insufficient consideration of human existential experience in carrying out research projects.

In the conciliar call to return to the sources (*redditio ad fontes*), Schillebeeckx sees the postulate to appreciate the entire complex set of current Christian and non-Christian experiences in a critical conjunction with the great tradition of Judeo-Christian experiences contained in the Bible. The history of theology confirms the validity of respecting the essential relationship between faith and experience. In the past, more attention was paid to the elite experience of clerical intellectuals in creating new theological systems and adopting new methods. Currently, one should appreciate the cognitive value of the everyday experience of people living in the world along with their broadly understood feelings, experience and desire for good.

---

467 OTh, 288.

468 Schillebeeckx, *Mensen als verhaal van God*, 33.

469 "Deze aardse structuur van onze persoonlijke gemeenschap met God bepaalt de theologische methode van de dogmatiek. De uitdrukking van de geloofsinhoud, die in zijn eigenheid hier op aarde onuitdrukbaar blijft, gebeurt in geloofsbegrippen die in een zekere ervaring wortelen: in de ervaring van de heilsgeschiedenis." OTh, 289.

The creation of contemporary Mariology must take into account the phenomenon of the alienation of religious individuals in the secularized world.[470]

Modern man does not experience religious reality in the manner of a sublime high-experience. Religious human behavior is rather a personal and reflective response to the pluralism of everyday experience, which is frequently of an ambivalent nature (experience of infinity and experience of the finite). Everyday experiences share a double dimension of meaning and the lack thereof, and they provoke man to make the final interpretative decision of a religious nature. Thanks to the theological outline of the ambivalent experience of everyday life, there is a real possibility of achieving a new type of a clearly religious experience.[471]

According to Schillebeeckx, every person, including the recipient of theological content, participates in an experience of experience (*in der Erfahrung-mit-Erfahrungen*) or experiences experience. The content of faith is not accepted on the basis of external authority, but on the basis of personal conviction. Hence, credible theology cannot present the ancient tradition of Christian experience in an outdated conceptual system which is incompatible with the modern mentality. According to Schillebeeckx, the best method is to construct theology as a historical science in which the event of Jesus and the history of His life lead contemporary people to authentic Christian experience. Therefore, one of the most important tasks of modern theology is to develop the theme of God's presence in the tradition of human experience.[472]

The Flemish theologian completes Paul's statement about faith born from listening (*fides ex auditu*) with the formula that faith grows also from the peculiar ecclesial and Christian *praxis*.[473] The meeting of particular people with the historical Jesus became for them an existential experience of salvation, liberation and reconciliation, which was then reflected upon, interpreted and passed on in the Church tradition of experience.[474] For Jesus, life *praxis* was inseparable from experiencing God as the Father (*Abba-ervaring*). On the other hand, teaching served to interpret redemptive deeds. The story of Jesus in the New Testament clearly shows that theological reflection on faith must take place not only in the ecclesial environment, but also in everyday human experience of the world.[475] The question arises: to what

---

470 Schillebeeckx, *Menschliche Erfahrung und Glaube an Jesus Christus*, 13–7.

471 Schillebeeckx, *Menschliche Erfahrung und Glaube an Jesus Christus*, 20.

472 Schillebeeckx, *Menschliche Erfahrung und Glaube an Jesus Christus*, 20–3; cf. Schillebeeckx, *Interim Report on the Books Jesus & Christ*, 5–7.

473 Schillebeeckx, *Menschliche Erfahrung und Glaube an Jesus Christus*, 24–5.

474 E. Schillebeeckx, *Interim Report on the Books Jesus & Christ*, 10.

475 Schillebeeckx, *Menschliche Erfahrung und Glaube an Jesus Christus*, 66–8; cf. Robert Schreiter, *The Praxis of Christian Experience. An Introduction to the Theology of Edward Schillebeeckx* (San Francisco: Harper & Row, 1989).

extent can the story of Jesus, His life and teaching inspire contemporary people who live in completely different social and cultural conditions and face different questions and problems?

According to Schillebeeckx, there are various conflicting theological approaches in history, which in turn lead to the purification of faith. A peculiar development by demolition takes place. Dogmatic formulations always contain secondary, representational elements related to a specific epoch, which must be eliminated in particular interpretative models in order to preserve the core of truth. There is a difference between the wording borrowed from a specific cultural circle and the essential content of faith. By changing borrowings, one makes progress in thinking about faith.[476] According to the Flemish theologian, each generation of Christians takes the trouble to express the Redemption experienced in Jesus with adequate modern concepts and images. However, there is a risk of depreciating redemptive reality by the improper use of new models of interpretation which take into account contemporary culture, problems, expectations and needs of people. As the history of experience continues to unfold, what is experience for contemporaries today will become tradition for others tomorrow. Therefore, it is necessary to work out the basic principles that can be applied in the process of structuring the contemporary world of experience. Schillebeeckx suggests four principles:

1) The theological and anthropological principle emphasizing the truth that God wants to be the salvation of man and for man (*Gott Heil von und für Menschen*) and wants to offer it in the context of history that seeks its meaning. Finding redemption in God is at the same time man's self-understanding (*Zu-sich-selbst-Kommen des Menschen*).

2) The principle of Christological mediation which shows that in Jesus of Nazareth the reality of God meets the reality of man in a perfect way.

3) The principle of ecclesiological *praxis* which indicates that the history of God in Jesus is still prophesied, and that every human being, through the possibility and necessity to follow Jesus, should become the next chapter of the still unfolding history of the Living One.

4) The principle of eschatological fulfillment which expresses the truth that human history, stretched between "already" (*Schon*) and "not yet" (*Noch-nicht*), does not attain the ultimate perfection of temporal structures, but heads for the eschatic end of history.[477]

---

476 Mark Schoof, *Przełom w teologii katolickiej* (Kraków: Znak, 1972), 212–3.

477 Schillebeeckx, *Menschliche Erfahrung und Glaube an Jesus Christus*, 42–3; cf. Schillebeeckx, *Gerechtigheid en liefde. Genade en bevrijding*, 584–89; I. D'hert, *Een spoor voor ons getrokken. De Jezustrilogie van Edward Schillebeeckx*, 49–50.

The following question arises: what areas of modern human experience should undergo such structuring? Schillebeeckx pays special attention to two trends in contemporary societies. The first one is expressed in the anticipation of a better future, while the second illustrates the fear of the future. In connection with these tendencies, the salvation and self-liberation of man in the individual and collective aspect has ceased to be of interest to a small group of clergymen only. Now, it appears as an important matter also for the humanities, technology and all practical activities.[478]

The question of redemption and a better human future associated with it arises in the context of social disintegration and alienation. In this situation, redemption itself ceases to be a purely religious and theological subject and becomes an ideological "ferment" of the modern man's existence. Now, Redemption takes on more social forms and being aware of the great impulse for the development of all human history. Opening theology to the world of new experiences and problems allows modern man to discover the truth that Christianity is not a relic of the past, but a credible and understandable reality in which one can experience God as the redemption of man and for man (*Heil von und für Menschen*).[479] Theology which respects experience as the "environment" for the Divine Revelation (*locus revelationis*) is able to show Christian redemption in a holistic way, emphasizing that it concerns the individual and community dimensions of man, and covers the ecological, social and political aspects of the created reality.[480]

Appreciation for the importance of current experience in the process of renewing theological thinking does not mean, for Schillebeeckx, an uncritical admission of an equal epiphanic value to all experiences the contemporary man undergoes. By analogy, with the hierarchy of theological truths (*een hiërarchie van waarheden*), the Flemish professor adopts the hierarchy of experiences (*een hiërarchie van ervaringen*) which constitute a specific historical and social matter for the Divine Revelation.[481] In the melting-pot of often contradictory experiences, the process of authentic human liberation, which takes place, above all, in history, deserves the name of the medium and matter of the Divine Revelation (*het bevrijdend proces in de menselijke geschiedenis als medium en materiaal van goddelijke openbaring*).

---

478 "What once seemed only to be of interest to religious people has now become a concern of all kinds of human sciences, techniques and actions: all strive for the healing, the making whole or the salvation of man and his society." Schillebeeckx, *Interim Report on the Books Jesus & Christ*, 57.

479 Schillebeeckx, *Menschliche Erfahrung und Glaube an Jesus Christus*, 46–7.

480 Schillebeeckx, *Interim Report on the Books Jesus & Christ*, 58.

481 "Vanuit het opzicht van openbaringsdichtheid mag men dus spreken van een hiërarchie van ervaringen; van een hiërarchie van waarheden in onze menselijke ervaringen binnen de sociaal-historische context van die ervaringen." Schillebeeckx, *Mensen als verhaal van God*, 43.

Consequently, in all events and activities aimed at freeing humanity from the dominion of evil and suffering, one can discover also theophanic and redemptive meaning, in addition to the purely temporal dimension. Therefore, according to Schillebeeckx, the universal history of the world becomes an irreplaceable space of meeting and dialogue for both believers who see the face of God in history, and non-believers who see only temporal value in the process of liberation.[482] Hence, theology, open to reality and co-created in confrontation with experience, takes on a kerygmatic character.

Schillebeeckx's gradual depreciation of the value of pure speculation and the departure from great philosophical systems has led to the emphasis on the problems of human act, action and practice. Due to the radical pluralism in understanding the world and man, the Flemish theologian no longer sees the possibility of achieving a common prior understanding of the Gospel (Bultmann's *Vorverständnis*) based on philosophical anthropology.[483] By abandoning Gadamer's humanistic and philosophical hermeneutics and Bultamann's existential interpretation, Schillebeeckx turns to the reality of an act, action and dynamic *praxis* that mounts resistance and stages protest against evil.[484] In his opinion, the current attitude of negative dialectics, understood as opposition to the existing reality, may constitute a common prior understanding of the Gospel and its promise of a meaningful fate which belongs to the absolute future. Instead of a purely theoretical interpretation of religious reality, there is a specific theory of Christian *praxis* in which man's self-realization through action and the humanization of earthly life have primacy.[485]

On the basis of elementary experiences, including the ambivalence of the world, the phenomenon of radical contrast, the coexistence of values and anti-values (e. g. truth-falsehood, justice-injustice, good-evil, meaning-nonsense), Schillebeeckx intends to demonstrate the essence of ecclesial *praxis,* which aims at a positive transformation of the world, and whose current model is still the new practice of life revealed in Jesus.[486] Each praxeological reinterpretation, which evaluates the old practice in the light of the promise of the future, not only kindly explains the past, but also effectively transforms it, showing how theory is related to practice.[487] Furthermore, new interpretations in the field of Mariology must arise not so much

---

482 Ibid., 26–7.

483 "Ich komme immer mehr zu der Überzeugung, daß sich heute eine Theologie nicht mehr auf einer Anthropologie errichten läßt, denn jede Deutung des Menschen ist pluralistisch." Schillebeeckx, *Die Theologie*, 21.

484 Schillebeeckx, *Mensen als verhaal van God*, 24–6.

485 Schoof, *Przełom w teologii katolickiej*, 279–280.

486 Cf. Schillebeeckx, *Menschliche Erfahrung und Glaube an Jesus Christus*, 66.

487 Edward Schillebeeckx, "Het «rechte geloof», zijn onzekerheden en zijn criteria," *Tijdschrift voor Theologie* 9 (1969): 141.

from a specific philosophical system, but rather from a critical negation of the evil that exists in the world, creating, in a further instance, a praxeological icon of Mary that inspires contemporary people to live like the Mother of God. The hitherto static metaphysical Mariology, which remains at the level of purely interpretative reflection, should, according to the Flemish theologian, be complemented with a praxeological way of thinking that takes into account the dynamics of the human person and contemporary experiences.[488] According to Schillebeeckx, this is how orthodoxy can express itself in orthopraxy because "the practice of universal human liberation is not a secondary superstructure or merely a consequence of a theoretically known universal truth, but it is a historical mediation of the manifestation of the universal truth that applies to all people."[489]

Schillebeeckx sees the basic method of contemporary Mariology in the exegetical and historical study of the Bible. When creating new Mariology, he does not take into account the need to apply any particular philosophical type or system that would constitute a systematizing factor. This function is performed by the results of modern exegesis. Schillebeeckx is against theological anthropology because, in his opinion, Christian revelation adds nothing new to the human sciences except for the simple fact that man has been introduced to the mystery of the Divine Grace.[490] This position, however, is wrong and actually contradictory, because introducing a person into the mystery of grace produces ontic effects in him or her and is the basis for the construction of a specifically Christian anthropology. In fact, all theology is a kind of anthropology through the prism of the Revelation and does not deal with God *in abstracto*. Similarly, it can be said that Mariology is a theological reflection on the person of Mary in her relationship to God, Christ, the Church and the world. As the spiritual Mother of all believers, Mary is constantly and inspiringly present in the Church, which Benedict XVI rightly calls "God's family in the world" (*familia Dei*) and a "community of love" (*communio caritatis*).[491]

In the absence of a philosophical and anthropological structure, Mariological issues seem to be considered by Schillebeeckx as if separately and without being put in a theological and dogmatic whole. Instead of a broad, coherent, universalis-

---

488 Cf. MGVM, 53–6.

489 "Deze universeel bevrijdende praxis is niet een bovenbouw achteraf op, of louter een consequentie van, een theoretisch reeds als universeel erkende waarheid, maar ze is de historische bemiddeling van de manifestatie van waarheid juist als universele, voor alle mensen geldende waarheid." Schillebeeckx, *Mensen als verhaal van God*, 196.

490 "Das Christentum weiß deshalb nicht mehr über die menschliche Anthropologie, als daß das, was auch immer der Mensch ist, in das gnadenvolle Mysterium Gottes aufgenommen ist; also: daß das Mysterium, das der Mensch ist, zutiefst eben das Mysterium Gottes ist." Schillebeeckx, *Gott, Kirche, Welt*, 290.

491 Benedict XVI, Encyclical letter *Deus caritas est*, no. 20, 25.

tic Mariological vision of a dogmatic nature, there is atomized Mariology of the hermeneutical type, which focuses on individual Marian issues not related to a holistic structure, the explanation of which is based solely on biblical exegesis. Such an approach can lead to a biblicism in which Mariology will not achieve the status of dogmatic systematization, but will remain at the level of biblical Mariology. With such reductionist methodological assumptions, Mariology ceases to treat Mary in her essential connection with the reality of Christ, the Church, the Holy Spirit, community and history. Instead, it is limited to a minimizing scripturistic version by answering only the question: "What does the Bible say about Mary?" According to the Dominican theologian, future Mariology in its formal aspect will head towards the development of exegetical, literary, philological and hermeneutic methods, while at the same time omitting the philosophical dimension and, consequently, eliminating abstract language in favor of the colloquial one.

Schillebeeckx also has a tendency to reduce the ontological dimension.[492] According to the Flemish theologian, Mary should be shown in a dynamic relationship to modern man who asks fundamental questions about the importance of the Mother of God, her life and history for human existence. As a result, the problem of answering the question: "Who is Mary in her essence?" becomes unimportant in contemporary Mariology which is all about exposing functional and significative approaches to Mary.[493]

***

To conclude, from the point of view of hermeneutics, the method used is extremely interesting, but insufficient to present *mysterium Mariae* in a more comprehensive way. The reduction of ontological thinking, typical of the Dutch school of theology, may result in the erroneous treatment of Mary as a purely verbal, scripturistic figure that can be arbitrarily assigned various meanings depending on the changing social and cultural conditions. There is also the risk of accepting Mary as merely a symbol or literary model of human perfection and functional prowess. Reducing Mary to the linguistic category inevitably leads to the idealization of her person, and understanding her as an idea, image, meaning, norm, or convention.

Summing up, it should be emphasized that Schillebeeckx was aiming at developing a meta-dogmatic Mariology which shows the very genesis of Mariological dogmas rather than presenting a positive theological and dogmatic vision. Finally,

---

492 Cf. Haight, "Engagement met de wereld als zaak van God. Christologie & postmoderniteit," 87–88; Antoni Nadbrzeżny, "Deus semper novus. Kontekstualna chrystologia Edwarda Schillebeeckxa," in *Współczesne kontrowersje chrystologiczne*, ed. Bogdan Ferdek (Wrocław: PWT, 2016), 96–8.

493 Cf. MGVM, 44; Ted Schoof, "Geschiedenis en theologie: een haat-liefde-verhouding?," *Tijdschrift voor Geschiedenis* 4 (1988): 510–24; Snijdewind, *Leeswijzer bij "Jezus, het verhaal van een Levende" van Edward Schillebeeckx*, 12–5.

it must be said that the methods proposed by Schillebeeckx, despite the appreciation for the biblical aspect and the category of experience, rather open the way to functional Mariology, while neglecting the subjective aspect.

Conclusion

The renaissance of interest in Mariology among Western theologians leads to the problem of determining the type of Mariology practiced today. Currently, theologies of a linguistic nature are shaped under the pressure of analytical philosophy, structuralism and hermeneutics. They aim to reduce all theological problems to the analysis of language itself. As a result, one-sided theology arises, one that recognizes the primacy of language over person and redemptive event. When faced with the minimizing tendencies of linguistic trends, contemporary Mariology must strive to develop realistic concepts.

The goals of this study were to critically present the Mariology of Edward Schillebeeckx, to show its genesis and development from pre-conciliar concepts to contemporary approaches, to demonstrate its relationship with the transformations characteristic of our time, and to indicate the area for further research. The Theology of the Flemish Dominican perfectly reflects the multiplicity of contemporary ideological trends which seek a permanent right to interpret the content of the Catholic faith. Research into the thought of the professor from Nijmegen permitted the creation of a coherent and complete structure of Mariology and to highlight its most characteristic features.

Edward Schillebeeckx's Mariology has a **personalistic character**. It deals primarily with Mary as a person and not only with her functions and role in the history of salvation. Thanks to this, the one-sidedness of the relationalist approach, which makes us perceive Mary only in relation to Christ, the Church, and people, is overcome. The Flemish theologian presents Mary as a human person of deep, mysterious holiness, discovering in her, first of all, inalienable value and dignity, and only then perceiving the historico-salvific relations the Mother of God is part of. It seems that the concept of appreciation for the personal value of Mary results from Schillebeeckx belonging to the so-called Christological School of Antioch which promotes the theological outline of the Word-man (*Logos-anthropos*) as opposed to the Alexandrian views of the Word-body (*Logos-sarks*).

As a consequence of adopting the Antiochian approach, Schillebeeckx recognises the human Person in Christ, which is in conflict with the traditional Chalcedonian concept of one and the same Christ and two natures. In this Christological context, Mary appears in the first place as the mother of Jesus of Nazareth, and secondarily as the Mother of God. As the parent of Jesus, the historical man, she must therefore be theologically presented as a real human being. Jesus is born of Mary as a person from a specific person, not as a person from the substantive Marian relation. In this way, the Flemish theologian recognizes the primacy in theological explanations of the person over the relationship.

A thorough analysis of Schillebeeckx's texts permits the description of his Mariology as **historical and phenomenological**. Although initially the Flemish theologian relies mainly on Thomistic ontology, with time he moves on to phenomenology which does not concern ontic depth but deals with the essence of surface phenomena. As a result, Mary is presented as an extraordinary human phenomenon, and her life is interpreted through the prism of a sequence of phenomena, not metaphysics. Schillebeeckx emphasizes event-related, existential, conscious, descriptive, one-time, empirical elements in the person of Mary, while avoiding a priori systemic assumptions. The description of events takes the place of philosophical deduction which is the basis of scholastic dogmatics. The salvation history reorientation of current Mariology is the consequence of adopting phenomenology. The emphasis placed by Schillebeeckx on Mary's historical dimension is an important objectifying factor that overcomes idealistic tendencies resulting from phenomenological intuition.

In Schillebeeckx's interpretation, Mary is the embodiment of an **active sensitivity of faith** (*actieve geloofsontvankelijkheid*). As a representative of humanity, she is best summed up by the idea of receiving God's gift of redemption (*receptivitas*). Unlike Christ, she only represents the "bottom-up" aspect of the Incarnation and the Redemption. Therefore, she is not an intermediary in the full sense. Mary is not a medium from God to man, but rather from the side of man to God, whereby her mediation is completely subordinated to the primary redemptive mediation of Christ, the Son of God. Mary symbolizes humanity awaiting the Redemption and takes an attitude of total openness to the gift from God. She is a partner (*deelgenote*) in the dialogue with God, uttering *fiat* also on behalf of all mankind. Consequently, Mary is presented as the first person to accept the Divine Revelation, the gift of the Redemption and the fullness of grace, as the first hearer and disciple of the Master, the first fruit of the Redemption and Christ's most beautiful creation (*Maria Christus' mooiste wonderschepping*).

An important *novum* of this work lies in the discovery of **the sacramentological concept of Mary's motherhood** in Schillebeeckx's thought. Unconditional availability, faithful openness and active receptivity are related to the mystery of Mary's motherhood which is a fundamental Mariological principle and an essential interpretative key. Mary's motherhood is not limited to the biological, natural and functional level, but is the deepest personal way of participating in the reality of objective and subjective redemption. Mary's motherhood was presented by the Flemish theologian as a dynamic, progressive reality, which results in a transition from the historical and individual level (the historical Mother of Jesus of Nazareth) to the trans-historical and social level (The Assumed Mother of all people). Pursuing her maternal vocation, Mary participates in a unique dialogue with Christ Who is the primordial sacrament. The Mother's dialogue with the Son is not limited to the exchange of words and thoughts, or to the communication of mutual desires, but reaches the deepest sphere of existence, taking the form of a non-verbal exchange of gifts of personality and grace. In the mystery of realized motherhood, Mary develops the grace of holiness received at the moment of her coming into existence. The subsequent stages of motherhood are related to the development of holiness thanks to the cooperation with Grace which reaches her mediated by the humanity of Jesus the Savior. As a result, all of Mary's earthly life is sacramental.

Influenced by theistic existentialism of G. Marcel, S. Kierkegaard, and R. Guardini, Schillebeeckx's Mariology manifests **high anthropological sensitivity**, a sense of drama of life, existential pain, the importance of subjective experiences, being toward death (*Sein zum Tode*), and the domination of fear. In shaping the theological icon of Mary, Schillebeeckx avoids Gnostic, Manichaean, Docetic, and idyllic ideas. He presents the Mother of God as an authentic personal being, who is seeking God, who is embedded in the drama of the world, and who is developing the awareness of her mission in the history of salvation. Mary participates in the universal fate of human sufferings, revealing at the same time their supernatural meaning. She survives the night of faith and, believing against all hope, she is present by the cross at the very peak of the Redemption. Schillebeeckx's thought aims to overcome the dualism characteristic of the Alexandrian school, e. g. Clement of Alexandria, Eusebius of Caesarea, Cyril of Alexandria, or Origen, which absolutely separates and juxtaposes body and soul, matter and spirit, secular and sacred history. The Flemish theologian strongly emphasizes the positive meaning of earthly life. The human person and his or her temporal history become the privileged place of the Divine Revelation. Hence, an essential epiphany dimension becomes visible in Mary. Due to her belonging to the order of the Revelation, Mary's earthly existence penetrates and shapes the inner and profound flow of sacred history. Within human history, Mary experiences specific stages of growth in faith, in awareness of her mission and in her role in the drama of salvation.

Schillebeeckx's Mariology clearly echoes the **philosophy of dialogue** (M. Buber, E. Levinas, G. Marcel, R. Guardini), which emphasizes the truth that the human person is fully realized in relation to God, to other people and to society. Mary perceives her "I" more and more through constant dialogue with the Divine "You." Thanks to her maternal and inherently dialogic relationship with Jesus, Mary achieves the highest degree of self-understanding and awareness of the meaning of her existence in the temporal, historico-salvific, ecclesial and eschatic dimensions.

According to Schillebeeckx, **Mary's historicity** (*zoeken naar de historische Maria*) seems to be an extremely important idea for the development of contemporary Mariology. Thanks to an in-depth biblical exegesis, it is possible to reconstruct the Mary of history. The return to the historical image of Mary is the necessary basis for any subsequent theological interpretation as it averts the dangers of mythologism.

In the 1990s, the thesis about the **universal nature of Mary's spiritual motherhood** (*geestelijk moederschap van Maria ten aanzien van alle gelovigen*) comes to the fore. Schillebeeckx clearly distances himself from the previously promoted title "Mary, Mother of the Redemption" (*Maria moeder van de verlossing*), preferring the new expression: "Mother of all believers" (*Maria moeder van alle gelovigen*). In this way, he wants to link what is specific and singular (the individual story of Mary) with what is universal (the universal history of salvation). Bethlehem motherhood gradually turns into Calvary motherhood and takes the final form of universal social motherhood that covers all humanity. Mary is presented here more as the mother of all humanity than the Mother of the Church, the Mystical Body of Christ. In the development of Schillebeeckx's Mariological thought there is an evident transition from the traditional scholastic concept of Mary as a mediator to Christ (*mediatrix ad Christum*) towards historico-salvific approaches in which the Mother of God is recognized as a representative of humanity, an existential and moral model, and a symbol of the bond between man and God. The departure from ontologism has led to the exposure of the relationships between Mary and the Church, Mary and the world, or Mary and the communities of other religions. Typical of Schillebeeckx's thought is the intellectual confrontation of the theological image of *Madonna of the Catholic tradition* with the biblical image of *Mary of history*, and then, the creation of a contemporary portrait of *Miriam of general religious faith*, which undoubtedly entails an idealizing tendency.

When it comes to Marian devotions (*Mariaverering*), Schillebeeckx firstly justifies them theologically, and then formulates the norms that are the basis of practical pastoral solutions. Based on the analysis of the *Magnificat*, he proposes a **theocentric orientation of Christian Marian piety**, which has its source in the structure of the history of salvation. He also postulates a more biblical character of Marian liturgical piety and its supplementation with existential imitation, in accordance with the principle of verifying orthodoxy through orthopraxy. Integrally understood Marian devotions should always include thanksgiving for the person of the Mother of God and for the redemptive work done by God in her life. Ultimately, in Christian piety, we should thank God for Mary, with Mary and like Mary.

In Schillebeeckx's work, we encounter a **positive evaluation of the experience of Marian apparitions and the phenomenon of popular piety**. He emphasizes the importance of strong expression in Marian popular piety (*mariale volksdevotie*) in the context of universal human symbolic activity (*symboolactiviteit*). Marian apparitions that have the status of private revelations must be interpreted through the prism of the prophetic and charismatic dimension of the Church. In terms of the content, private revelations do not bring any radical novelty. Instead, they play a motivating role in the deepening of the faith and constitute the *hic et nunc* specification of the general evangelical message.

The Flemish theologian, however, discerns several **negative tendencies in the practice of Marian piety**. The main causes of the irregularities include: misunderstanding of the principle *per Mariam ad Iesum*, uncritical use of human analogies, instrumental treatment of Christian worship and linguistic anachronism of prayer and dogmatic formulas. Schillebeeckx, like many contemporary theologians, e. g. John Paul II, Y. Congar, S. Napiórkowski, A. Czaja, M. Gilski, A. Nadbrzeżny, or K. Pek, puts forward a proposal to adopt a new Mariological principle: *per Iesum ad Mariam*, which will supplement the one-sided approach to Mary's mediation expressed in the formula: *per Mariam ad Iesum*. A clear departure from the "multi-level" model of mediation testifies to Schillebeeckx's innovative views which are close to the idea of Mary's maternal and intercessory mediation, subordinated to the sole, saving and absolute mediation of Christ.

Schillebeeckx's Mariology also has its **meta-theological side**, as far as cognitive methods, hermeneutic principles, verification system, and ways of constructing science are concerned. In the methodological aspect, there are particular elements of the so-called **moderate historicism** in Schillebeeckx's Mariology, similarly to other contemporary Catholic thinkers, including R. Guardini, H. Urs von Balthasar, Y. Congar, K. Rahner, or G. Thils. Schillebeeckx appreciates the categories of history, time and space, assigning them an important role in shaping the world and man. He also takes into account the historical dimension of human awareness. He has a tendency to present Mariology in a dynamic, developmental way, while recognizing permanent and transcendent elements.

Accepting **history as a theological category** does not mean accepting extreme subjectivism, immanentism, relativism, and lack of purpose or specificity. The history of the world contains an important transcendent dimension, becoming the environment of God's revelations and actions. Schillebeeckx tackles the problem of the relationship between temporal history and sacred history in an extremely interesting way. The thesis about the theophanic nature of Mary's earthly history is put forward boldly and creatively, becoming a solid basis for developing Mariology with a historico-salvific profile. Thanks to this, the Manichean view concerning the absolute separability of history and the transcendent world is overcome.

Schillebeeckx **avoids extremes** in historical thinking. On the one hand, he rejects the absolute determinism of the human person and does not reduce Mary to a purely passive, instrumental dimension. On the other hand, he opposes the indefiniteness and directionlessness of historical processes, i. e. the randomness and the arbitrariness of events in Mary's life, and the inability to know their deeper meaning. The historical process in which Mary participates is not an anonymous, unknowable reality, guided only by immanent laws, but an objective and meaningful sequence of events shaped by God and man in dialogue. Schillebeeckx's conscious resignation from the classical, too metaphysical and abstract way of constructing Mariology in favor of the introduction of historical methods resulted in the emergence of a realistic Mariology which is more specific and closer to life.

The Flemish scholar surpasses many contemporary thinkers in their views on the **role of experience in constructing theology.** Following the line of Gustaw Thils from Louvain, Schillebeeckx appreciates the "bottom-up" cognitive trend that respects the revelatory value of created reality (theology of earthly realities). In his opinion, theology arises from both proper revelation (the Bible, the Tradition) and humanistic, historical, praxeological and cultural knowledge which takes into account the dynamics of contemporary human experience. The category of experience (*ervaring*), understood in its basic and broadest, even undefined, sense, is recognized by Schillebeeckx as having cognitive and scientific value. The rich and varied world of human experiences is treated as a theological source (*locus theologicus*). The most difficult problems that need a satisfactory solution include the determination of the factors that objectify and structure the subjectivity of human experiences in the individual and social dimensions.

In the field of Mariology, Schillebeeckx **appreciates the knowledge of existential, psychological, singular and specific phenomena in the individual history of Mary of Nazareth.** He does not simply state the facts and describe events, but tries to relate a specific event to the universal dimension of the Redemption, while seeking a more general comprehensive vision. In contrast to the principles of metaphysics, the heterogeneous world of human experiences, which is extremely difficult to systematize, makes it possible to know religious reality in a more realistic, existential, detailed, dynamic and developmental way. Hence, Mariology which arises from contemporary human experience avoids schematism and apriorism. In the scientific method, Schillebeeckx strongly links intellectual knowledge with intuitive knowledge, which does not deny the objectivity of the presented propositions.

By analogy to contemporary Protestant theologians (O. Cullmann, J.A.T. Robinson, K. Barth, W. Pannenberg), Schillebeeckx proposes to **practice theology without the necessary connection to classical philosophy.** This position seems to be too extreme, because while it is correct to reduce excessive abstractionism in theology, it cannot be realized by completely resigning from specific philosophical terminology, cognitive methods and ways of understanding the world and man. The absolute breach of the relationship between theology and philosophy diminishes the scientific nature of theological knowledge, reducing it to the area of common methodically disorganized knowledge. Theology cannot be bound forever with one philosophical system (Thomism) either, because philosophical concepts themselves get old and become obsolete. Hence, openness to new philosophical trends usually serves theology well in terms of content and methodology.

Influenced by the wave of linguistic philosophies, Schillebeeckx addresses **the problem of Mariological language,** which is extremely important from the point of view of theological methodology. In his opinion, the excess of abstraction in creating theological language should be abandoned in favor of a more specific existential way of expressing the content. The language of contemporary Mariology should constitute a creative synthesis, firstly, of the biblical language as a scripturistically established religious experience; secondly, of the experience of the encounter between Jesus and Mary interpreted by specific people (apostles, disciples, evangelists, witnesses); and thirdly, of the language of contemporary experiences which takes into account the entire Tradition of the Church. In constructing an adequate language of Mariology, semantic (meaning), syntactic (language structure) and pragmatic (language use) relations should be taken into account.

From the methodological point of view, the innovative concept of **"sacramentological" Mariology**, developed by the Flemish theologian, deserves special attention. It consists in emphasizing Mary's relationship with Christ, the primordial sacrament, whose main implication is the sacramental interpretation of her motherhood (*het geestelijk-lichamelijk, concreet moederschap met zijn sacramentele voorafwerking en zijn sacramentele innerlijke vruchtbaarheid*). Taking into account the thesis about the sacramental structure of the Revelation, one can, according to Schillebeeckx, perceive in Mary's motherhood a kind of "sacrament," understood as a real historical encounter with God through the humanity of Jesus, the Son of God. The inclusion of the sacramentological context in research on Mariology complements the previously exposed links between Mariology and Christology, ecclesiology or pneumatology. Moreover, the principle of interdisciplinarity in theology (*interdisciplinariteit in de theologie*), promoted by Schillebeeckx, creates the basis for building an "up-to-date" Mariology which takes into account contemporary horizons of understanding in the hermeneutic process of revising the content of faith.

In Schillebeeckx's Mariology, a wide range of **positive elements characteristic of Western mindsets** can be discerned. These include: a clear personalistic and humanistic attitude, deep respect for the biblical icon of Mary, dynamism of Mary's relationship to Christ, the Church and the world, the idea of Mary's universal motherhood, emphasis on the exemplary value in the cult of Mary, Augustinian emphasis on the subjective and conscious dimensions of the human person, distance from excessive doctrinal objectivization, appreciation for everyday experience, giving up metaphysical issues, promoting historico-salvific approach, emphasizing the idea of universal unity of humanity, dialogic and sociological concept of the Church, taking into account the ambivalence of the world and man, and special emphasis on Christian *praxis*.

Not all of Schillebeeckx's ideas are free from one-sidedness. The weakness of his Mariological project lies in the gradual **departure from ontological issues**, like Mary's participation in the work of the Redemption, immaculate conception, Assumption, or virginity, and the focus on functional approaches, i. e. Mary's social motherhood, Mary's relationship to the Church and the world. Pushing ontic issues to the periphery of theological reflection leads to the fragmentation of Mariology which is then difficult to harmonize with other fields of theology. The study of Mary presented by Schillebeeckx does not sufficiently analyze the relationship between Mary and the Holy Trinity. It does not take into account Mary's culture-forming role and does not see deeper connections between Mariology and the science of freedom (eleuterology). In addition, the Flemish professor does not elaborate on more actual topics, like Mary and feminism, or Mary as a model of implementing the highest values of love, good, peace, social service, or Christian spirituality. There is also no theological presentation of Mary in terms of beauty (Aesthetic Mariology of H. Urs von Balthasar and P. Evdokimov).

The rich theological output of Edward Schillebeeckx; the original type of Christology and ecclesiology he practiced; the acceptance of human experience as *locus theologicus;* the reception of the basic ideas of existentialism, phenomenology, philosophy of dialogue, and structuralism; avoiding the hermeticism of thought and openness to the results of modern sciences – all these provide an intellectual inspiration to undertake further research in the field of Mariology. From the substantive point of view, it would be valuable to elaborate on the **Mariological implications of functional Christology and the dialogic concept of the Church** developed by the Flemish theologian. For the purposes of theological methodology, it would be worth presenting more broadly the **updating function of experience in the construction of contemporary Mariology**.

In the context of the individualistic culture developing in European societies today, it would be worthwhile to make an original attempt to portray Mary from the perspective of the values sought by modern men and women. It would be valuable to outline an **axiological type of Mariology** inspired by the theological thought of Edward Schillebeeckx, who wishes to portray the person and lifestyle of Mary as an intriguing response to the contemporary crisis of values, in which existential flight from the world, loneliness, indifference, selfishness and despair can be overcome by presence, encounter with others, care, sacrifice and hope. Such an axiological Mariology could, to some extent, help overcome the cultural pessimism caused by the modern phenomena of the "eclipse of God" (M. Buber), as well as the "eclipse of man" (A. J. Heschel).

Personalistic Mariology created by Edward Schillebeeckx, which is deeply rooted in the Bible and, at the same time, remains open to dialogue with contemporary human experience, is at the very center of theology and ecclesial awareness, and constitutes a strong argument against the erroneous theories of Docetism, monophysitism and Christological idealism. The historico-salvific Mariology presented by the Flemish theologian shows Mary in dynamic relations to Christ, the Holy Spirit, the Church and the whole world. It should be considered as a serious proposal, which is able to replace previous projects of an overly abstract, idealizing, biographical, fabulous and privileged nature. In the gallery of contemporary Mariological systems, the theological icon of Mary by Edward Schillebeeckx delights with the beauty of its universalism and the splendor of the evangelical truth about the Mother of all believers.

Abbreviations

CCC	Catechism of the Catholic Church
DCE	Benedict XVI, Encyclical Letter *Deus caritas est*
EN	Paul VI, Apostolic Exhortation *Evangelii nuntiandi*
GS	Second Vatican Council, Pastoral Constitution on the Church in the Modern World *Gaudium et spes*
HK	*Glaubensverkündigung für Erwachsene. Deutsche Ausgabe des Holländischen Katechismus*
LF	Francis, Encyclical Letter *Lumen fidei*
LG	Second Vatican Council, Dogmatic Constitution on the Church *Lumen gentium*
MC	Paul VI, Apostolic Exhortation *Marialis cultus*
MCMW	E. Schillebeeckx, *Maria, Christus' mooiste wonderschepping. Religieuze grondlijnen van het Maria-mysterie*
MGVM	E. Schillebeeckx, *Mariologie: gisteren, vandaag, morgen*, Baarn 1992.
MMV	E. Schillebeeckx, *Maria, moeder van de verlossing. Religieuze grondlijnen van het Maria-mysterie*
MThS	E. Schillebeeckx, *Maria. Theologische synthese*
OTh	E. Schillebeeckx, *Openbaring en Theologie*
RM	John Paul II, Encyclical Letter *Redemptoris Mater*
RVM	John Paul II, Apostolic Letter *Rosarium Virginis Mariae*
SC	Second Vatican Council, Constitution on the Sacred Liturgy *Sacrosanctum concilium.*
SM	Paul VI, Apostolic Exhortation *Signum magnum*

Bibliography

1.   Church Documents

Pius XII. Encyclical Letter *Mediator Dei* (20 November 1947).

Second Vatican Council, Constitution on the Sacred Liturgy *Sacrosanctum concilium* (4 December1963).

Second Vatican Council, Dogmatic Constitution on the Church *Lumen gentium*, (21 November 1964).

Second Vatican Council, Pastoral Constitution on the Church in the Modern World *Gaudium et spes* (7 December 1965).

Paul VI. Apostolic Exhortation *Signum magnum* (13 May 1967).

Paul VI. Apostolic Exhortation *Marialis cultus* (2 February 1974).

Paul VI. Apostolic Exhortation *Evangelii nuntiandi* (8 December 1975).

John Paul II. Encyclical Letter *Redemptoris Mater* (25 March 1987).

Catechism of the Catholic Church (Città del Vaticano: Libreria Editrice Vaticana, 1994).

John Paul II. Apostolic Letter *Rosarium Virginis Mariae* (16 October 2002).

Benedict XVI. Encyclical Letter *Deus caritas est* (25 December 2005).

Francis. Encyclical Letter *Lumen fidei* (29 June 2013).

2.   Mariological Works of Edward Schillebeeckx

"Rozenkrans bidden in nuchtere werkelijkheid." 33, no. 1 *De Bazuin* (October 1st, 1949): 4–6.

"De gezinsrozenkrans." *Tijdschrift voor Geestelijk Leven* 6 (1950): 523–532.

"Het wonder dat Maria hee." *Thomas* 7, no. 7 (1953/54): 5–7.

Maria, Christus' mooiste wonderschepping. Religieuze grondlijnen van het Maria-mysterie. Antwerpen: Apostolaat van de Rozenkrans, 1954.

"Beata quae credidisti." *Biekorf* 36 (1954): 1–23.

"Betekenis en waarde van de Maria-verschijningen." In *Hoe preken wij over O. L. Vrouw.* Edited by Ambrosius M. Bogaerts, 30–48. Antwerpen: Apostolaat van de Rozenkrans, 1954.

"Het geloofsleven van de *dienstmaagd des Heren.*" *Tijdschrift voor Geestelijk Leven* 10 (1954): 242–269.

"Maria onze hoop." *Thomas* 8, no. 1 (1954/55): 4–6.

"De bruid van de Heilige Geest." *Thomas* 8, no. 3 (1954/55): 3–5.

"De zware strijd van Maria's geloof." *Thomas* 8, no. 2 (1954/55): 6–7.

"De Schrift zwijgt over Maria!" *De Bazuin* 38, no. 16 (January 15th, 1955): 2–3.

"De leer van het Rozenkransgebed." *De Rozenkrans* 82 (1955/56): 53–54.

"Providentieel Redmiddel." *De Rozenkrans* 82 (1955/56): 18–21.

Maria, moeder van de verlossing. Religieuze grondlijnen van het Maria-mysterie. Antwerpen: Apostolaat van de Rozenkrans, 1955.

"Maria. Theologische synthese." In *Theologisch Woordenboek.* Vol. II. Edited by H. Brink, 3124–3154. Roermond en Maaseik: J.J. Romen & Zonen, 1957.

"Mutua correlatio inter redemptionem obiectivam eamque subiectivam B. M. Virginis in ordine ad eius maternitatem erga Christum et nos, ut principium fundamentale mariologiae." In *Virgo Immaculata. Acta Congressus Mariologici-Mariani Romae anno MCMLIV celebrati.* Vol. IX: *De immaculata conceptione aliisque privilegis B. V. Mariae pro statu Christum natum antecedente et concomitante,* 305–321. Roma: Academia Mariana Internationalis, 1957.

"De Mariaverschijningen in het leven van de kerk." *De Rozenkrans* 84 (1957/58): 131–133.

"Rozenkransgebed: verantwoord gebed." *De Rozenkrans* 84 (1957/58): 4–7.

"Maria, meest-verloste moeder." *De Linie* 13, no. 641 (July 12th, 1958): 2.

"Het charisma der verschijningen." *De Bazuin* 41, no. 19 (February 8th, 1958): 1–2.

"Het Lourdes-dossier." *Tijdschrift voor Geestelijk Leven* 14 (1958): 256–260.

"De eigen techniek van de rozenkrans." *De Rozenkrans* 85 (1958/59): 208–211.

"Maria." In *Catholica. Geïllustreerd encyclopedisch vademecum voor het katholiek leven.* Edited by A. M. Heidt, col. 1040–4. Den Haag: Pax 1961.

"Verschillend standpunt van exegese en dogmatiek." In *Maria in het boodschapsverhaal. Verslagboek der zestiende Mariale dagen 1959,* 53–74. Tongerlo: Secretariaat der Mariale dagen – Norbertijner Abdij, 1960.

"Het mensdom is reeds verheerlijkt in Christus en Maria." *De Rozenkrans* 88 (1961/62): 136–137.

Evangelie verhalen, 25–31. Baarn: Nelissen, 1982.

"Mariologie: gisteren, vandaag, morgen." In Edward Schillebeeckx, and Catharina Halkes. *Maria: gisteren, vandaag, morgen.* Baarn: Nelissen, 1992, 23–66.

3. Other Works of Edward Schillebeeckx

"De sacramentaire structuur van de openbaring." *Kultuurleven* 19 (1952): 785–802.

De sacramentele heilsekonomie. Theologische bezinning op S. Thomas' sacramentenleer in het licht van de traditie en van de hedendaagse sacramentsproblematiek. Antwerpen: Nelissen, 1952.

"Het gebed, centrale daad van het menselijk leven." *Tijdschrift voor Geestelijk Leven* 10 (1954): 469–490.

"Lex orandi, lex credendi." In *Theologisch Woordenboek.* Vol. II. Edited by H. Brink, col. 2926–2928. Roermond en Maaseik: J.J. Romen & Zonen, 1957.

"Loci theologici." In *Theologisch Woordenboek*. Vol. II. Edited by H. Brink, col. 3004–3006. Roermond en Maaseik: J.J. Romen & Zonen, 1957.

"Gebed als daad van geloof, hoop en liefde." *De Heraut van het Heilig Hart* 92 (1961): 186–188.

"Het gebed als liefdesgesprek." *De Heraut van het Heilig Hart* 92 (1961): 153–156.

"Gebedsdialoog." *De Heraut van het Heilig Hart* 92 (1961): 121–125.

"Het mysterie van het gebed." *De Heraut van het Heilig Hart* 92 (1961): 91–93.

Het Tweede Vaticaans Concilie, I. Tielt: Lannoo, 1964.

Openbaring en Theologie. Bilthoven: Nelissen, 1964.

God en mens. Bilthoven: Nelissen, 1965.

"Kościół a ludzkość." *Concilium* 1–10 (1965/66): 27–40.

Het Tweede Vaticaans Concilie, II. Tielt: Lannoo, 1966.

Christus sacrament van de Godsontmoeting. Bilthoven: Nelissen, 1964.

"Zasięg znaczenia teologicznego wypowiedzi Urzędu Nauczycielskiego Kościoła w sprawach społecznych i politycznych." *Concilium* 1–10 (1968): 296–310.

"O katolickie zastosowanie hermeneutyki. Tożsamość wiary w toku jej reinterpretacji." *Znak* 20 (1968): 978–1010.

"Katholiek leven in de Verenigde Staten." *De Bazuin* 51, no. 17 (January 21st, 1968): 1–6.

"Z hermeneutycznych rozważań nad eschatologią." *Concilium* 1–5 (1969): 31–41.

God the Future of Man. London: Sheed & Ward, 1969.

"Het «rechte geloof», zijn onzekerheden en zijn criteria." *Tijdschrift voor Theologie* 9 (1969): 125–149.

Gott, Kirche, Welt. Mainz: Matthias-Grünewald Verlag, 1970.

"Die Theologie." In Edward Schillebeeckx et al. *Kirche in Freiheit. Gründe und Hintergründe des Aufbruchs in Holland*, 9–27. Freiburg im Breisgau: Herder, 1970.

"Krytyczny status teologii." In *Concilium*. "Materiały Kongresu *Przyszłość Kościoła*, Brussels, September 12–17, 1970," special issue (Poznań: 1971): 46–51.

"De schok van de toekomst in Amerika." *De Bazuin* 41, no. 41 (special issue; July 11th, 1971): 1–8.

"The crisis in the Language of Faith as a Hermeneutical Problem." Concilium 9, no. 5 (1973): 31–45.

Jezus, het verhaal van een levende. Bloemendaal: Nelissen, 1974.

"Interdisciplinarity in theology." *Theology Digest* 24 (1976): 137–142.

Gerechtigheid en liefde. Genade en bevrijding. Bloemendaal: Nelissen 1977.

Menschliche Erfahrung und Glaube an Jesus Christus. Freiburg im Breisgau: Herder, 1979.

Kerkelijk ambt. Voorgangers in de gemeente van Jezus Christus. Bloemendaal: Nelissen, 1980.

Interim Report on the Books Jesus & Christ. New York: Crossroad, 1981.

Pleidooi voor mensen in de kerk. Christelijke identiteit en ambten in de kerk. Baarn: Nelissen, 1985.

Glaubensverkündigung für Erwachsene. Deutsche Ausgabe des Holländischen Katechismus. Nijmegen-Utrecht 1968.

"Die Rolle der Geschichte im dem, was das neue Paradigma genannt wird." In *Das neue Paradigma von Theologie, Strukturen und Dimensionen*. Edited by Hans Küng, and David Tracy, 75–86. Zürich: Benziger, 1986.

Een demokratische Kerk. Utrecht: Impress, 1989.

Mensen als verhaal van God. Baarn: Nelissen, 1989.

"In memoriam M.-D. Chenu (1995–1990)." *Tijdschrift voor Theologie* 30 (1990): 184–185.

Theologisch testament. Notarieel nog niet verleden. Baarn: Nelissen, 1994.

"In memoriam Yves Congar (1904–1995)." *Tijdschrift voor Theologie* 35 (1995): 271–273.

Je suis un théologien heureux. Paris: Cerf, 1995.

"Over vergeving en verzoening: De kerk als verhaal van toekomst." *Tijdschrift voor Theologie* 37 (1997): 368–383.

4. Works on Edward Schillebeeckx

Ambaum, Jan. *Glaubenszeichen. Schillebeeckx' Auffassung von den Sakramenten*. Regensburg: Pustet, 1980.

Auwerda, Richard. *Dossier Schillebeeckx. Theoloog in de kerk der conflicten*. Bilthoven: Nelissen, 1969.

Boeve, Lieven, Frederiek Depoortere and Stephan van Erp, eds. *Edward Schillebeeckx and Contemporary Theology* (London: T&T Clark International, 2010).

Borgman, Erik. "Op zoek naar Maria … en verder! Schillebeeckx' mariologie en haar actuele betekenis." *Tijdschrift voor theologie* 33 (1993): 241–266.

Borgman, Erik. *Edward Schillebeeckx: een theoloog in zijn geschiedenis*. Baarn: Nelissen, 1999.

Borgman, Erik. *Edward Schillebeeckx. A Theologian in His History*. London: Bloomsbury, 2006.

Borgman, Erik. "… als het ware een sacrament – Naar een theologische visie op de reëel bestaande kerk." *Tijdschrift voor Theologie* (2010): 123–143.

Bosschaert, Dries and Stephan van Erp. "Schillebeeckx's Metaphysics and Epistemology: The Influence of Dominicus De Petter." In *T&T Clark Handbook of Edward Schillebeeckx*. Edited by Stephan van Erp, and Daniel Minch, 29–44. London: Bloomsbury, 2019.

Bowden, John. *Edward Schillebeeckx. Portrait of a Theologian*. London: SCM Press, 1983.

Bowden, John. *Who's Who in Theology*. London: SCM Press, 1990.

Brambilla, Franco Giulio. *La cristologia di Schillebeeckx. La singolarità di Gesù come problema di ermeneutica teologica*. Brescia: Morcelliana, 1989.

Bullivant, Stephen. "The Myth of Rahnerian Exceptionalism: Edward Schillebeeckx's *Anonymous Christians*." *Philosophy and Theology* 22, no. 1–2 (2010): 339–351.

Cavadini, John C., and Danielle M. Peters, eds. *Mary on the Eve of the Second Vatican Council*. Notre Dame: University of Notre Dame Press, 2017.

Chamoso, Roman Sánchez. *La teoría hermenéutica de E. Schillebeeckx. La reinterpretación de la fe: contexto, presupuestos, principios y criterios.* Salamanca: Universidad Pontificia de Salamanca, 1978.

Depoorter, Annekatrien. "Tussen denken en leven. Een beknopte biografie van Edward Schillebeeckx." *Tijdschrift voor Geestelijk Leven* 1 (2009): 5-12.

D'hert, Ignace. *Een spoor voor ons getrokken: de Jezustrilogie van Edward Schillebeeckx.* Baarn: Nelissen, 1997.

De Fiores, Stefano. *Maria nella teologia contemporanea.* Roma: Centro di Cultura Mariana "Mater Ecclesiae," 1987.

de Jong, Marijn. *Metaphysics of Mystery. Revisiting the Question of Universality through Rahner and Schillebeeckx.* London: Bloomsbury, 2021.

Feder, Julia. "Mary, Model of Eschatological Faith." In *T&T Handbook of Edward Schillebeeckx.* Edited by Stephan van Erp and Daniel Minch, 326-339. London: Bloomsbury 2019.

Fernández, Domiciano. "María en las recientes cristologías holandesas." *Estudios Marianos* 47 (1982): 47-72.

Geldhof, Joris and Leo Kenis. "The World and History as Sacrament: Schillebeeckx on the Eve of the Second Vatican Council." In *T&T Handbook of Edward Schillebeeckx.* Edited by Stephan van Erp and Daniel Minch, 111-120. London: Bloomsbury 2019.

Gibellini, Rosino. *La teologia del XX secolo.* Brescia: Queriniana, 1992.

Gibellini, Rosino. "Préface. Honnêtes envers le monde. La théologie de frontière d'Edward Schillebeeckx." In Edward Schillebeeckx, *Je suis un théologien heureux,* 7-16. Paris: Cerf, 1995.

Grelot, Pierre. *Église et ministères. Pour un dialogue critique avec E. Schillebeeckx.* Paris: Cerf, 1983.

Haar, Huub ter, ed. *Mensen maken de kerk. Verslag van het symposion rond 75e verjaardag van Edward Schillebeeckx.* Baarn: Nelissen, 1989.

Haight, Roger. "Engagement met de wereld als zaak van God. Christologie & postoderniteit." *Tijdschrift voor Theologie* 1 (2010): 73-94.

Häring, Hermann. "Met mensen op weg, voor mensen op weg. Over het theologisch denken van Edward Schillebeeckx." In *Mensen maken de kerk. Verslag van het symposion rond 75e verjaardag van Edward Schillebeeckx.* Edited by Huub ter Haar, 27-46. Baarn: Nelissen, 1989.

Hilkert, Mary Catherine. "Hermeneutics of History in the Theology of Edward Schillebeeckx." *The Tomist* 51, no. 1 (1987): 97-145.

Hilkert, Mary Catherine and Robert Schreiter, eds. *The Praxis of the Reign of God. An Introduction to the Theology of Edward Schillebeeckx.* New York: Fordham University Press, 2002.

Hilkert, Mary Catherine. "Nieuwe paden in een oude tuin. Sacramentele theologie en antropologie." *Tijdschrift voor Theologie* 1 (2010): 108-122.

Houdijk, Marinus. "Edward Schillebeeckx." In *Modern Theologians. Christians and Jews*. Edited by Thomas E. Bird, 84–107. Notre Dame (Indiana): University of Notre Dame Press, 1967.

Iammarrone, Luigi. *La cristologia di E. Schillebeeckx*. Genova: Quadrivium, 1985.

Kennedy, Philip. *Schillebeeckx*. Collegeville: Liturgical Press, 1993.

Kennedy, Philip. *Deus humanissimus: The Knowability of God in the Theology of Edward Schillebeeckx*. Fribourg: University Press, 1993.

Logister, Wiel. "De passie van en voor Jezus Christus." *Tijdschrift voor Geestelijk Leven* 1 (2009): 43–53.

Mettepenningen, Jürgen. *Nouvelle Théologie – New Theology. Inheritor of Modernism, Precursor of Vatican II*. London: T&T Clark, 2010.

Minch, Daniel. *Eschatological Hermeneutics. The Theological Core of Experience and Our Hope For Salvation*. London: Bloomsbury, 2020.

Mondin, Battista. "Schillebeeckx." In Battista Mondin, *Dizionario dei teologii*, 530–9. Bolonia: Edizioni Studio Domenicano, 1992.

Nadbrzeżny, Antoni. "Kościół jako sakrament dialogu według Edwarda Schillebeeckxa," *Roczniki Teologiczne* 50, no. 2 (2003): 229–242.

Nadbrzeżny, Antoni. "Teolog w świecie konfliktów. *In memoriam* Edward Schillebeeckx (1914–2009)." *Roczniki Teologii Dogmatycznej*, 57, no. (2010): 119–129.

Nadbrzeżny, Antoni. *Sakrament wyzwolenia. Zbawcze posłannictwo Kościoła w posoborowej eklezjologii holenderskiej*. Lublin: Wydawnictwo KUL, 2013.

Nadbrzeżny, Antoni. "Deus semper novus. Kontekstualna chrystologia Edwarda Schillebeeckxa." In *Współczesne kontrowersje chrystologiczne*. Edited by Bogdan Ferdek, 95–107. Wrocław: PWT, 2016.

Nadbrzeżny, Antoni. "Kerk en bevrijding in het denken van Edward Schillebeeckx." *Roczniki Teologiczne* 64, no. 7 (2017): 97–107.

Nadbrzeżny, Antoni. "Tussen sacralisatie en banalisering. Lijden in de theologie van Edward Schillebeeckx." *Roczniki Teologiczne* 45, no. 2 (2018): 47–61.

Nadbrzeżny, Antoni. "Schillebeeckx." In *Encyklopedia Katolicka*. Vol. 17, col. 1224–1226. Lublin: Towarzystwo Naukowe KUL, 2012.

Nadbrzeżny, Antoni. *Filozofia zbawienia. Soteriologia egzystencjalna Paula Tillicha i Edwarda Schillebeeckxa*. Kraków: Wydawnictwo WAM, 2020.

Nadbrzeżny, Antoni. "De receptie van de de theologie van Edward Schillebeeckx in Polen (1965–2016)." In *De Lage Landen en de religie. De positie van de religie in verschillende culturele aspecten*. Edited by Bas Hammers and Muriel Waterlot, 65–76. Lublin: Wydawnictwo KUL, 2017.

Nadbrzeżny, Antoni. "Edward Schillebeeckx OP (1914–2009) als een pionier van de hermeneutische theologie." In *Plurima sub falso tegmine vera latent. The Embarrassments of Interdisciplinarity*. Edited by Agnieszka Flor-Górecka, 183–192. Lublin: Towarzystwo Naukowe KUL, 2022.

Oosterhuis, Huub, and Piet Hoogeveen. *God is ieder ogenblik nieuw. Gesprekken met Edward Schillebeeckx*. Baarn: Ambo, 1982.

Rossum, Pieter van. "La christologie du R. P. Schillebeeckx." *Esprit et Vie* 85 (1975): 129–135.

Rossum, Pieter van. "L'epistemologia di Schillebeeckx e la dottrina della fede." *La Rivista del Clero Italiano* 57 (1976): 988–999.

Schoof, Mark. *Przełom w teologii katolickiej*. Kraków: Znak, 1972.

Schoof, Mark. "The later theology of Edward Schillebeeckx. The New Position of Theology after Vatican II." *The Clergy Review* 55 (1970): 943–960.

Schoof, Ted. "Edward Schillebeeckx – De laatste twintig jaar." *Tijdschrift voor Theologie* 50, no. 1 (2010): 144–152.

Schoof, Ted. *De zaak Schillebeeckx*. Bloemendaal: Nelissen, 1980.

Schoof, Ted, and Jan van de Westelaken. *Bibliography (1936–1996) of Edward Schillebeeckx O. P.* Nijmegen: Nelissen, 1997.

Schoonenberg, Piet. "Schillebeeckx en de exegese. Enige gedachten bij *Jezus, het verhaal van een levende*." *Tijdschrift voor Theologie* 15 (1975): 255–268.

Schreiter, Robert. "Schillebeeckx." In *The Modern Theologian*. Edited by David F. Ford, 152–61. Cambridge: Blackwell, 1997.

Schreiter, Robert. *The Praxis of Christian Experience. An Introduction to the Theology of Edward Schillebeeckx*. San Francisco: Harper & Row, 1989.

Silvestre, Giuseppe. *Quale salvezza fuori dalla chiesa? Il Cristianesimo anonimo nella teoria di Edward Schillebeeckx*. Cosenza: Progetto, 1995.

Snijdewind, Hadewych. *Leeswijzer bij "Jezus, het verhaal van een Levende" van Edward Schillebeeckx*. Baarn: Nelissen, 1994.

Straeter, Carl. *La mariologia secondo la <nuova teologia> olandese*. Roma: Edizioni Paoline, 1972.

Valkenberg, Pim. *Leeswijzer bij "Mensen als verhaal van God" van Edward Schillebeeckx*. Baarn: Nelissen, 1991.

van Erp, Stephan. "Tussen traditie en situatie. Edward Schillebeeckx voor een volgende generatie." *Tijdschrift voor Theologie* 1 (2010): 8–18.

van Erp, Stephan, Martin G. Poulsom, and Lieven Boeve, eds. *Grace, Governance and Globalization*. London: T&T Clark, 2018.

van Erp, Stephan. "*Sign and Precursor God's Grace for All*: Schillebeeckx's Ecclesiology During the Second Vatican Council." In *T&T Clark Handbook of Edward Schillebeeckx*. Edited by Stephan van Erp and Daniel Minch, 122–134. London: Bloomsbury, 2019.

van Erp, Stephan, and Daniel Minch, eds. *T&T Clark Handbook of Edward Schillebeeckx*. London: Bloomsbury, 2019.

Van Wiele, Jan. "Edward Schillebeeckx' theologie van de religies." *Tijdschrift voor Theologie* 1 (2010): 95–107.

Walle, Ambroos Remi van de. "Theologie over werkelijkheid. Een betekenis van het werk van Edward Schillebeeckx." *Tijdschrift voor Theologie* 14 (1974): 463–490.

Willems, Boniface. "Edward Schillebeeckx." In *Tendenzen der Theologie im 20. Jahrhundert. Eine Geschichte in Porträts.* Edited by Hans Jürgen Schulz, 602–607. Stuttgart: Kreuz-Verlag, 1966.

Winling, Raymond. *Teologia współczesna 1945–1980.* Kraków: Wydawnictwo ZNAK, 1990.

5. Selected Literature

Adamiak, Elżbieta. *Błogosławiona między niewiastami. Maryja w feministycznej teologii Cathariny Halkes.* Lublin: Redakcja Wydawnictw KUL, 1997.

Altizer, Thomas and William Hamilton. *Radical Theology and the Death of God.* New York: Bobbs-Merrill, 1966.

Altizer, Thomas. *The Gospel of Christian Atheism.* Philadelphia: Westminster Press, 1966.

Asmussen, Hans. *Maria, die Mutter Gottes.* Stuttgart: Evangelisches Verlagswerk, 1950.

Balter, Lucjan. "Duch Święty w tajemnicy Maryi i Kościoła." In *Matka Jezusa pośród pielgrzymującego Kościoła.* Edited by Jan S. Gajek and Kazimierz Pek, 243–257. Warszawa: Wydawnictwo Księży Marianów, 1993.

Bartnik, Czesław. "Możliwość stosowania analizy strukturalistycznej w teologii." *Znak* 25 (1973): 720–738.

Bartnik, Czesław. *Hermeneutyka personalistyczna.* Lublin: Wydawnictwo "Polihymnia", 1994.

Bartnik, Czesław. *Poznanie teologiczne.* Lublin: Pracownia Poligraficzna PKLO, 1998.

Bartnik, Czesław. *Matka Boża.* Lublin: Wydawnictwo KUL, 2012.

Beinert, Wolfgang, ed. *Cześć Maryi dzisiaj. Propozycje pastoralne.* Warszawa: Wydawnictwo Księży Marianów, 1992.

Beinert, Wolfgang. *Maria in der Feministichen Theologie.* Kevelaer: Butzon & Bercker, 1988.

Boff, Leonardo. *Ave Maria. Das Weibliche und der Geist.* Düsseldorf: Patmos-Verlag, 1982.

Boff, Leonardo. *Das mütterliche Antlitz Gottes.* Düsseldorf: Patmos-Verlag, 1985.

Boff, Leonardo. *Der dreieinige Gott.* Düsseldorf: Patmos-Verlag, 1987.

Bolewski, Jacek. *Misterium Mądrości. Traktat sofio-mariologiczny.* Kraków: Wydawnictwo WAM, 2012.

Bonhoeffer, Dietrich. *Letters and Papers from Prison.* New York: Macmillan, 1963.

Budzik, Stanisław. "Odnowa kultu maryjnego według adhortacji *Marialis cultus.*" *Resovia Sacra* 3 (1996): 59–74.

Budzik, Stanisław. *Maryja w Tajemnicy Chrystusa i Kościoła.* Tarnów: Biblos, 1997.

Cantalamessa, Raniero. *Mary: Mirror of the Church.* Collegeville: The Liturgical Press, 1992.

Cecchin, Franco. *W poszukiwaniu Maryi. Komentarz egzystencjalny do encykliki "Redemptoris Mater."* Warszawa: Wydawnictwo Księży Marianów, 1989.

Cox, Harvey. *The Secular City. Secularization and Urbanization in Theological Perspective.* Princeton: University Press, 2013.

Congar, Yves. *Wierzę w Ducha Świętego. Vol. 1: Duch Święty w ekonomii. Objawienie i doświadczenie Ducha.* Warszawa: Wydawnictwo Księży Marianów 1995.

Cullmann, Oscar. *Christus und die Zeit.* Zürich: Evangelischer Verlag A.G., 1948.

de la Potterie, Ignace. *Mary in the Mystery of the Covenant.* New York: Alba House, 1992.

de Lubac, Henri, *The Splendor of the Church,* San Francisco: Ignatius Press, 1999.

de Lubac, Henri. *Petite catéchèse sur nature et grâce.* Paris: Fayard, 1980.

De Petter, Dominicus. *Begrip en werkelijkheid. Aan de overzijde van het conceptualisme.* Antwerpen: Paul Brand, 1964.

De Petter, Dominicus. "De oorsprong van de zijnkennis volgens de H. Thomas van Aquino." *Tijdschrift voor Philosophie* 17 (1955): 199–254.

De Petter, Dominicus. "Een geamendeerde phenomenologie." *Tijdschrift voor Philosophie* 22 (1960): 286–306.

Durlak, Ewa. "Antropologiczna droga odnowy kultu maryjnego." In *Nauczycielka i Matka. Adhortacja Pawła VI "Marialis cultus" na temat rozwoju należycie pojętego kultu maryjnego. Tekst i komentarze.* Edited by Stanisław C. Napiórkowski, 405–426. Lublin: Redakcja Wydawnictw KUL, 1991.

Ferdek, Bogdan. *Nasza Siostra – Córą i Matką Pana. Mariologia jako przestrzeń syntezy dogmatyki.* Świdnica: Świdnicka Kuria Biskupia, 2007.

Ficek, Ryszard. "Mariological Dimension of the Theological and Pastoral Concepts of Cardinal Stefan Wyszyński, Primate of Poland." *Studia Sandomierskie* 27 (2021): 229–249.

Forte, Bruno. *Maria, Mutter und Schwester des Glaubens.* Zürich: Benziger, 1990.

Forte, Bruno. *Maryja Ikona Tajemnicy. Zarys mariologii symboliczno-narracyjnej.* Warszawa: Wydawnictwo Księży Marianów, 1999.

Gajek, Jan Sergiusz, and Kazimierz Pek, eds. *Matka Jezusa pośród pielgrzymującego Kościoła.* Warszawa: Wydawnictwo Księży Marianów, 1993.

Gambero, Luigi. *Mary in the Middle Ages. The Blessed Virgin Mary in the Thought of Medieval Latin Theologians.* San Francisco: Ignatius Press, 2005.

Gellner, Ernest. *Thought and Change.* Chicago: University of Chicago Press, 1964.

Ghidelli, Carlo. *Magnificat. Il cantico di Maria, la donna che ha creduto.* Milano: Edizioni Paoline, 1990.

Gilkey, Langdon. *Naming of Whirlwind: The Renewal of God-Language.* Indianapolis: The Bobbs-Merrill Company, 1969.

Gilski, Marek. *Mariologia kontekstualna św. Augustyna.* Lublin: Wydawnictwo KUL, 2006.

Góźdź, Krzysztof. *Jesus Christus als Sinn der Geschichte bei Wolfhart Pannenberg.* Regensburg: Verlag Friedrich Pustet, 1988.

Góźdź, Krzysztof. *Teologia historii zbawienia według Oscara Cullmanna.* Lublin: Redakcja Wydawnictw KUL, 1996.

Grabner-Haider, Anton. *Glaubenssprache. Ihre Struktur und Anwendbarkeit in Verkündigung und Theologie.* Wien: Herder, 1975.

Gręś, Stanisław. *Maryja wzorem życia w Duchu Świętym.* Włocławek: Włocławskie Wydawnictwo Diecezjalne, 1995.

Grignion de Monfort, Ludwik Maria. *Traktat o prawdziwym nabożeństwie do Najświętszej Maryi Panny.* Warszawa: Wydawnictwo Księży Marianów, 1996.

Gusdorf, Georges. *La parole*. Paris: Presses universitaires de France, 1956.

Halkes, Catharina. *Zoekend naar wat verloren ging. Enkele aanzetten voor feministische theologie*. Baarn: Ten Have, 1984.

Halkes, Catharina. *Maria*. In *Wörterbuch der feministischen Theologie*. Gütersloh: Verlagshaus Gerd Mohn, 1991.

Hammans, Herbert. "Recent Catholic Views on the Development of Dogma." *Concilium* 21 (1967): 109–131.

Howe, Reuel. *The Miracle of Dialogue*. New York: Seabury Press, 1963.

Hünermann, Peter. "Theologischer Kommentar zur dogmatischen Konstitution über die Kirche *Lumen gentium*." In *Herders Theologischer Kommentar zum Zweiten Vatikanischen Konzil II*. Edited by Peter Hünermann and Bernd Jochen Hilberath, 263–563. Freiburg im Breisgau: Herder, 2004.

Ilzo, Daniel Lázaro, *La mediazione materna di Maria in Cristo negli insegnamenti di Giovanni Paolo II* (Collana di Mariologia 9). Lugano – Gavirate: Eupress-FTL, 2011.

Jagodziński, Marek. "Communional Marian Anthropology." *Roczniki Teologiczne* 62, no. 7 (2015): 75–87.

Johnson, Elizabeth. *Truly Our Sister: A Theology of Mary in the Communion of Saints*. New York – London: Continuum, 2006.

Kasper, Walter. *Glaube und Geschichte*. Mainz: Matthias-Grünewald-Verlag, 1970.

Kluz, Marek. "Mary as a Model of Faith and Moral Life for the Contemporary Disciples of Christ." *The Person and the Challenges* 1 (2018): 155–170.

Kubiś, Adam. *Jezus Oblubieniec. Metafora małżeńska w Ewangelii Janowej*, Rzeszów: Bonus Liber, 2023.

Kudasiewicz, Józef. *Matka Odkupiciela*. Kielce: Wydawnictwo "Jedność," 1996.

Langella, Alfonso. *Maria e lo Spirito nella teologia cattolica post-conciliare*. Napoli: D'Auria, 1993.

Langkammer, Hugolin. *Maria in der Bibel. Was will die Offenbarung von der Mutter Jesu sagen?* Wien: Rozenkranz-Sühnekreuzzug, 1988.

Langkammer, Hugolin. *Maryja w Nowym Testamencie*. Gorzów Wielkopolski: Gorzowskie Wydawnictwo Diecezjalne, 1991.

Laurentin, René. *La Madonna. Questione di teologia*. Brescia: Morcelliana, 1964.

Laurentin, René. *The Apparitions of the Blessed Virgin Mary Today*. Dublin: Veritas, 1990.

Levine, Amy-Jill, and Maria Mayo Robbins. *A Feminist Companion to Mariology*. New York – London: T&T Clark, 2005.

Logister, Wiel. *Maria, een uitdaging*. Averbode: Gooi en Sticht, 1995.

Masciarelli, Michele Giulio. "Maria «figlia di Sion» e «Chiesa nascente» nella riflessione di Joseph Ratzinger." *Marianum* 68 (2006): 321-415.

McBrien, Richard. *The Church. The Evolution of Catholicism*. New York: HarperCollins Publishers, 2008.

Miczyński, Jan Krzysztof, ed. *Maryja i Kościół*. Lublin: Wydawnictwo KUL, 2018.

Mielcarek, Krzysztof. "Mary in the Apostolic Church in the Light of Lucan Writings." *Biblical Annals* 10, no. 4 (2020): 599–614.

Milbank, John. *The Suspended Middle. Henri de Lubac and the Debate Concerning the Supernatural.* London: SCM Press, 2012.

Moltmann, Jürgen. *The Coming of God. Christian Eschatology.* Minneapolis: Fortress Press, 1996.

Moltmann, Jürgen. *Theologie der Hoffnung.* München: Kaiser, 1965.

Monden, Luis. *Le miracle signe de salut.* Bruges-Paris: Desclée de Brouwer, 1960.

Napiórkowski, Andrzej. *Maryja jest piękna. Zarys mariologii i maryjności.* Kraków: Wydawnictwo Naukowe UPJPII, 2016.

Napiórkowski, Stanisław Celestyn. "Natura współodkupieńczej zasługi Maryi." *Roczniki Teologiczno-Kanoniczne* 12, no. 2 (1965): 69–83.

Napiórkowski, Stanisław Celestyn. "Où en est la mariologie?" *Concilium* 3, no. 29 (1967): 97–112.

Napiórkowski, Stanisław Celestyn. *Jak uprawiać teologię.* Wrocław: Wydawnictwo Wrocławskiej Księgarni Archidiecezjalnej, 1996.

Napiórkowski, Stanisław Celestyn. "Ku odnowie kultu maryjnego." *Ateneum Kapłańskie* 110, no. 475 (1988): 416–429.

Napiórkowski, Stanisław Celestyn. *Matka naszego Pana.* Tarnów: Biblos, 1992.

Napiórkowski, Stanisław Celestyn. "O mariologii eklezjotypicznej" In *Matka Jezusa pośród pielgrzymującego Kościoła.* Edited Sergiusz J. Gajek and Kazimierz Pek, 19–36. Warszawa: Wydawnictwo Księży Marianów, 1993.

Napiórkowski, Stanisław Celestyn. "O właściwe miejsce Bogarodzicy w pobożności katolickiej. Pytania o hierarchię prawd." In *Maryja w tajemnicy Chrystusa.* Edited by Stanisław C. Napiórkowski and Stanisław Longosz, 187–197. Niepokalanów: Wydawnictwo Ojców Franciszkanów, 1997.

Napiórkowski, Stanisław Celestyn, and Stanisław Longosz, eds. *Maryja w tajemnicy Chrystusa.* Niepokalanów: Wydawnictwo Ojców Franciszkanów, 1997.

Napiórkowski, Stanisław Celestyn, and Jan Usiądek. *Matka i Nauczycielka. Mariologia Soboru Watykańskiego II.* Niepokalanów: Wydawnictwo Ojców Franciszkanów, 1992.

Napiórkowski, Stanisław Celestyn, Teofil Siudy, and Krzysztof Kowalik, eds. *Duch Święty a Maryja. Materiały z sympozjum zorganizowanego przez Katedrę Mariologii KUL oraz Oddział PTT w Częstochowie, Częstochowa, 22–23 maja 1998 roku.* Częstochowa: Wydawnictwo "Regina Poloniae," 1999.

Napiórkowski Stanisław Celestyn, *Spór o Matkę. Mariologia jako problem ekumeniczny.* Lublin: Wydawnictwo KUL, 2011.

Napiórkowski, Stanisław Celestyn. *Mariologia polsko-syberyjska.* Lublin: Wydawnictwo KUL, 2023.

Pannenberg, Wolfhart. *Offenbarung als Geschichte.* Göttingen: Vandenhoeck & Ruprecht, 1982.

Pek, Kazimierz. *Per Spiritum ad Mariam. Implikacje mariologiczne pneumatologii Y. Congara.* Lublin: Wydawnictwo KUL, 2000.

Pek, Kazimierz, and Teofil Siudy, eds. *Trójca Święta a Maryja.* Częstochowa: Wydawnictwo "Regina Poloniae," 2000.

Pek, Kazimierz, Stanisław Celestyn Napiórkowski, and Wacław Siwak. *The Debate about Mariology of John Paul II.* Stockbridge, MA: Marian Heritage, 2018.

Pek, Kazimierz. *Totus Tuus Renewed – John Paul II.* Lublin: Towarzystwo Naukowe KUL, 2021.

Perrella, Salvatore. "Concilio Vaticano II." In *Mariologia.* Edited by Stefano de Fiores, Valeria Ferrari-Schiefer, and Salvatore Perella, 308–319. Cinisello Balsamo: Edizioni San Paolo, 2009.

Pesch, Rudolf. *Jesu ureigene Taten? Ein Beitrag zur Wunderfrage.* Freiburg im Breisgau: Herder, 1970.

Philips, Gérard. *Dogmatische Constitutie over de Kerk "Lumen gentium." Geschiedenis, Tekst, Kommentaar.* Vol. II. Antwerpen: Patmos, 1968.

Rahner, Karl. "Kirche und Parusie Christi." *Catholica* 17 (1963): 113–128.

Rahner, Karl. *Visions and prophecies.* London: Burns & Oates, 1963.

Rahner, Karl. "Die anonymen Christen." In Karl Rahner. *Schriften zur Theologie.* Vol. VI, 545–554. Einsiedeln: Benziger, 1965.

Ratzinger, Joseph. *Die Tochter Zion. Betrachtungen über den Marienglauben der Kirche.* Einsiedeln: Johannes Verlag, 1978.

Ratzinger, Joseph. *Bilder der Hoffnung. Wanderungen im Kirchenjahr.* Freiburg im Breisgau: Herder, 1999.

Ratzinger, Joseph. "The Ecclesiology of the Constitution *Lumen Gentium*." In Joseph Ratzinger. *Pilgrim Fellowship of Faith. The Church as Communion*, 123–152. San Francisco: Ignatius Press 2005.

Ratzinger, Joseph. *The Sign of the Woman: An Introductory Essay on the Encyclical "Redemptoris Mater."* In Joseph Ratzinger, and Hans Urs von Balthasar. *Mary. The Church at the Source*, 37–60. San Francisco: Ignatius Press, 2005.

Richardson, Peter, Charles Mueller, and Stephen Pihlaja. *Cognitive Linguistics and Religious Language.* New York: Routledge 2021.

Ricoeur, Paul. *Hermeneutics and the Human Sciences: Essays on Language, Action and Interpretation.* Cambridge: Cambridge University Press, 1981.

Ruether, Rosemary. *Mary – The Feminine Face of the Church.* Philadelphia: The Westminster Press, 1977.

Ruddy, Christopher. "*A Very Considerable Place in the Mystery of Christ and the Church? Yves Congar on Mary*." In *Mary on the Eve of the Second Vatican Council.* Edited by John C. Cavadini and Danielle M. Peters, 113–132. Notre Dame: University of Notre Dame Press, 2017.

Salij, Jacek. "Maryja eschatologiczną Ikoną Kościoła (refleksja na marginesie KKK 972)." In *Maryja w Katechizmie Kościoła Katolickiego.* Edited by Stanisław C. Napiórkowski, and Bogusław Kochaniewicz, 89–95. Kraków: Bratni Zew, 1996.

Shea, John. *Religious Language in a Secular Culture. A Study in the Theology of Langdon Gilkey.* Mundelein, IL: University of St. Mary of the Lake, 1976.

Scheffczyk, Leo and Ziegenaus Anton. *Maria in der Heilsgeschichte. Mariologie.* Achen: MM-Verlag, 1998.

Schiwy, Günther. *Neue Aspekte des Strukturalismus.* München: Kösel Verlag, 1971.

Schlier, Heinrich. *Die Zeit der Kirche. Exegetische Aufsätze und Vorträge.* Freiburg im Breisgau: Herder, 1956.

Schoof, Ted. "Geschiedenis en theologie: een haat-liefde-verhouding?" *Tijdschrift voor Geschiedenis* 4 (1988): 510–524.

Schoonenberg, Piet. "Wierzę w życie wieczne." *Concilium* no. 5 (1969): 60–9.

Schottroff, Luise. "Das Magnificat und die älteste Tradition von Jesus von Nazareth." *Evangelische Theologie* 38 (1978): 298–313.

Serra, Aristide. *Myriam, fille de Sion.* Paris: Mádiaspaul, 1999.

Siwak, Wacław. *Fiat mihi secundum verbum. Maryja w Tajemnicy Wcielenia według Jana Pawła II.* Lublin: Redakcja Wydawnictw KUL, 2001.

Smith, Wilfred. *The Meaning and End of Religion.* New York: New American Library, 1964.

Spinetoli, Ortensio da. *Maryja w Biblii.* Niepokalanów: Wydawnictwo Ojców Franciszkanów, 1997.

Sroka, Józef. "Liturgiczna droga odnowy kultu maryjnego." In *Nauczycielka i Matka. Adhortacja Pawła VI "Marialis cultus" na temat rozwoju należycie pojętego kultu maryjnego. Tekst i komentarze.* Edited by Stanisław Celestyn Napiórkowski, 285–324. Lublin: Redakcja Wydawnictw KUL, 1991.

Steiger, Lothar. *Die Hermeneutik als dogmatisches Problem.* Gütersloh: Verlagshaus Gerd Mohn, 1961.

Thompson, Daniel Spedd. "Epistemological Frameworks in the Theology of Edward Schillebeeckx." *Philosophy and Theology* 15, no. 1 (2003): 19–56.

Thurian, Max. *Maryja Matka Pana. Figura Kościoła.* Warszawa: Wydawnictwo Księży Marianów, 1990.

Tyrell, George. *Lex orandi, or Prayer and Creed.* London: Longmans, Green & Co., 1903.

van Erp, Stephan, Christopher Cimorelli, and Christiane Alpers, eds. *Salvation in the World. The Crossroads of Public Theology.* London: Bloomsbury, 2017.

van Schaik, Ton H.M. *Alfrink: Een biografie.* Amsterdam: Anthos, 1997.

von Balthasar, Hans Urs. "The Marian Mold of the Church." In J. Ratzinger, H. Urs von Balthasar, *Mary. The Church at the Source,* 125–144. San Francisco: Ignatius Press, 2005.

Wąsek, Damian. "Interdisciplinarity in Theology." In *Perspectives on Interdisciplinarity.* Edited by Bartosz Brożek, Marek Jakubiec and Piotr Urbańczyk, 155–173. Kraków: Copernicus Center Press, 2020.

Winter, Gibson. *The New Creation as Metropolis.* New York: Macmillan, 1963.

Wojtkowski, Julian, and Stanisław Celestyn Napiórkowski, eds. *Nosicielka Ducha. Pneumato-fora. Materiały z Kongresu Mariologicznego Jasna Góra 18–23 sierpnia 1996 r.* Lublin: Redakcja Wydawnictw KUL, 1998.

Życiński, Józef. *Three Cultures: Science, the Humanities and Religious Values.* Tuckson: Pachart Publishing House, 1990.

Życiński, Wojciech. *Matka, która pozostała Dziewicą.* Kraków: Scriptum, 2017.

Author Index